THE ART
OF
MICROWAVE
COOKING

Produced by Copyright Studio, Paris
Editor : Jean-Paul Paireault
Cooking Editor : Catherine Monnet
Art Director : Jacques Hennaux
Design : Sandrine Desbordes

Recipes created by : Frédéric Lebain
Photographs by : Jean-Paul Paireault

MALLARD PRESS

An imprint of BDD Promotional Book Company, Inc.,
666 Fifth Avenue, New York, N.Y. 10103
Mallard Press and its accompanying design and logo
are trademarks of BDD Promotional Book Company, Inc.

CLB 2374
© 1990 Colour Library Books Ltd., Godalming, Surrey, England.
Color separations by Coloursplendor Graphics Ltd., Hong Kong.
Printed and bound in Hong Kong by Leefung Asco Printers Ltd.
All rights reserved.
ISBN 0 792 45230 5

THE ART

O F

MICROWAVE COOKING

MALLARD PRESS

CONTENTS

Introduction 6

Microwave techniques 8

Food characteristics 10

Utensils 12

Appetizers 14

Rice, pasta and potatoes 78

Fish and seafood 98

Poultry and game   138

Meat   170

Desserts   222

Index   270

INTRODUCTION

This is a wonderful new microwave cookbook for creating classic and original gourmet cuisine in your microwave oven. Step-by-step photographs and simple concise directions make this book suitable for the beginner as well as the experienced cook. This collection of recipes was especially selected by a competent French chef, tested and retested to ensure your success in reproducing each delicious gourmet preparation at home.

Included in the book is important information on the use of the microwave cooking utensils, cooking times for different foods so that regardless of the type of oven you own, you may reproduce these recipes without fail.

Some of the dishes appearing in this book are quick and easy to prepare for a simple home meal. Others are more elaborate and time-consuming but impressive for special dinners. Each one of these delicious recipes, from first course to dessert, is guaranteed to bring gourmet pleasure to your family and friends.

MICROWAVE TECHNIQUES

What is a Microwave ?

Microwaves are very short high frequency electro-magnetic waves similar to radio and television waves. Microwaves are constantly vibrating and are differentiated by the number of vibrations per second. All electromagnetic waves are measured by the number of oscillations per unit of time. The frequency of microwaves is approximately 2,450 megahertz.

Microwave Ovens

The microwave oven is called an oven because that is the appliance it must resembles. The interior consists of a metallic cavity and a door. When the door is closed, and the oven is turned on, a transmitter called a magnetron sends signals to a receiver within the oven. The moment the door is opened, the microwave oven stops broadcasting just as a radio will not play if the station has signed off. Once the door is closed, the receiver deflects the microwave energy into the metal-lined oven cavity where it agitates the food molecules. All the energy remains inside the oven, where it turns to heat in the food.

How do microwaves heat food?

When high frequency microwaves come into contact with food or liquid they activate the minute food particles or molecules, so that they move quickly against each other, causing friction. The vibrations are so fast and the friction so great that enough heat is produced to cook the food. The microwave cooking process spreads from the surface to the center of the food by conduction.

Microwave equipment

Microwaves cook by provoking a rise in temperature within the mass of the food itself. Nothing should inhibit this process. Glass, china, pottery and plastic dishes are all suitable for use in microwave cooking. These materials do not act as a barrier to microwaves. Traditional metal cooking utensils are not suitable as they reflect the microwaves. Nor should utensils with metallic decorations, gold or silver designs, for example be used. Since such materials are flammable, they should not be used at high temperatures or for prolonged cooking. The same holds true for semi-rigid plastics, which should be reserved for reheating or short cooking. With the growing popularity of microwave cookery, there is now a wide range of utensils on the market, casseroles, trivets, baking dishes etc, which are especially adapted for microwave cooking.

FOOD CHARACTERISTICS

All recipes in this book were prepared using a 700 watt oven. If using an oven with a lower maximum output, cooking times should be increased as follows:

300 watt-add 40 seconds for every minute stated in the recipe,
600 watt-add 20 seconds for every minute stated in the recipe,
650 watt-only a slight increase in the overall time is necessary.

RICE and PASTA	QUANTITY	COOKING TIME	OBSERVATIONS
RICE	300g/12oz	10 to 12 minutes on HIGH	Cook in salted boiling water (twice the volume of rice). St twice during cooking.
PASTA	300g/12oz	8 to 12 minutes, depending on type, on HIGH	Cover the pasta with salted boiling water in a covered di Stir during cooking.

FRUITS	QUANTITY	COOKING TIME	OBSERVATIONS
PEARS	4 pears	6 to 8 minutes on HIGH	Cook the pears, cut into even sized pieces, without water, in a little butter and sugar if desired. Stir during cooking.
APPLES	4 apples	5 to 6 minutes on HIGH	Peel and quarter the apples and cook with a little sugar and butter. Ideal for making an apple compote quickly.
RASPBERRIES STRAWBERRIES	250g/10oz	5 minutes on HIGH	Add sugar to make a "coulis" (sauce), stir during cooking and reduce the mixture to a purée with a hand-held electric blender.
PINEAPPLE	1 small	4 to 6 minutes on HIGH	Peel the pineapple and cut it into even sized pieces. Cook it in a dish with a little sugar. Stir during cooking.
CHERRIES	300g/12oz	4 minutes on HIGH	Stone the cherries, place them in a cooking dish with a little sugar and cook stirring once.
MANGO	1 at 400g/14oz	3½ minutes on HIGH	Peel the mango, remove the seed and cut the flesh into pieces. Place in a cooking dish with a little sugar and stir once during cooking.

VEGETABLES	QUANTITY	COOKING TIME	OBSERVATIONS
CARROTS	500g/1lb	8 to 10 minutes on HIGH	Cook the carrots, covered, w little water or with a knob of butter. Stir the carrots from ti to time. They can be cut into sticks or slices.
POTATOES	4 large	6 to 7 minutes on HIGH	Bake the potatoes placed on outside edge of the plate on a turntable. (Remember to pric them before cooking).
CAULIFLOWER	1 cauliflower	8 to 10 minutes on HIGH	Break the cauliflower into flo and place in a cooking dish w a little water and lemon juice Cook, covered, stirring once.
COURGETTES	300g/12oz	3 to 5 minutes depending upon shape and size	Cut the courgettes into any shape, place in a cooking dis with a little water and if desir knob of butter.
PEAS	300g/12oz	10 to 12 minutes on HIGH	Cook the peas, covered, in w to cover.
ASPARAGUS	500g/1lb	8 to 10 minutes, depending upon size, on HIGH	Cook the asparagus in a cove dish with water to cover. Stir once or twice during cooking
SPINACH	300g/12oz	4 to 6 minutes on HIGH	Wash and stem the spinach. Place in a dish with a knob o butter, and cook, covered, stirring once.
STRING BEANS	300g/12oz	10 to 14 minutes, depending upon variety, on HIGH	Trim the string beans. Cook i a covered dish with water to cover. Stir twice during cooki

OULTRY	QUANTITY	COOKING TIME	OBSERVATIONS
OUSSIN	400g/14oz	6 minutes on HIGH	Split the poussins in half, sear on a browning dish with a little oil and butter, cooking for 3 minutes on each side. Allow to rest for 5 minutes.
HICKEN	whole 1.2kg/2lbs 8oz	20 minutes on HIGH	Cook the chicken in chicken stock to cover on high for 10 minutes and Medium 10 minutes. Allow to rest for 10 minutes after cooking.
HICKEN	in pieces	7 to 10 minutes according to method	Cook the chicken pieces with 50 ml/2 fl oz/¼ cup chicken stock or sear the pieces on a browning dish with a knob of butter.

FISH	QUANTITY	COOKING TIME	OBSERVATIONS
URBOT	600g/1lb 4oz fillets	6 minutes on HIGH	Place the seasoned fillets on a cooking tray with a little butter. Rotate the fish during cooking.
ADDOCK	800g/1lb 12oz fillets	6 to 7 minutes on HIGH	Place the haddock fillets in a cooking tray. Cover with milk and cook. If necessary soak the haddock in milk before cooking to remove excess salt.
TROUT	150g/6oz fillet	1 minute 30 seconds on HIGH	Preheat a browning dish. Sear the trout fillets in a little butter, then finish cooking. Allow to rest for 1 minute.
ALMON	180g/7oz pieces	2 to 2½ minutes on HIGH.	Preheat the browning dish. Sear the fish pieces in a little oil and a knob of butter. Cook for 1 to 1½ minutes on each side.
SOLE	100g/4oz fillets	1 minute on HIGH	Place the fillets in a buttered dish with several drops of lemon; or roll up the fillets and cook in a microwave steam cooker for 7 minutes. Allow to rest, covered, for 5 minutes.
COD	180g/7oz fillets	1½ minutes on HIGH	Sear the cod fillets in a browning dish for 1 minute on the first side and 30 seconds on the second side.

MEATS	QUANTITY	COOKING TIME	OBSERVATIONS
LEG OF LAMB	2kg/4½lbs roast	28 minutes on HIGH	Sear the lamb on all sides in a browning dish with a knob of butter. Insert a meat thermometer. Remove from the oven when it has reached 60°C/140°F. Allow to rest for 10 minutes.
ROAST PORK	1kg/2lbs 8oz	10 minutes on HIGH	Sear the pork on all sides in a browning dish with a knob of butter. Insert a meat thermometer and remove from the oven when it has reached 70°C/160°F. Allow to rest for 10 minutes.
ROAST BEEF	1kg/2lbs 8oz	3 minutes on HIGH	Sear the beef evenly in a browning dish with a knob of butter. Insert a meat thermometer and cook according to taste (60°C/140°F for a rare roast). Allow to rest for 5 minutes.
LAMB CHOPS	70g/3½oz per chop	3 minutes on HIGH	Preheat a browning dish and sear the lamb chops in a knob of butter for 1½ minutes on each side.

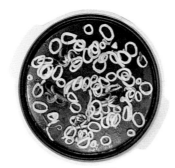

BROWNING DISH

This utensil allows you to sear or brown various foods : meat, onions, fish etc. Preheating times vary according to your oven type. Follow the manufacturer's instructions.

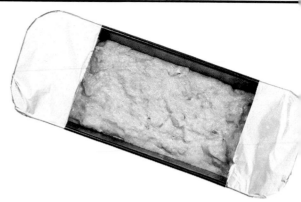

MICROWAVE CAKE DISH

This utensil is specially used for microwave cooking. Its non-stick surface allows easy unmolding. When cooking certain cakes, it is necessary to cover the ends with aluminum foil during the first part of cooking.

THE UTENSILS

A cook's utensils, like a workman's tools, can often determine his success or failure. Well constructed pots and pans, sharp knives and proper cooking tools, greatly facilitate food preparation. Today we have the added advantage of time saving machines, mixers, processors, etc.

ROUND MICROWAVE CASSEROLE

For cooking, stewing or defrosting larger portions of food. Equipped with a cover, it allows you to reheat food alongside other dishes.

MEAT THERMOMETER

Place the thermometer into the center of the roast to verify the meat is properly cooked. After removing the meat from the oven, allow the meat to rest for a while as it continues to cook outside the oven.

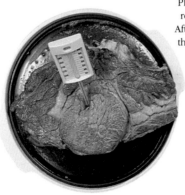

RECTANGULAR MICROWAVE BAKING DISH

Used for cooking rectangular shaped pastries or cakes. It is necessary to line it with wax paper for certain preparations.

SMALL WHISK

For mixing relatively liquid mixtures, such as vinaigrette dressing, also for lightly whipping creams and egg whites.

ROUND MICROWAVE COOKING DISH

For cooking, stewing and defrosting various foods. By superimposing two round dishes, one can create a "bain marie" for cooking certain sauces and custards.

MICROWAVE SPATULA

Made from a special plastic, it allows you to mix and stir any mixture without damaging your dishes.

LARGE MICROWAVE CASSEROLE

For cooking or stewing (if used with a cover) larger quantities of food.

MICROWAVE BROILER

When placed over a round cooking dish, this broiler (made from a special plastic) allows you to cook roasts, sausages etc, without stewing them in the juices. Used alone, a broiler is ideal for defrosting certain products more evenly and efficiently.

MICROWAVE TART OR FLAN DISH

Specially designed for microwave ovens, this tin allows you to cook and remove tarts, flans and pies without sticking.

VEGETABLE SOUP

SERVES : 6

PREPARATION TIME : 35 minutes
COOKING TIME : 30 minutes
PREHEATING: 8 minutes

An ever popular soup of fresh vegetables cooked in chicken stock, this is low in calories but rich in flavor. The vegetables can be varied with the season and if desired, cooked pasta can be added at the last minute.

INGREDIENTS

- ☐ 2 carrots
- ☐ ¼ green cabbage
- ☐ ½ leek
- ☐ 14oz fresh peas
- ☐ 6oz bacon
- ☐ 1 slice ham
- ☐ 2 large potatoes
- ☐ 2 large turnips
- ☐ Bouquet garni (parsley, thyme, bay leaf)
- ☐ 1 tbsp olive oil
- ☐ 2 tsps butter
- ☐ 4 cups chicken stock
- ☐ Fresh chervil
- ☐ Salt and pepper

1 Peel and dice the carrots.

2 Remove the outer leaves and core of the cabbage. Cut the cabbage into slices.

3 Quarter the leek, wash and chop finely. Shell the peas.

4 Steam the peas on HIGH for 8 minutes.

5

Remove the rind of the bacon and dice. Finely slice the ham.

9

Turn this mixture into a casserole, and add the cabbage, carrots, peas, and 4 tbsps water. Cook on HIGH for 4 minutes.

6

Peel the potatoes and turnips, and dice. Cover the potatoes in water until cooking.

10

Add the drained potatoes, the turnip, and bouquet garni and season with salt.

7

Make the bouquet garni, by tying together the parsley, thyme and bay leaf. Set aside.

11

Add the chicken stock, stir and cook, covered, on HIGH for 20 minutes. Allow to rest 5 minutes. Season with salt and pepper to taste.

8

Preheat the browning dish for 8 minutes. Add the olive oil with the butter. Sauté the leek, bacon and ham, on HIGH for 2 minutes.

12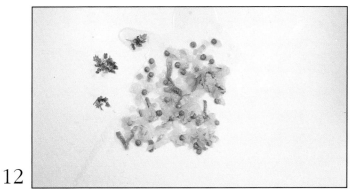

Serve the soup garnished with chopped fresh chervil.

ONION SOUP

SERVES : 4

PREPARATION TIME : 25 minutes
COOKING TIME : 26 minutes
BROWNING: 20 minutes

A French classic adapted to modern microwave cooking, this is a hearty and flavorful soup, wonderful for winter evenings. Serve it garnished with fresh garlic croutons.

INGREDIENTS

- ☐ 4 large onions
- ☐ 2 tbsps olive oil
- ☐ 4 cups chicken stock
- ☐ Bouquet garni (parsley, thyme, bay leaf)
- ☐ 1 clove garlic (central shoot removed)
- ☐ 4 slices white bread
- ☐ 1½ tbsps butter
- ☐ ½ bunch chives
- ☐ 1 egg, beaten
- ☐ Salt and pepper

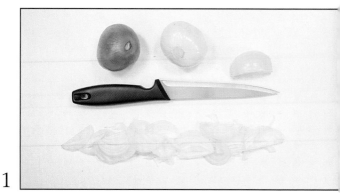

1 Peel and slice the onion. Chop finely.

2 Preheat the browning dish 8 minutes on HIGH. Remove and add 1 tbsp olive oil. Sauté half the onion for 2 minutes on HIGH. Repeat with the rest of the onion (preheat for 4 minutes).

3 Place the onions in a casserole, stir in the stock, and season with salt and pepper. Cook on HIGH for 5 minutes.

4 Make the bouquet garni, by tying together the parsley, thyme and bay leaf.

5 Chop the garlic finely.

9 Melt the butter in the hot tray, then brown the croutons on one side, turning quickly to brown on the other side.

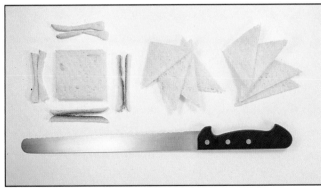

6 Add the garlic and bouquet garni to the soup, and cook on HIGH for 15 minutes.

10 Chop the chives finely.

7 Make the croutons : remove the crusts from the bread and cut the bread into triangles.

11 Using a fork, drizzle the beaten egg into the boiling Soup. Cook on HIGH for 1 minute.

8 Preheat a browning dish for 8 minutes on HIGH and have ready the butter and croutons.

12 Serve the soup with the croutons and the fresh chives.

CHINESE NOODLE SOUP

SERVES : 4

PREPARATION TIME : 35 minutes
COOKING TIME : 25 minutes

*An Oriental-inspired dish, in which Chinese
vegetables and noodles are cooked in chicken
stock enriched with aromatic seasonings and
herbs. Add a little lemon grass to flavor
the soup, if it is available.*

INGREDIENTS

- [ ] 10g black Chinese mushrooms
- [ ] 12oz fresh peas
- [ ] 4oz bamboo shoots
- [ ] 8 jumbo shrimp
- [ ] 2 tsps butter
- [ ] 4oz Chinese vermicelli
- [ ] 3 cups chicken stock
- [ ] 2 tbsps soy sauce
- [ ] Tabasco to taste
- [ ] ½ bunch fresh chives
- [ ] Salt and pepper

1 Reconstitute the mushrooms in water for 15 minutes. Rinse and drain. Chop into fine julienne. Blanch them for 3 minutes on HIGH in a little water, and drain again.

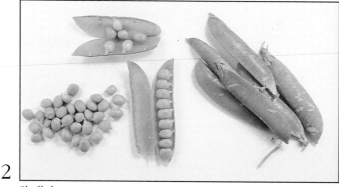

2 Shell the peas.

3 Steam the peas for 10 to 12 minutes on HIGH. Rinse, drain and set aside.

4 Cut the bamboo shoots into strips, then chop into fine julienne. Blanch in water for 5 minutes on HIGH.

Drain the bamboo shoots, rinse thoroughly and set aside.

9

Cook the vermicelli in a dish of boiling water for 1 minute on HIGH. Rinse and drain.

Shell and devein the shrimp. Cut in half lengthwise.

10

Pour the stock into a large casserole, then add the mushrooms, bamboo shoots and peas. Cook for 6 minutes on HIGH.

Preheat the browning dish for 8 minutes on HIGH. Spread in the butter, then sear the jumbo shrimp.

11

Combine the jumbo shrimp with the soy sauce, tabasco and vermicelli. Cook 3 minutes on HIGH.

Cook the shrimp for 1½ minutes, turning after 1 minute. Season with salt and pepper.

12

Serve the soup garnished with the chopped fresh chives.

CREAM

OF

ASPARAGUS SOUP

SERVES : 6

PREPARATION TIME : 25 minutes
COOKING TIME : 33 minutes

≈ ≈

A creative version of a delicious cream soup made from fresh asparagus. It is flavoured and garnished with sliced bacon and fresh peas. Use frozen peas if fresh are out of season.

INGREDIENTS

- ☐ 1lb 8oz asparagus
- ☐ 3 cups chicken stock
- ☐ 5 slices bacon
- ☐ 14oz fresh peas
- ☐ 3½ tbsps heavy cream
- ☐ 1 bunch chives
- ☐ Fresh chervil
- ☐ Salt and pepper

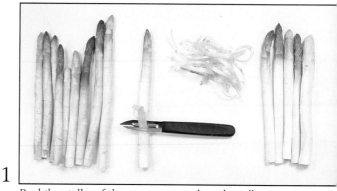

1 Peel the stalks of the asparagus and wash well.

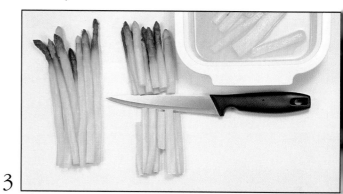

2 Cook the asparagus in a large, flat casserole with 1 cup chicken stock, covered, on HIGH for 10 minutes. Add salt as necessary.

3 After cooking, drain the asparagus, cut off the tips and set them aside. Continue cooking the stalks, covered, in the stock on HIGH for 5 minutes more.

4 After cooking add the remaining stock, and purée in a food processor (in two batches) to chop the asparagus stalks finely.

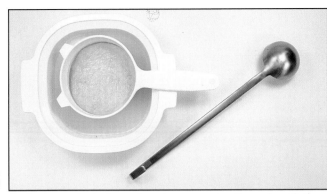

Strain the contents through a sieve, pressing through with the back of a spoon, to eliminate any fibers.

9

Cover the peas in salted water and cook, covered, on HIGH for 10 minutes, then drain.

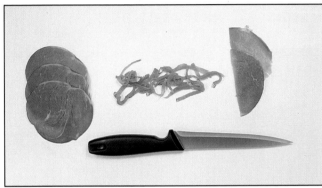

Dice the bacon evenly.

10

Mix together the asparagus purée, the peas, and the bacon and cook, covered, on HIGH for 5 minutes.

Cut half of the asparagus tips into round slices and cut the other half lengthwise. Set aside.

11

Add the cream and the asparagus tips to the soup and cook, covered, at MEDIUM for 3 minutes. Finely chop the chives and the chervil leaves.

Shell the peas.

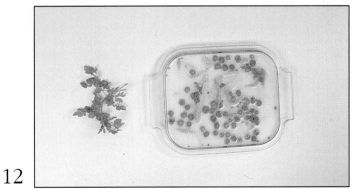

12

Serve the soup hot, garnished with the chives and chervil.

CREAM

OF

CHICKEN SOUP

SERVES : 6

PREPARATION TIME : 35 minutes
COOKING TIME : 28 minutes

≈≈≈

A rich and elegant, yet inexpensive and simple-to-prepare soup. Ground chicken and chopped mushrooms enhance a cream soup. Serve with cheese-topped croutons.

INGREDIENTS

- ☐ 1 carrot
- ☐ 1 onion
- ☐ Bouquet garni ($^1/_2$ leek, thyme, bay leaf)
- ☐ 3 chicken thighs
- ☐ 4 cups water
- ☐ 8oz mushrooms
- ☐ $^1/_2$ cup heavy cream
- ☐ 1 small loaf whole wheat bread
- ☐ 4 tbsps Gruyère cheese, shredded
- ☐ 2 tbsps chopped chives
- ☐ Salt and pepper

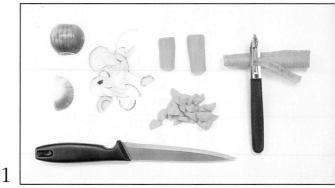

1 Peel the carrot and onion, and chop coarsely.

2 Prepare the bouquet garni : quarter the leek and clean well ; tie it together with the thyme and bay leaf.

3 In a casserole, combine the chicken thighs, onion, carrot and bouquet garni and cover with 4 cups water. Salt lightly. Cook, covered, on HIGH for 20 minutes.

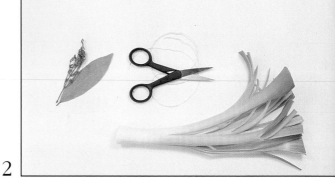

4 Trim the mushrooms, wash quickly and dry on a kitchen towel.

Finely chop the mushrooms.

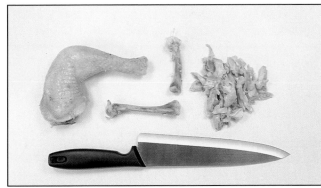

After cooking the chicken, drain and strain the stock through a sieve. Discard the vegetables and herbs.

Allow the chicken thighs to cool, remove the bones and shred the meat.

Cook the stock with the chopped mushrooms on HIGH for 5 minutes. Salt lightly.

9

Remove the stock from the oven, add the cream and mix with a hand-held blender. Add the shredded chicken and cook on HIGH for 2 minutes.

10

Finely slice the bread.

11

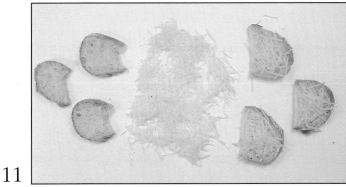

Sprinkle each slice with grated Gruyère and cook on HIGH for 1 minute.

12

Serve the chicken soup with the cheese croutons, and garnished with chopped chives.

SPRING ROLLS

SERVES : 6

PREPARATION TIME : 45 minutes
COOKING TIME : 15 minutes
PREHEATING : 8 minutes
RESTING TIME : 30 minutes

Delicate rice paper is stuffed with Chinese vegetables, pineapple and surimi (crab flavored fish sticks found in Oriental supermarkets). The rolls are quickly browned then served with a spicy soy sauce dip. If surimi is not available, use cooked crab or shrimp.

INGREDIENTS

- [ ] 1 carrot
- [ ] 2oz bamboo shoots
- [ ] 10g dried black mushrooms
- [ ] 4oz bean sprouts
- [ ] 1 slice pineapple
- [ ] 1 clove garlic (central shoot removed)
- [ ] 2 slices fresh ginger root
- [ ] 6 sticks surimi (fish sticks)
- [ ] 4 tbsps soy sauce
- [ ] Few drops tabasco
- [ ] 12 sheets rice paper
- [ ] 1 tbsp butter
- [ ] 1 tbsp vinegar
- [ ] ½ tsp sesame oil
- [ ] ½ tsp sugar
- [ ] 12 lettuce leaves
- [ ] Fresh mint

1 Reconstitute the mushrooms, then blanch on HIGH for 4 minutes. Dry and cut into fine julienne.

2 Peel the carrots, slice then cut into fine julienne. Do the same with the bamboo shoots, and blanch on HIGH for 4 minutes. Rinse and drain.

3 Trim the bean sprouts, and blanch on HIGH for 4 minutes, covered. Rinse and drain. Cut the pineapple into small pieces and set aside.

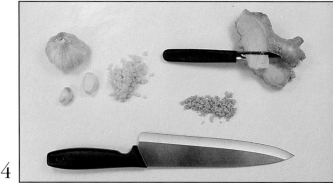

4 Peel and finely chop the garlic. Cut 2 slices from the fresh ginger with a vegetable peeler, and chop finely.

Cut the surimi sticks in half lengthwise, then shred with your fingers.

9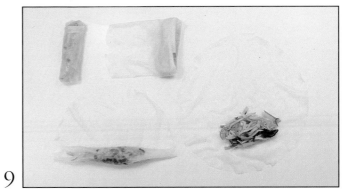

Place a bit of vegetable mixture on each sheet of rice paper. Fold in the sides, then roll up. Allow to rest in the refrigerator for 30 minutes.

Combine the bean sprouts, the surimi, carrots, bamboo, mushrooms and pineapple, mixing well.

10

Preheat the browning dish on HIGH for 8 minutes. Melt the butter and brown the spring rolls. Cook on HIGH for 3 minutes, turning once.

Add 2 tbsps soy sauce, half the chopped ginger and a few drops tabasco.

11

In a bowl mix the remaining 2 tbsps soy sauce, the vinegar, 2 tbsps water, the sugar, a few drops tabasco and the sesame oil. Mix thoroughly with a whisk.

Moisten the rice paper with warm water, using a brush.

12

Serve the spring rolls with the lettuce leaves and mint, accompanied with the above sauce.

VEGETABLE QUICHE

SERVES : 6

PREPARATION TIME : 25 minutes
COOKING TIME : 22 minutes

This is an easy-to-prepare variety of quiche. Grated zucchini and carrot are precooked, then added to a cheese custard base, and cooked in a pie shell. You may vary the quiche by using other cooked vegetables, such as broccoli or celery.

INGREDIENTS

- ☐ 2¹/₂ cups all (purpose flour)
- ☐ 1 egg yolk
- ☐ 4 tbsps water
- ☐ ¹/₂ cup butter
- ☐ 2 carrots (12oz)
- ☐ 1 zucchini (14oz)
- ☐ ¹/₂ cup milk
- ☐ ¹/₂ cup heavy cream
- ☐ 2 eggs
- ☐ 1 tsp butter
- ☐ Nutmeg
- ☐ Fresh chervil
- ☐ Salt and pepper

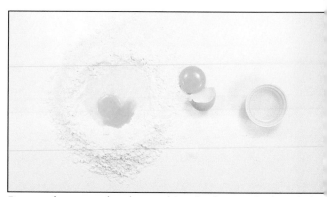

1 Prepare the pastry dough : combine the flour and salt with the egg yolk and water.

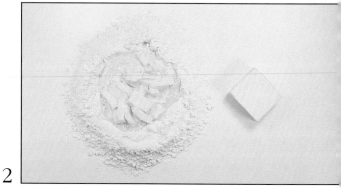

2 Add the butter (at room temperature), gradually incorporating it with your fingers.

3 Once you have obtained a homogeneous mixture, form it into a ball and set aside in a cool place for 30 minutes.

4 Peel the carrots and grate them rather finely.

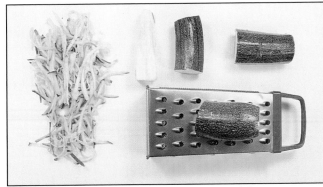

5 Finely grate the zucchini, having first removed the center core.

6 Steam the grated vegetables in a casserole over hot water on HIGH for 3 minutes. Allow to drain well.

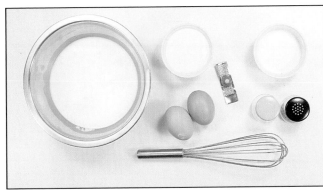

7 In a bowl mix together the milk, cream, and eggs and season with salt, pepper and grated nutmeg.

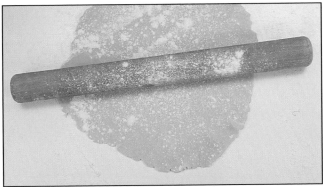

8 Roll out the pastry dough to fit a tart or pie pan.

9 Line a buttered pie pan with the dough. Trim off any excess dough.

10 Prick the dough with a fork. Cut a circle of wax paper to fit the bottom of the tart and cover with a plate. Cook on HIGH for 3 minutes.

11 Spread the drained grated vegetables in the bottom of the precooked pie shell. Top with the egg and cream filling. Cook on MEDIUM for 10 minutes and on HIGH for 6 minutes.

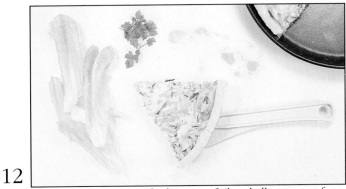

12 After cooking, cover with aluminum foil and allow to rest for 10 minutes. Garnish with the fresh chervil.

VEGETABLE MOLDS

SERVES : 6

PREPARATION TIME : 1 hour
COOKING TIME : 8 minutes
CHILLING : 6 Hours

These molds of diced cooked vegetables and poached quail eggs in a chicken flavored aspic make an attractive first course. They are served with a creamy chive sauce. If quail eggs are not available, use half the quantity of chicken eggs.

INGREDIENTS

- [ ] 2 carrots
- [ ] 12oz green beans
- [ ] 1 zucchini
- [ ] 2 turnips
- [ ] 4oz celeriac
- [ ] 1 sprig tarragon
- [ ] 3 cups chicken stock
- [ ] 2 packages powdered gelatin
- [ ] 1 tbsp vinegar
- [ ] 12 quail eggs
- [ ] ½ cup sour cream
- [ ] 4 tbsps chopped chives
- [ ] 2 tbsps vinegar
- [ ] Salt and pepper

1 Wash and peel the carrots, and cut into sticks, then dice. Wash and trim the green beans.

2 Cut the zucchini and turnips into sticks, then dice (discard the soft center of the zucchini).

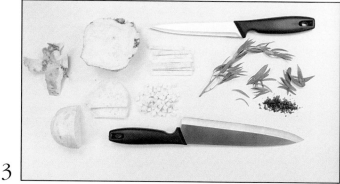

3 Peel the celeriac with a small knife. Cut into sticks, then dice. Trim and chop the tarragon.

4 Cook the turnips and zucchini in 3 tbsps salted water, covered, on HIGH for 3 minutes. Cook the celery and carrots separately in 3 tbsps water covered on HIGH for 4 minutes.

5

Cook the green beans in boiling salted water to cover on HIGH for 10 minutes. Drain, freshen in cold water and cut into small dice. Rinse and refresh the other diced vegetables. Drain.

6

Bring to a boil the stock, strain through a sieve covered with cheesecloth. Soften the gelatin in a little water ; add the hot stock and the tarragon. Mix well.

7

To poach the quail eggs, in a small casserole, boil water with the vinegar and salt. Once the water is simmering, break in 6 eggs and cook on HIGH covered for 40 seconds. Repeat.

8

Remove the eggs with a perforated spoon and drain on paper towels. Mix the diced vegetables together.

9

Spoon a layer of chicken stock into the bottom of 6 ramekins. Chill in the refrigerator until firm, add a layer of diced vegetables and another layer of stock. Chill slightly.

10

Place the eggs over the aspic, add more stock and refrigerate until firm. Add another layer of vegetables, cover with the remaining stock and chill at least 6 hours in the refrigerator.

11

Mix together the sour cream and chopped chives, salt, pepper and 2 tbsps vinegar (Reserve 1 tbsp chopped chives as a garnish.)

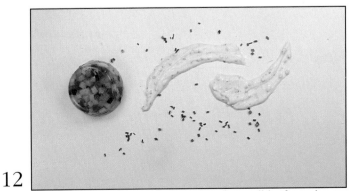

12

Unmold the ramekins with the point of a small knife, and serve the molds with the sour cream sauce. Garnish with chopped chives.

BELL PEPPER SAUTÉ

WITH

EGGS

SERVES : 4

PREPARATION TIME : 30 minutes
COOKING TIME : 26 minutes
BROWNING : 8 minutes

A colorful dish which can serve as a light lunch entrée or as a first course. Red and green peppers, onions and garlic are topped with poached eggs. If you wish, add zucchini and eggplant to the sautéed peppers.

INGREDIENTS

- [ ] 2 shallots
- [ ] 2 red peppers
- [ ] 2 green peppers
- [ ] 2 garlic cloves (central shoot removed)
- [ ] 2 onions
- [ ] 2 slices ham
- [ ] 1 small hot red pepper
- [ ] 1 tbsp olive oil
- [ ] ½ cup chicken stock
- [ ] 8 eggs
- [ ] 1 tbsp vinegar
- [ ] 2 tbsps olive oil
- [ ] ½ bunch chives
- [ ] 4 portions salad
- [ ] Fresh chervil
- [ ] Salt and pepper

1 Peel and finely chop the shallots.

2 Cut open the bell peppers, remove the pith and seeds, then chop into fine slices.

3 Peel the garlic and onion. Finely chop.

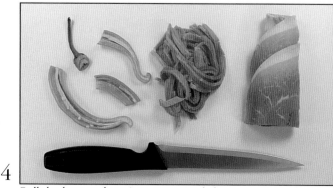

4 Roll the ham and cut into even-sized slices. Cut open the hot pepper, and remove the seeds (use only ¼ of the pepper).

Preheat the browning dish 8 minutes on HIGH. Add the 1 tbsp olive oil, sauté the onion, hot pepper, shallot, garlic for 4 minutes on HIGH, stirring twice. Turn into a large plate after cooking.

Add the pepper slices. Cook covered for 4 minutes on HIGH, then uncovered for 3 minutes at MEDIUM, stirring twice.

Add the slices of ham. Mix and cook 5 minutes on HIGH, stirring twice.

Add the stock, and season with salt and pepper. Cook for 3 minutes on HIGH, stirring twice.

9

Break the eggs into small ramekins, then top with the bell pepper and ham mixture. Pierce the egg yolks with a needle (to prevent bursting in the oven). Cook for 6 minutes at MEDIUM.

10

Make a vinaigrette dressing : mix together the vinegar, salt and pepper ; gradually beat in the 2 tbsps olive oil.

11

Finely chop the chives. Wash and trim the salad.

12

Serve the bell pepper sauté after allowing it to rest 5 minutes. Accompany with a salad tossed in the vinaigrette and garnished with fresh chervil.

BAKED EGGS

WITH

RED WINE SAUCE

SERVES : 4

PREPARATION TIME : 20 minutes
COOKING TIME : 18 minutes

This Lyons specialty, well known in France, makes an interesting first course. A red wine sauce is made with shallots, ham and mushrooms to accompany poached eggs garnished with garlic croutons.

INGREDIENTS

- ☐ 6oz button mushrooms
- ☐ 2 slices ham
- ☐ 2 shallots
- ☐ Bouquet garni (parsley, thyme, bay leaf)
- ☐ 1 cup red wine
- ☐ 1½ tbsps butter
- ☐ 8 eggs
- ☐ ½ loaf French bread
- ☐ 1 clove garlic (central shoot removed), chopped
- ☐ Fresh chervil
- ☐ Salt and pepper

1 Trim the mushrooms. Wash them quickly and dry on a kitchen towel.

2 Finely slice the mushrooms.

3 Cut the ham into fine julienne.

4 Peel the shallots and chop finely.

5

Prepare the bouquet garni, by tying together the parsley, thyme and bay leaf.

6

Combine the red wine, chopped shallots and mushrooms and bouquet garni. Cook on HIGH for 10 minutes.

7

Melt 2 tsps of the butter on HIGH for 30 seconds, and grease the bottoms of 4 ramekins.

8

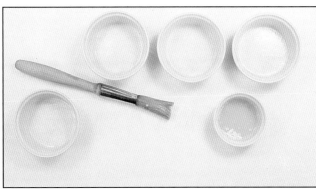

Break the eggs into the ramekins, season and prick each egg yolk with a needle. Cook at MEDIUM for 3 minutes. Cook the eggs in 2 operations, setting them around the edge of the turntable.

9

Remove the bouquet garni from the red wine sauce, add the cream and ham and season again. Mix well and cook on HIGH for 1 minute.

10

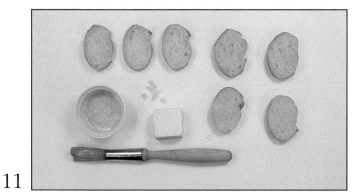

Slice the French bread.

11

Add the chopped garlic to the remaining 2 tsps butter, and cook on HIGH for 30 seconds. Brush the bread slices with the garlic butter.

12

Serve the eggs in the ramekins topped with the wine sauce and garnished with fresh chervil. Accompany with the garlic croutons.

PIQUANT CHORIZO OMELET

SERVES : 4

PREPARATION TIME : 10 minutes
COOKING TIME : 6 minutes
PREHEATING : 20 minutes

*For an interesting first course or lunch dish,
eggs are cooked omelet style and flavored with
onions, chorizo, and exotic spices. The omelet is
rolled up and served with a salad tossed in a
vinaigrette dressing.*

INGREDIENTS

- ☐ 2 onions
- ☐ ½ chorizo sausage, or other spicy cooked sausage
- ☐ 2½ tbsps oil
- ☐ 2 tbsps butter
- ☐ 12 eggs
- ☐ 1 tsp curry powder
- ☐ 1 pinch saffron
- ☐ ½ tsp turmeric
- ☐ 1 tbsp vinegar
- ☐ 3 tbsps oil
- ☐ 4 portions salad
- ☐ 2 tbsps chives, chopped
- ☐ Fresh chervil
- ☐ Salt and pepper

1 Peel the onions, cut in half, then chop finely. Set aside.

2 Remove the casing of the chorizo sausage, if necessary, then cut the sausage into even, round slices.

3 Preheat the browning dish on HIGH for 8 minutes. Add ½ tbsp oil, 1½ tsps butter and sauté the onion.

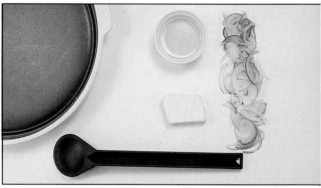

4 Cook the onion on HIGH for 2 minutes, stirring twice.

5 Break open the eggs in a bowl and beat with a fork.

9 After cooking, roll up the omelet. Cook and roll up the second omelet in the sauce way.

6 Add the sausage and the onion to the eggs, and mix well.

10 Prepare the vinaigrette dressing : dissolve a little salt in the vinegar, and add the pepper. Beat in the oil. Chop the chives.

7 Add to this mixture the curry powder, turmeric and saffron. Season with salt and pepper, and mix thoroughly.

11 Trim and wash the salad. Dry well.

8 Preheat the browning dish on HIGH for 8 minutes. Add 1 tbsp oil and 1½ tsps butter, and pour in half the omelet mixture. Stir and cook on HIGH for 2 minutes.

12 Serve the omelets with the salad, seasoned with the vinaigrette dressing, and garnished with the chopped chives and chervil.

SPINACH FLAN

WITH

NUTMEG

SERVES : 6

PREPARATION TIME : 20 minutes
COOKING TIME : 20 minutes

A healthy first course or lunch dish. Eggs, cream and cooked fresh spinach are combined and flavored with a hint of grated nutmeg. Other spices could replace the nutmeg and you could substitute another vegetable for the spinach.

INGREDIENTS

- [ ] 12oz fresh spinach
- [ ] 1 clove garlic (central shoot removed)
- [ ] 8oz ricotta or cottage cheese, sieved
- [ ] 4 eggs
- [ ] 1 tbsp flour
- [ ] 2 tbsps butter
- [ ] Nutmeg
- [ ] 4oz bacon
- [ ] 1¹/₂ cups heavy cream
- [ ] Fresh chervil
- [ ] Salt and pepper

1 Remove the stems of the spinach. Wash well and dry.

2 Finely chop the spinach.

3 Peel the garlic and chop finely.

4 Combine the ricotta or cottage cheese, the eggs, flour and garlic.

Cook the spinach with the butter in a small casserole for 5 minutes on HIGH.

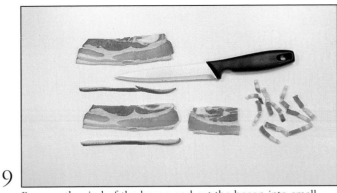

9

Remove the rind of the bacon and cut the bacon into small, even-sized pieces.

During cooking, remove the casserole twice, stir the spinach and season with salt and pepper.

10

Mix together the cream, bacon and a little grated nutmeg in a small dish. Season and cook on HIGH for 4 minutes, stirring twice.

Add the egg and cheese mixture to the cooked spinach, and season with a little grated nutmeg. Season with salt and pepper to taste.

11

After cooking, allow the spinach flan to rest for 5 minutes, covered with aluminum foil, then slice into serving portions.

Pour the mixture into a buttered pie pan. Cook for 1 minute on HIGH, remove, stir the edges towards the center. Cook on HIGH for 4 minutes. Reduce the power to MEDIUM, cook 10 minutes.

12

Serve each portion with a little cream sauce, garnished with fresh chervil.

ROQUEFORT-NUT QUICHE

SERVES : 6

PREPARATION TIME : 25 minutes
COOKING TIME : 20 minutes

*This makes a unique and flavorful first course.
A pie shell is stuffed with chopped apple,
Roquefort cheese, and chopped walnuts and
baked with an egg custard. Accompany with an
endive salad tossed in a vinaigrette dressing.*

INGREDIENTS

- ☐ 2¹/₂ cups flour
- ☐ 1 egg yolk
- ☐ ¹/₄ cup water
- ☐ ¹/₂ cup butter, softened to room temperature
- ☐ 1 cup heavy cream
- ☐ 1 cup milk
- ☐ 5oz Roquefort cheese
- ☐ 3 eggs
- ☐ ¹/₄ cup walnuts, chopped
- ☐ 2 tsps butter, for greasing
- ☐ 2 apples
- ☐ 3 endives
- ☐ 4 tbsps vinaigrette dressing
- ☐ Nutmeg
- ☐ Fresh chervil
- ☐ Salt and pepper

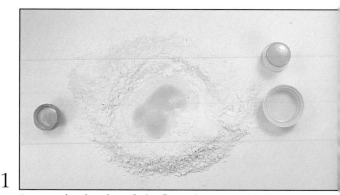

1 Prepare the dough : sift the flour, then mix with the egg yolk, the water and a pinch of salt.

2 Add the butter cut in small pieces, incorporating it thoroughly with your fingers.

3 Form the dough into a ball, and allow to rest in the refrigerator for 30 minutes.

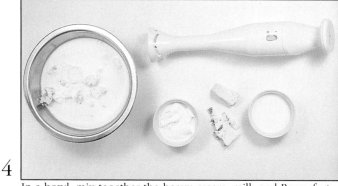

4 In a bowl, mix together the heavy cream, milk and Roquefort cheese. Blend with a hand-held blender to obtain a smooth cream.

Add the eggs, and chopped walnuts to the cream, and season with salt and pepper, and a little grated nutmeg. Mix together well and set aside.

Remove the dough from the refrigerator and roll out to fit a pie pan, flouring as you go.

Line a buttered pie pan with the dough ; remove any excess. Prick the base of the pie shell with a fork.

Cut a piece of wax paper to fit the base of the pan, lay it in and place a small plate on top. Cook on HIGH for 3 minutes.

9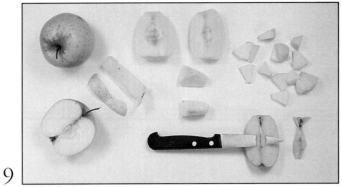

Peel the apples, quarter, remove the seeds and core. Cut into small, even-sized pieces.

10

Once the pie shell is cooked, remove the plate and paper, and distribute the chopped apples everly over the base.

11

Pour the Roquefort cream mixture over the apples and cook at MEDIUM for 10 minutes. Stir gently after 5 minutes without touching the dough. Cook on HIGH another 7 minutes.

12

Allow the quiche to rest, covered with a kitchen towel, for 10 minutes. Serve with the endives finely chopped and tossed in the vinaigrette dressing. Garnish with fresh chervil.

SQUID AND VEGETABLE RAGOUT WITH CHORIZO

SERVES : 6

PREPARATION TIME : 30 minutes
COOKING TIME : 23 minutes
PREHEATING : 8 minutes

A variety of fresh vegetables are cooked with sliced squid and spicy chorizo in this unique seafood dish. The vegetables may be varied to suit your taste.

INGREDIENTS

- ☐ 1lb 4oz squid
- ☐ 6oz carrots
- ☐ 1 zucchini, medium-sized
- ☐ 14oz fresh peas
- ☐ 6oz green beans
- ☐ 2 tbsps olive oil
- ☐ 4 tbsps butter
- ☐ 5oz canned corn
- ☐ 1 (6oz) chorizo, or other spicy cooked sausage
- ☐ Fresh chervil
- ☐ Salt and pepper

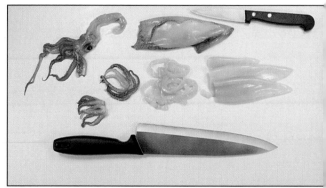

1 Skin and clean the squid. Rinse well. Slice and drain on paper towels.

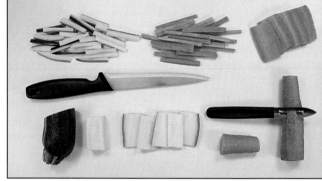

2 Peel the carrots and slice into matchsticks. Slice the zucchini into matchsticks, eliminating the spongy core.

3 Shell the peas and trim the green beans.

4 Cook the carrots in ½ cup water with 2 tsps butter. Season, cover and cook on HIGH for 3 minutes. Drain the carrots after cooking.

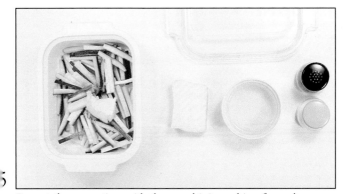

5 Repeat the operation with the zucchini, cooking for only 2 minutes.

9 Place all the drained vegetables in a casserole, including the corn, and dot with remaining butter.

6 Cook the peas, covered, in ½ cup salted water with 2 tsps butter on HIGH for 10 minutes. Cook the green beans in the same water on HIGH for 10 minutes. Drain the vegetables on paper towels.

10 Remove the casing of the chorizo and slice the sausage.

7 Preheat the browning dish on HIGH for 8 minutes. Meanwhile, dry the squid with paper towels.

11 Add the chorizo and sautéed squid to the vegetables. Cover and cook on HIGH for 4 minutes.

8 Sear the squid on the browning dish in 1 tbsp olive oil and 1 tsp butter. Cook on HIGH for 2 minutes, stirring once. Season with salt and pepper.

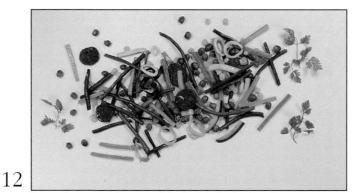

12 Serve the ragout hot, garnished with fresh chervil.

VEGETABLE-STUFFED FENNEL BULBS

SERVES : 6

PREPARATION TIME : 45 minutes
COOKING TIME : 38 minutes

This is a rather elaborate vegetable dish but worth the preparation time. Fennel bulbs are halved, poached in milk and stuffed with diced vegetables and ham in a béchamel sauce. They are baked and served with a fresh red pepper and cream sauce.

INGREDIENTS

- [ ] 2 red peppers
- [ ] 3 medium-sized fennel bulbs
- [ ] 3 cups milk
- [ ] 1 carrot
- [ ] 4oz green beans
- [ ] 2 thick slices ham
- [ ] 1 tbsp butter
- [ ] 1 tbsp flour
- [ ] 3 tbsps corn
- [ ] 3 tbsps shredded Gruyère cheese
- [ ] 6 fl oz heavy cream
- [ ] ½ lemon
- [ ] 1 tsp vinegar
- [ ] Tabasco
- [ ] Nutmeg
- [ ] Fresh dill
- [ ] Salt and pepper

1 Cut open the peppers, remove the pith and seeds and purée the pepper in a food processor in order to extract the juice. Allow to rest for 30 minutes.

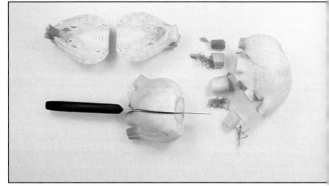

2 Halve the fennel bulbs lengthwise and wash.

3 Cook the fennel in a small casserole covered with 2 cups milk (add water if necessary to cover the fennel). Season. Cook, covered, on HIGH for 20 minutes, turning once. Drain.

4 Peel the carrots and trim the green beans. Dice both finely.

Cook the carrots in 3 tbsps water, covered on HIGH, for 3 minutes. Cook the green beans in water on HIGH for 8 minutes. Drain and rinse after cooking.

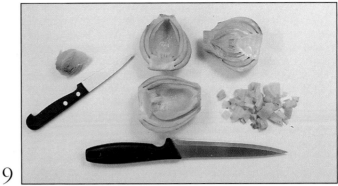

9 After cooking the fennel, remove the core with a small knife and cut it into small cubes.

Slice the ham into strips, then cut into cubes.

10 Combine the béchamel sauce, diced carrot and green beans, ham, corn and diced fennel. Mix well and use to stuff the hollowed fennel bulbs. Sprinkle with grated Gruyère.

7 Prepare the béchamel sauce : melt the butter on HIGH for 30 seconds, add the flour, mix and cook on HIGH for 30 seconds. Add 1 cup boiling milk and beat well.

11 Skim the foam from the red pepper purée, add the cream, several drops of lemon juice, the vinegar, salt, pepper and tabasco. Cook on HIGH for 2 minutes. Mix well and set aside.

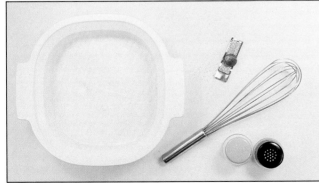

8 Cook on HIGH for 1 minute, stirring twice. Season with salt, pepper and a little grated nutmeg.

12 Heat the stuffed fennel on HIGH for 3 minutes. Serve with the red pepper sauce and fresh herbs (dill). Serve any leftover vegetables on the side.

CAULIFLOWER

AND

HAM AU GRATIN

SERVES : 6

PREPARATION TIME : 15 minutes
COOKING TIME : 20 minutes

*This makes a good lunch or supper dish ;
it is easy to prepare and the ingredients are
inexpensive. Cooked cauliflower and ham
are baked in a béchamel sauce topped with
breadcrumbs and shredded Gruyère cheese.*

INGREDIENTS

- ☐ 1 cauliflower
- ☐ 6 slices ham
- ☐ 4 slices white bread
- ☐ 2 tbsps parsley
- ☐ 2 tbsps butter
- ☐ 2 tbsps flour
- ☐ 2 cups milk
- ☐ 6oz Gruyère cheese, shredded
- ☐ 6 portions salad
- ☐ 6 tbsps vinaigrette dressing
- ☐ Nutmeg
- ☐ Fresh basil
- ☐ Salt and pepper

1 Remove the stalk and leaves from the cauliflower, then break the rest into flowerets.

2 Cook the cauliflower in 4 tbsps salted water on HIGH for 10 minutes, stirring once. Drain and set aside.

3 Roll up the ham and slice evenly.

4 Remove the crust from the bread and grind the bread in a food processor.

Stem and wash the parsley, then chop finely. Set aside.

9 In a bowl, mix the cauliflower with the béchamel sauce.

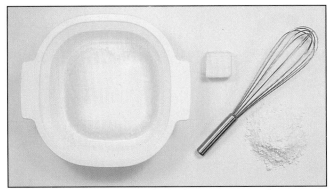

Make a béchamel sauce : melt the butter on HIGH for
1 minute, mix in the flour, and cook on HIGH for 1 minute.
Boil the milk on HIGH for 3 minutes.

10 Add the ham and chopped parsley. Mix well.

Gradually stir the milk into the butter and flour mixture. Stir
well and cook on HIGH for 30 seconds.

11 Turn the cauliflower mixture into a large casserole. Top with
the shredded Gruyere and the breadcrumbs. Cook on HIGH
for 5 minutes.

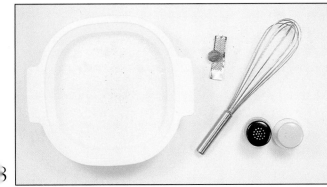

Once the béchamel sauce thickens, season with salt and
pepper and a little grated nutmeg.

12 Once the gratin is cooked, serve accompanied with the salad,
tossed in the vinaigrette dressing, and garnished with fresh
basil.

FRESH PASTA

WITH

HAM, CREAM

AND BASIL

SERVES : 6

PREPARATION TIME : 40 minutes
COOKING TIME : 10 minutes

*This is a delicious recipe for home-made
tagliatelle. They are enriched with egg yolk, and
accompanied with a garlic-flavored cream
sauce and garnished with fresh basil.*

INGREDIENTS

- ☐ 14oz flour
- ☐ 4 eggs
- ☐ 6 slices smoked ham
- ☐ 2 cloves garlic (central shoot removed)
- ☐ 20 basil leaves
- ☐ 1 cup heavy cream
- ☐ 2 egg yolks
- ☐ Fresh basil
- ☐ Salt and pepper

1 In a bowl mix together the flour, a pinch salt and the eggs and work into a hall of dough. Set aside in the refrigerator for 10 minutes.

2 Quarter the dough and pass each quarter through a pasta machine or roll out using a rolling pin. Flour throughout the operation

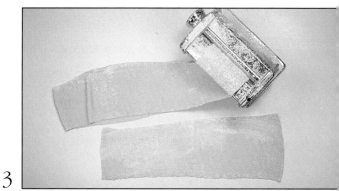

3 Continue to thin the dough, flouring continuously, to obtain thin strips.

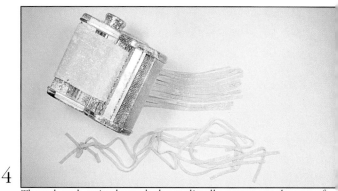

4 Thread each strip through the tagliatelle cutter attachment of the pasta machine, or roll the strip up and slice thinly using a sharp knife.

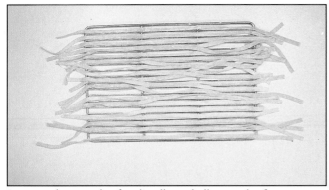

Separate the strands of tagliatelle and allow to dry for approximately 2 hours.

9

After cooking, drain the tagliatelle, rinse and set aside.

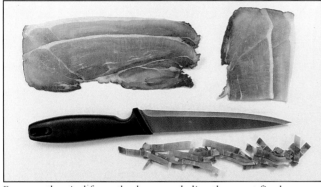

Remove the rind from the ham, and slice the meat finely.

10

In a casserole, combine the cream, ham, garlic, and salt and pepper. Cook on HIGH for 2 minutes.

Peel the garlic and chop finely. Remove the basil leaves and cut into fine julienne. Reserve several whole leaves for decoration.

11

Add the pasta together with the fresh basil and egg yolks. Mix well and cook on HIGH for 2 minutes, stirring once.

Cook the pasta in boiling salted water on HIGH for 5 to 7 minutes (depending on thickness of pasta).

12

Serve the pasta garnished with the reserved basil leaves.

BEEF MACARONI AU GRATIN

SERVES : 6

PREPARATION TIME : 40 minutes
COOKING TIME : 27 minutes
PREHEATING : 12 minutes

This is an economical dish wich uses readily available ingredients. Ground beef is cooked with chopped onions, peppers ham and ketchup, then mixed with a home-made white sauce and layered with cooked macaroni. The casserole is topped with shredded Gruyère cheese and quickly baked in the microwave.

INGREDIENTS

- ☐ 1lb beef
- ☐ 3 sprigs parsley
- ☐ 2 slices ham
- ☐ 2 onions
- ☐ 2 cloves garlic (in method)
- ☐ 2 bell peppers (1 green, 1 red)
- ☐ 5 tbsps butter
- ☐ 3 tbsps ketchup
- ☐ 1 tbsp butter
- ☐ 1 cup milk
- ☐ 14oz macaroni
- ☐ 6oz Gruyère cheese, shredded
- ☐ 6 portions salad
- ☐ 6 tbsps vinaigrette dressing
- ☐ Nutmeg
- ☐ Salt and pepper

1 Finely grind the meat in a food processor.

2 Wash and dry the parsley, and chop finely. Stack the ham slices together and chop finely.

3 Peel the onion, and finely chop. Peel the garlic, halve and remove the central shoot.

4 Halve the bell peppers, remove the pith and seeds and chop the flesh finely.

Preheat the browning dish on HIGH for 8 minutes. Melt 1 tbsp butter and sauté half the onion and bell pepper. Cook on HIGH for 2 minutes. Repeat with the remaining onion and bell pepper.

Put the onion and bell peppers, the ground meat, garlic and ketchup into a casserole. Mix thoroughly and cook on HIGH for 15 minutes, stirring 3 times. Season with salt and pepper.

Melt the remaining butter on HIGH for 30 seconds. Add 1 tbsp flour, stir and pour in the milk, which has been brought to a boil. Mix thoroughly, cook on HIGH for 1 minute, stirring twice.

Once the béchamel has cooked, season with salt, pepper and a little grated nutmeg.

9

Bring a large casserole of salted water to a boil; cook the macaroni on HIGH for 8 to 10 minutes, according to the size of the macaroni (taste during the cooking). Drain and rinse.

10

In a bowl, mix the béchamel sauce with the cooked meat. Reheat the macaroni with the remaining butter on HIGH for 2 minutes. Season with salt and pepper.

11

In a casserole, alternate layers of macaroni, meat and shredded Gruyère. End with a layer of Gruyère. Cook on HIGH for 5 minutes. Allow to rest 5 minutes before serving.

12

Serve the macaroni au gratin hot with the vinaigrette dressed salad.

CHINESE NOODLES

WITH

DUCK

SERVES : 4

PREPARATION TIME : 30 minutes
COOKING TIME : 18 minutes
PREHEATING : 12 minutes

A delicious Oriental-style dish. Duck breast is sliced and sautéed, then tossed with Chinese noodles in a sweet and sour sauce containing pineapple, honey, ginger and soy sauce. If you like, replace the pineapple with mango and add a few Chinese mushrooms.

INGREDIENTS

- ☐ ¼ pineapple
- ☐ 2 duck breasts (1lb 8oz)
- ☐ 1 zucchini
- ☐ 1 clove garlic (in method)
- ☐ 1-inch piece fresh ginger root
- ☐ 2 tbsps olive oil
- ☐ 2 tbsps butter
- ☐ 3 tbsps soy sauce
- ☐ 1 tbsp honey
- ☐ ½ cup chicken stock
- ☐ 14oz Chinese noodles
- ☐ Fresh coriander
- ☐ Salt and pepper

1 Remove the ends of the pineapple, peel and core.

3 Cut ¼ of the pineapple into even-sized pieces.

2 Remove the eyes of the pineapple with a vegetable peeler.

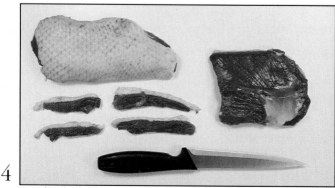

4 Cut the duck breast into even-sized slices.

5 Trim off the ends of the zucchini and cut into matchsticks. Discard the spongy core.

9 Place the duck and pineapple in a casserole, add the soy sauce, garlic, ginger, honey and stock. Stir and cook on HIGH for 4 minutes, stirring twice.

6 Steam the zucchini on HIGH for 2 minutes over salted water. Refresh in cold water after cooking.

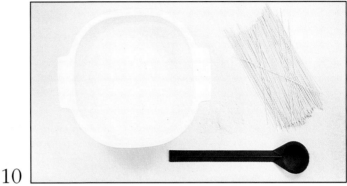

10 Cook the noodles in a casserole of salted water. Drain and rinse. Cook the noodles on HIGH 4 to 8 minutes, depending on the thickness of the noodles.

7 Peel the garlic, remove the central shoot and chop finely. Peel the fresh ginger root and cut 5 slices with a vegetable peeler. Chop finely.

11 Toss the noodles with the duck and vegetable preparation. Season with pepper and cook on HIGH for 2 minutes, stirring once.

8 Preheat the browning dish on HIGH for 8 minutes. Melt 1 tbsp olive oil with 1 tbsp butter, and sear half the duck slices. Cook on HIGH for 2 minutes. Repeat with the remaining duck.

12 Serve the noodles hot, garnished with fresh coriander.

SPAGHETTI BOLOGNESE

SERVES : 6

PREPARATION TIME : 50 minutes
COOKING TIME : 20 minutes

*The microwave speeds production of
home-made pasta with Bolognese sauce. If you
are limited for time, buy commercially prepared
spaghetti, and save even more time by
using ready-ground beef.*

INGREDIENTS

- [ ] 3½ cups flour
- [ ] 4 small eggs
- [ ] 6 tomatoes
- [ ] Bouquet garni (parsley, thyme, bay leaf)
- [ ] 2 cloves garlic (central shoot removed)
- [ ] 2 shallots
- [ ] 1 onion
- [ ] 2 carrots
- [ ] 1lb braising beef
- [ ] 2 tbsps heavy cream
- [ ] 3 tbsps butter
- [ ] Fresh basil
- [ ] Salt and pepper

1 Sift the flour into a bowl, add salt and the eggs. Mix well. Form into a ball and set aside for 10 minutes.

2 Quarter the ball of dough, flattening each quarter slightly before passing it through the pasta machine, or rolling out with a rolling pin.

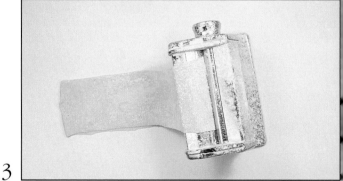

3 Roll out the pieces of dough gradually, flouring as you work, to obtain strips of pasta dough, to your preferred thickness.

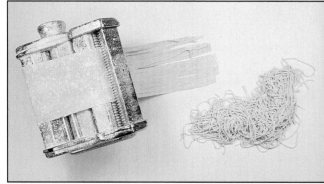

4 Pass the strips of pasta through a cutting machine, or roll up the strips and slice, to obtain spagetti. Flour lightly and set aside.

5

Core the tomatoes and plunge in boiling water for 1 minute.

6

Freshen in cold water and peel. Cut in half and squeeze out the seeds. Chop the flesh finely.

7

Prepare a bouquet garni, by tying together the parsley, thyme and bay leaf. Peel the garlic and shallot, and finely chop the shallot.

8

Peel the onion and carrot, and dice.

9

In a food processor, finely grind the meat.

10

In a casserole, combine the meat, tomato, bouquet garni, onion, garlic, shallot and carrot. Cook on HIGH for 15 minutes, stirring. Remove excess liquid. Add the cream, season and set aside.

11

Cook the pasta in boiling salted water, covered, on HIGH for 3 to 5 minutes. Drain and rinse. Cook on HIGH for 2 minutes in a casserole with the butter, salt and pepper.

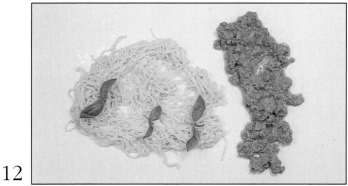

12

Reheat the tomato sauce on HIGH for 2 minutes. Serve with the hot spagetti, garnished with fresh basil.

VEGETABLE RISOTTO

SERVES : 6

PREPARATION TIME : 35 minutes
COOKING TIME : 34 minutes

This is an elegant side dish or vegetarian main course. Diced cooked vegetables are mixed with cooked rice, then baked with fresh herbs. The risotto is served with a tarragon flavored cream sauce.

INGREDIENTS

- □ ¹/₂ cup canned corn
- □ 6oz green beans
- □ 4 tbsps butter
- □ ¹/₂ bunch radishes
- □ 3 shallots
- □ ¹/₂ bunch chives
- □ 14oz rice
- □ 1 sprig tarragon
- □ ¹/₂ cup white wine
- □ 1 tbsp wine vinegar
- □ 1¹/₂ cups heavy cream
- □ Salt and pepper

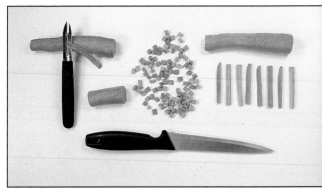

1 Peel the carrots, cut in slices, sticks, and then dice.

2 Trim the green beans, rinse. Drain the corn in a sieve.

3 Cook the green beans in salted water on HIGH for 8 to 10 minutes, stirring once. Cook the carrots with 4 tbsps water and 1 tbsp butter, covered, on HIGH for 4 minutes, stirring once.

4 Trim the radishes, wash and cut into rounds. Cook the radishes with 1 tsp butter, and 4 tbsps water, covered, on HIGH for 3 minutes, stirring once.

Peel the shallots, halve and finely chop. Chop the chives.

9 Add all the vegetables to the rice. Mix and cook, covered, on HIGH for 2 minutes, stirring once.

Bring a large dish of water to a boil and cook the rice on HIGH for 12 to 13 minutes, stirring twice.

10 In a small dish, reduce the shallots, white wine, vinegar and half the tarragon on HIGH for 3 minutes.

Drain the green beans when cooked and dice. Finely chop the tarragon sprig.

11 Add the heavy cream to this reduced sauce, and cook on HIGH for 2 minutes. Blend with a hand mixer. Season with salt and pepper.

Drain the rice when cooked, rinse and place in a dish with the remaining butter cut in small pieces, salt and pepper to taste and the chopped chives.

12 Arrange the rice in a circle on the plates (or in another attractive shape) and serve with the tarragon sauce. Garnish with the remaining tarragon.

HADDOCK

WITH

GREEN

PEPPERCORNS

SERVES : 6

PREPARATION TIME : 15 minutes
COOKING TIME : 20 minutes
MARINADE : 2 hours
PREHEATING : 12 minutes

*Smoked haddock is first soaked in milk to
remove the excess salt, then poached and served
with a creamy green peppercorn sauce. It is
accompanied with carrot pancakes flavored
with a dash of cinnamon.*

INGREDIENTS

- ☐ 2lbs haddock
- ☐ 4 cups milk
- ☐ 1lb 8oz carrots
- ☐ 3 eggs
- ☐ 2 tbsps crème fraiche, or heavy cream
- ☐ 2 tbsps olive oil
- ☐ 1½ tbsps butter
- ☐ 1 small sprig thyme
- ☐ ½ bay leaf
- ☐ 1 cup heavy cream
- ☐ 1 tsp green peppercorns
- ☐ Cinnamon
- ☐ Fresh dill
- ☐ Salt and pepper

1 Carefully remove the skin from the haddock.

2 Cut the haddock into large pieces and soak in 2 cups milk for 2 hours.

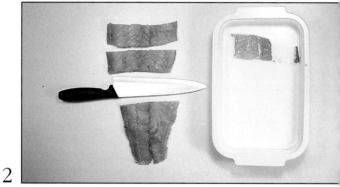

3 Peel the carrots and grate coarsely.

4 Mix the grated carrots with the eggs and beat well.

Add 2 tbsps heavy cream, season with salt and pepper and a little cinnamon.

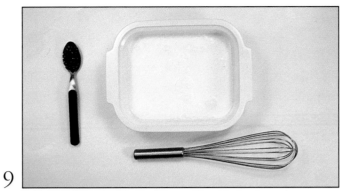

9 Combine ½ cup of the cooking milk with the 1 cup heavy cream and the green peppercorns. Cook at MEDIUM for 3 minutes.

Preheat the browning dish on HIGH for 8 minutes. Remove and add 1 tbsp oil and 2 tsps butter. Spread in ½ the carrot mixture.

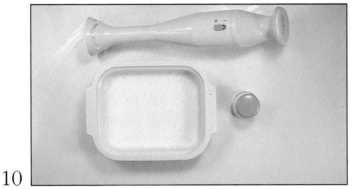

10 Beat the mixture with a hand mixer and set aside.

Cook the carrot mixture on HIGH for 3 minutes, turn with a large spatula, and cook on HIGH for another 2 minutes. Repeat the operation with the remaining carrot mixture. Set aside.

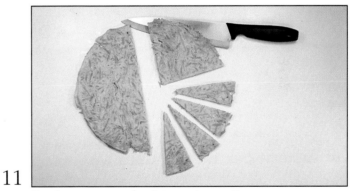

11 Cut the carrot pancakes into serving portions.

Drain the haddock and place in a casserole with the remaining milk, the thyme and bay leaf. Cook on HIGH for 6 minutes and drain on paper towels.

12 Reheat the haddock with the sauce, and the carrot pancakes. Serve garnished with the fresh dill.

SALT COD FRITTERS

WITH

PIQUANT SAUCE

SERVES : 4

PREPARATION TIME : 30 minutes
COOKING TIME : 14 minutes
SOAKING : 24 hours
PREHEATING : 8 minutes

Salt cod is first soaked, cooked and flaked, then dipped in a light batter. Rather than a being deep-fried, these fritters are cooked quickly like pancakes in the microwave on a buttered browning dish. They are served with a home-made mayonnaise flavored with tabasco and chopped gherkins.

INGREDIENTS

- ☐ 1lb salt cod, dried
- ☐ 1 clove garlic (in method)
- ☐ ½ bunch chives
- ☐ 4 tomatoes
- ☐ 2 eggs
- ☐ ½ cup milk
- ☐ 4 tbsps beer
- ☐ 1½ cups flour
- ☐ 1 egg yolk
- ☐ 1 tbsp mustard
- ☐ 1 cup oil
- ☐ 1 tbsp pickles, chopped
- ☐ 1 tbsp parsley, chopped
- ☐ 3 tbsps butter
- ☐ 5 tbsps vinaigrette dressing
- ☐ Tabasco
- ☐ Fresh chives
- ☐ Salt and pepper

1 Soak the salt cod in water for 24 hours, changing the water 2 or 3 times.

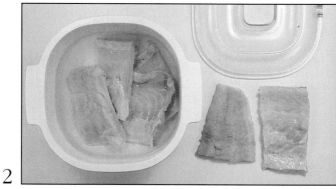

2 When the cod pieces are free of all salt, place them in a casserole, cover with water and cook, covered, on HIGH for 8 minutes. Drain on paper towels after cooking.

3 Remove the central shoot of the garlic and chop the rest finely. Core and quarter the tomatoes. Set aside.

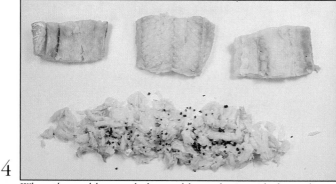

4 When the cod has cooled, crumble, and mix with the garlic and the chopped chives.

5 Prepare the batter : mix together the 2 egg yolks, the milk, the beer and add the flour gradually.

9 Prepare the mayonnaise : combine the 1 egg yolk with the mustard, salt and pepper, then beat in the oil gradually.

6 Beat the egg whites with a pinch of salt until stiff, using an hand-held electric blender.

10 Add a few drops tabasco, the pickles and the chopped parsley to the mayonnaise. Mix togother well.

7 Gently fold the egg whites into the batter, using a plastic spatula.

11 Preheat the browning dish on HIGH for 8 minutes. Add 1 tbsp butter and distribute little pancakes of batter on the tray. Cook each side on HIGH for 1 minute. Repeat twice more.

8 Add the crumbled cod to the batter. Mix thoroughly.

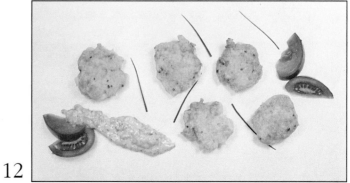

12 Drain the fritters on paper towels, and serve with the mayonnaise and the tomato quarters, seasoned with the vinaigrette. Garnish with the chopped chives.

SALMON TERRINE

WITH

SHELLFISH

SERVES : 6

PREPARATION TIME : 30 minutes
COOKING TIME : 21 minutes

*Fresh salmon is processed with eggs
and cream, then baked in a terrine with
mussels and cockles. The terrine can be eaten
hot as a main course or served cold with a salad
as a first course.*

INGREDIENTS

- [ ] 4 cups mussels
- [ ] ½ cup white wine
- [ ] 2 cups cockles
- [ ] 1lb fresh salmon
- [ ] 2 tbsps heavy cream
- [ ] 6 egg yolks
- [ ] ½ cup flour
- [ ] 4 egg whites
- [ ] 2 tsps melted butter
- [ ] ½ cup heavy cream
- [ ] ½ bunch chives
- [ ] Fresh chervil
- [ ] Salt and pepper

1 Scrub and debeard the mussels. Wash thoroughly in several changes of water to eliminate any sand.

2 Place the mussels in a large oven dish with 4 tbsps white wine and cook, covered, on HIGH for 5 minutes, stirring once.

3 After cooking, remove the mussels from the shells and strain the liquid. Set aside.

4 Thoroughly wash the cockles and proceed as for the mussels in step 2, cooking 3 or 4 minutes, and stirring after 2 minutes.

5 Remove the cockles from their shells, and strain the cooking liquid. Thoroughly rinse the cooked cockles to eliminate any sand.

9 Turn the salmon mixture into the terrine, cover the 2 ends of the dish with aluminum foil, cook at MEDIUM for 10 minutes. Remove the aluminum foil, cook on HIGH for another 3 minutes.

6 In a food processor, coarsely grind the skinned and boned salmon with the 2 tbsps cream. Season with salt and pepper.

10 Combine the reserved cooking liquids with the double cream and the chopped chives. Mix well and cook on HIGH for 3 minutes. Stir after removing from the oven.

In a bowl, mix together the ground salmon, the egg yolks, the flour and the well-drained shellfish, using a spatula.

11 After cooking the terrine, allow it to rest for 5 minutes, covered with aluminum foil. Unmold and slice with a serrated knife.

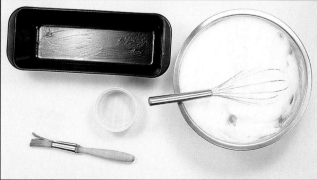

Beat the egg whites with a pinch of salt until stiff, and carefully incorporate into the salmon mixture. Butter a terrine pan.

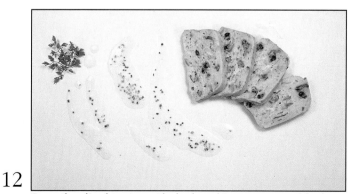

12 Serve the sliced terrine with the hot chive sauce, garnished with chervil. The terrine could also be accompanied with a mixed salad.

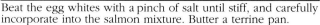

SEA TROUT

WITH

LEEKS

AND SHRIMP

SERVES : 6

PREPARATION TIME : 35 minutes
COOKING TIME : 10 minutes

This is a quick and delicious recipe for sea trout fillets breaded and sautéed with chopped fresh herbs. The fillets are served with a cream sauce containing finely chopped cooked leeks and shrimp.

INGREDIENTS

☐ 3 sea trout (12oz each)
☐ 3 leeks (1lb 4oz)
☐ 8oz shrimp
☐ 4 slices white bread
☐ 15 leaves fresh basil
☐ 1 sprig parsley
☐ 1 tbsp chopped chives
☐ 1 egg, beaten
☐ 1 cup heavy cream
☐ 2 tbsps butter
☐ Nutmeg
☐ Fresh dill
☐ Salt and pepper

1 Prepare the trout : cut off the fins ; scale ; gut and rinse.

2 Remove the trout fillets, working along the spine with a flexible knife.

3 Quarter the leeks. Wash thoroughly and chop finely.

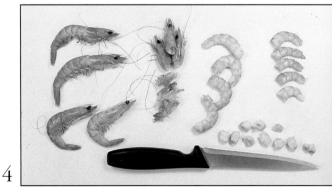

4 Shell the shrimp and devein. Cut into small pieces.

Remove the crusts from the bread and grind in a food processor.

9

Combine the chopped leek with the cream, salt, pepper and grated nutmeg, and cook on HIGH for 7 minutes, stirring 2 or 3 times. Add the shrimp after 4 minutes.

Trim the basil, parsley and chives. Chop finely.

10

Preheat the browning dish on HIGH 8 minutes. Add 1 tbsp butter, sear half the breaded trout fillets. Cook on HIGH 1¹/₂ minute, turning after 1 minute. Repeat with the remaining trout fillets.

Season the fish fillets and coat with the beaten egg. Sprinkle with the fresh herbs.

11

As soon as the fillets are cooked, drain on paper towels.

Coat the trout fillets with the bread crumbs.

12

Serve the trout with the leek and shrimp sauce, and garnished with fresh dill.

TURBOT

WITH

TOMATO

HOLLANDAISE

SERVES : 4

PREPARATION TIME : 25 minutes
COOKING TIME : 20 minutes

*This dish uses turbot, but any whitefish fillet
is suitable. It is accompanied with fresh wax
beans and served in a tomato hollandaise
sauce. The hollandaise is a delicate operation
in the microwave and needs close attention.*

INGREDIENTS

- [ ] 1 turbot (2lbs 8oz)
- [ ] 14oz fresh wax beans
- [ ] ½ lemon
- [ ] 6oz butter
- [ ] 3 egg yolks
- [ ] 1 tsp tomato paste
- [ ] 1 clovè garlic (central shoot removed)
- [ ] 2 sprigs parsley
- [ ] 2 tbsps butter
- [ ] Fresh dill
- [ ] Salt and pepper

1   Remove the turbot fillets.

2   Remove the skin.

3   String the beans, and trim the ends.

4   Cover the beans with salted water in a casserole. Cook, covered, on HIGH for 10 to 12 minutes stirring twice. After cooking, drain and freshen the beans. Set aside.

5 Prepare the hollandaise sauce : cook the juice of ¹/₂ lemon with salt and pepper on HIGH for 1 minute. Melt the (amount) butter separately on HIGH for 2 minutes.

9 Finely chop the garlic and parsley.

6 After removing the lemon from the oven, add 1 tbsp cold water, add the egg yolks and beat rapidly.

10 Place the wax beans in a casserole with the 2 tbsps butter, the parsley and garlic. Cook, covered, on HIGH for 3 minutes, stirring.

7 Gradually add the tepid melted butter to the egg yolks, beating constantly. Cook on HIGH for 10 seconds. Beat. Cook on HIGH for 15 seconds. Beat. Cook another 10 seconds. Beat again.

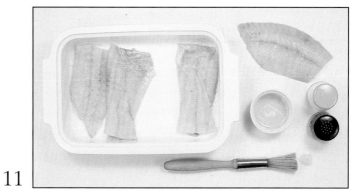

11 Cook the fish fillets, seasoned with salt and pepper, on a lightly buttered plate on HIGH for 3 minutes. Turn once during cooking.

8 Add the tomato paste to the hollandaise sauce and beat well.

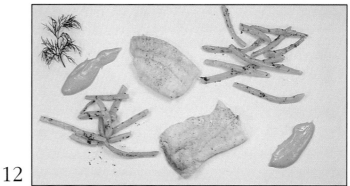

12 Serve the turbot fillets with the hollandaise sauce and the wax beans, and garnished with the fresh dill.

SALMON
À LA BASQUAISE

SERVES : 6

PREPARATION TIME : 40 minutes
COOKING TIME : 12 minutes
PREHEATING : 32 minutes

Basque-style vegetables of sautéed onions, bell peppers and zucchini accompany quickly seared and baked fresh salmon. This is a colorful and low-calorie main course. The recipe may be made with other types of fish.

INGREDIENTS

- [ ] 1 salmon (2lbs 8oz)
- [ ] 2 green peppers
- [ ] 2 red peppers
- [ ] 2 onions
- [ ] 2 cloves garlic (central shoot removed)
- [ ] Bouquet garni (parsley, thyme, bay leaf)
- [ ] 1 hot pepper
- [ ] 1 zucchini
- [ ] 1 tbsp butter
- [ ] Fresh basil
- [ ] Salt and pepper

1 Remove the salmon fillets, discarding all the bones.

2 Remove the skin. Slice the fillets into serving portions.

3 Cut open the bell peppers, remove the pith and seeds, then slice the peppers everly.

4 Peel the garlic and onion, and finely chop.

5

Prepare the bouquet garni, by tying together the parsley, thyme and bay leaf. Cut the hot pepper in half and eliminate the seeds. Use only ⅛ of the pepper.

6

Trim the ends of the zucchini and slice.

7

Preheat the browning dish 8 minutes. Remove and add 1 tbsp olive oil and half the bell peppers. Cook on HIGH for 2 minutes. Repeat with the remaining bell peppers and the hot pepper.

8

Wipe the browning dish, then preheat on HIGH for 4 minutes. Remove and add 1 tbsp olive oil. Add the onions and cook on HIGH for 2 minutes. Repeat the operation with the zucchini.

9

Add the zucchini and onion, garlic and bouquet garni to a casserole containing the bell peppers. Cook, covered, on HIGH for 10 minutes, stirring twice. Allow to rest 10 minutes. Season.

10

Preheat the browning dish on HIGH for 8 minutes. Melt ½ tbsp olive oil with the butter. Sear the seasoned salmon fillets.

11

Cook the salmon on HIGH 1 minute each side. Cook in batches, if necessary. Once cooked, drain on paper towels.

12

Serve the salmon fillets accompanied with the hot vegetables, and garnished with fresh basil.

LOBSTER À LA NAGE

SERVES : 4

PREPARATION TIME : 40 minutes
COOKING TIME : 30 minutes

Here is a truly elegant lobster dish. It is cooked in an aromatic court bouillon then served "swimming" in a rich cream sauce made with fish stock and julienne vegetables flavored with aniseed.

INGREDIENTS

- ☐ ¹/₂ leek, washed
- ☐ 1 sprig thyme
- ☐ 1 bay leaf
- ☐ 1 onion
- ☐ 2 lobsters (1lb each)
- ☐ 2 carrots
- ☐ 1 zucchini
- ☐ ¹/₄ cucumber
- ☐ 2 cups fish stock
- ☐ ¹/₂ tsp aniseed
- ☐ ¹/₂ cup heavy cream
- ☐ Fresh dill
- ☐ Salt and pepper

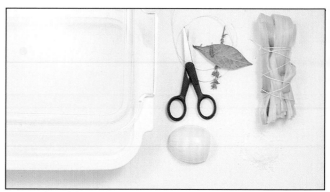

1 Tie up the ¹/₂ leek, the thyme and the bay leaf. Peel the onion, cut it in half. In a dish of water, place ¹/₂ the onion, the leek bundle, cook with a pinch of salt on HIGH for 12 minutes.

2 Prepare the lobsters : remove the heads (save for another recipe, such as lobster bisque), reserve the claws and the legs. Open the bodies with a pair of scissors.

3 Remove the vegetables from the stock, add the bodies, legs and claws of the lobsters and cook, covered, on HIGH for 7 minutes.

4 Meanwhile, prepare the carrots and zucchini : cut into thin strips, then into julienne with a chopping knife. Discard the sporgy core of the zucchini.

5

Peel the cucumber, then trim into a cylinder shape. Cut bands of flesh from around the central core of seeds. Cut these bands into fine julienne.

9
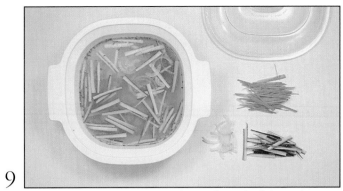
Prepare the sauce : in a casserole combine the fish stock, julienne of carrot, and zucchini and the chopped onion ; then add the aniseed. Cook on HIGH for 7 minutes.

6

Finely chop the second half of onion and reserve with the vegetable julienne.

10

Add the heavy cream, and season with salt and pepper.

7

After cooking, plunge the lobster pieces in cold water, then shell. Break open the claws with the aid of the flat edge of knife or nutcrackers and remove the meat..

11

Place the lobster pieces and the cucumber in the sauce, and reheat on HIGH for 2 minutes.

8

Cut the lobster meat into even-sized pieces.

12

Serve hot, garnished with the fresh dill.

COD

WITH

WATERCRESS
SAUCE

SERVES : 4

PREPARATION TIME : 35 minutes
COOKING TIME : 15 minutes
PREHEATING : 8 minutes

*A relatively quick and easy fish dish,
in which fresh cod is quickly sautéed,
accompanied with boiled potatoes, and served
in a sauce of puréed watercress and cream. You
will need a hand-held electric blender, or
food processor, for this dish.*

INGREDIENTS

☐ 2lbs cod
☐ 1 bunch watercress
☐ 1lb 12oz potatoes
☐ 1 tbsp butter
☐ 4 tbsps milk
☐ ³/₄ cup heavy cream
☐ Nutmeg
☐ Fresh dill
☐ Salt and pepper

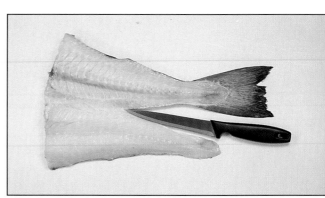

1 Fillet the cod, eliminating all the bones.

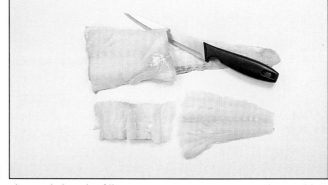

2 Skin and slice the fillets into serving portions. Dry thoroughly with paper towels or a kitchen towel.

3 Remove the watercress leaves. Wash and trim.

4 Cook the watercress in 2 tbsps water, covered, on HIGH for 4 minutes, stirring once.

5 After cooking, drain, rinse and squeeze out any excess water. Chop finely.

9 Preheat the browning dish on HIGH for 8 minutes. Season the fish with salt and pepper. Remove the browning dish and add the butter.

6 Peel the potatoes, slice lengthwise, and cover with water to prevent discoloration.

10 Sear the fish portions. Cook on HIGH 1 minute on one side and 30 seconds on the other side. Allow to rest 5 minutes after cooking, covered with aluminum foil.

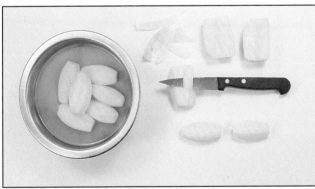

7 Trim the potatoes with a small knife into uniform oblong shapes.

11 Combine the watercress, milk and cream. Cook on HIGH for 3 minutes, then blend with a hand mixer to obtain a puree. Season to taste with salt, pepper and nutmeg.

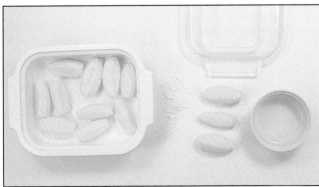

8 Cook the potatoes in salted water to cover on HIGH for 6 to 8 minutes. Stir once during cooking.

12 Serve the fish with the potatoes, and the watercress sauce, garnished with the fresh dill.

VEGETABLE

AND

PRAWN GALETTES

SERVES : 4

PREPARATION TIME : 45 minutes
COOKING TIME : 11 minutes
PREHEATING : 16 minutes

*These little vegetable pancakes
consist of grated potato, carrot or courgette
combined with finely chopped prawns, egg,
cream and chopped chives. They are served
with a curry flavoured mayonnaise containing
chopped apple. This dish makes an original
first course or a light lunch dish.*

VEGETABLE AND SHRIMP GALETTES

INGREDIENTS

- ☐ 1lb 12oz jumbo or large shrimp
- ☐ 3 carrots (8oz)
- ☐ 1 zucchini (8oz)
- ☐ 4 potatoes (8oz)
- ☐ 3 tbsps heavy cream
- ☐ ½ bunch chives, chopped
- ☐ 3 eggs
- ☐ 3 tbsps butter
- ☐ 2 tbsps flour
- ☐ 1 egg yolk
- ☐ 1 tsp mustard
- ☐ 1 tsp curry powder
- ☐ 1 cup oil
- ☐ ¼ apple
- ☐ Fresh chervil
- ☐ Salt and pepper

1 Shell the shrimp, then cut into small pieces. The heads may be set aside for anther recipe.

2 Peel and coarsely grate the carrots.

3 Peel and grate the zucchini, discarding the spongy core.

4 Peel the potatoes and cover in water to prevent discoloration. Then grate.

5 Preheat the browning dish on HIGH for 8 minutes. Meanwhile combine the grated potatoes with 1 tbsp heavy cream, $\frac{1}{3}$ the shrimp, $\frac{1}{3}$ the chopped chives and an egg. Season.

6 In the browning dish, melt 1 tbsp butter and shape 4 galettes out of the potato mixture. Cook on HIGH for 5 minutes, turning after 2 minutes. Drain the galettes on paper towels.

7 Preheat the browning dish on HIGH for 4 minutes. Meanwhile combine the grated zucchini with 1 tbsp flour, 1 egg, $\frac{1}{3}$ of the shrimp, chopped chives and 1 tbsp heavy cream. Season.

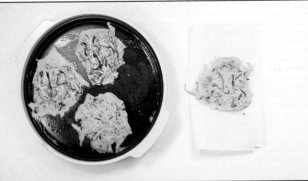

8 Melt 1 tbsp butter in the browning dish and shape 4 galettes out of the zucchini mixture. Cook on HIGH for 3 minutes, turning after 2 minutes. Drain on paper towels.

9 Preheat the browning dish another 4 minutes. Combine the grated carrots with the remaining chopped chives, heavy cream, shrimp, flour, and egg, and season with salt and pepper.

10 Melt 1 tbsp butter in the dish and form 4 carrot galettes. Cook on HIGH for 3 minutes, turning after 2 minutes.

11 Make the mayonnaise : in a bowl mix together the egg yolk, the mustard, salt, pepper, and the curry powder and gradually beat in the oil. Cut the $\frac{1}{4}$ apple into dice.

12 Add the diced apple to the mayonnaise. Serve the shrimp and vegetable galettes with the mayonnaise. The galettes may be served hot or at room temperature. Garnish with the chervil.

FILLET of SOLE

WITH

ASPARAGUS

SERVES : 4

PREPARATION TIME : 50 minutes
COOKING TIME : 21 minutes

This is an elegant and tasty dish, which is easy to prepare. Fillets of sole are rolled around a ground fish stuffing then steamed in the microwave. They are accompanied with fresh asparagus and served in a saffron-flavored cream sauce.

INGREDIENTS

- ☐ 2 sole fillets
- ☐ 10oz whitefish fillets
- ☐ 1 shallot, finely chopped
- ☐ 1 small egg
- ☐ 1 tbsp heavy cream
- ☐ Pinch saffron
- ☐ 1lb asparagus
- ☐ ½ red pepper (garnish)
- ☐ ¼ bunch chives
- ☐ ⅓ cup fish stock
- ☐ 1 cup heavy cream
- ☐ Salt and pepper

1 Pull the skins off the sole with the help of a small kitchen towel (or have the sole prepared by the fishmonger).

2 Remove the fillets, by working along the central bone, using a sharp knife.

3 Prepare the stuffing : combine the whitefish fillets, cut in pieces, with the chopped shallot, egg, salt and pepper in a food processor.

4 Place the stuffing in a bowl, add 1 tbsp cream and a small pinch of saffron. Mix together well with a spatula.

5

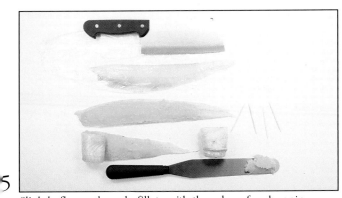

Slightly flatten the sole fillets with the edge of a chopping knife, first covering them with plastic wrap. Spread on the stuffing and roll up the fillets. Secure the rolls with toothpicks.

6

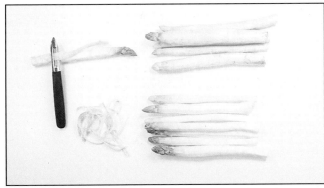

Peel the asparagus stalks up to the tips and wash well.

7

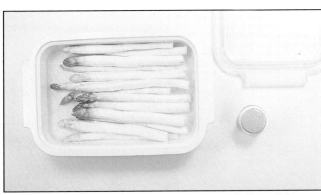

Cook the asparagus with water to cover in a shallow dish, covered, on HIGH for 10 minutes. Stir once. Drain and set aside.

8

Chop the ½ red pepper into small dice. Finely chop the chives.

9

Steam the sole fillets on HIGH, covered, for 7 minutes. Allow to rest, covered, for 5 minutes.

10

Prepare the sauce : bring the fish stock and cream to a boil (on HIGH for approximately 4 minutes). Add a small pinch of saffron, salt and pepper. Mix well and set aside.

11

Cut some of the sole fillets into round slices using a serrated knife, leaving the others whole.

12

Serve the sole fillets with the reheated asparagus, and the saffron sauce, and garnished with the chopped pepper and chives.

GLAZED CHICKEN

WITH

CHINESE VEGETABLES

SERVES : 6

PREPARATION TIME : 40 minutes
COOKING TIME : 34 minutes
PREHEATING : 12 minutes

This is an Oriental-inspired dish containing chicken and Chinese vegetables of bamboo shoots, bean sprouts and diced black mushrooms. It is cooked in a sauce flavored with garlic, ginger and honey.

INGREDIENTS

☐ 10g dried black Chinese mushrooms
☐ 6oz bamboo shoots
☐ 2 cloves garlic (central shoot removed)
☐ 1-inch piece fresh ginger root
☐ 1 large onion
☐ 1 medium chicken
☐ 1 red pepper
☐ 1 green pepper
☐ 4 tbsps butter
☐ 4 tbsps soy sauce
☐ 2 tbsps honey
☐ ½ cup chicken stock
☐ 12oz fresh bean sprouts
☐ Fresh chervil
☐ 1 tsp cornstarch (optional)
☐ Salt and pepper

1 Soak the black Chinese mushrooms in water, then blanch, covered, on HIGH for 4 minutes. Drain and slice finely.

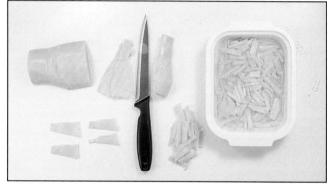

2 Cut the bamboo shoots into fine julienne. Blanch on HIGH for 4 minutes, covered with water.

3 Peel the garlic and ginger root, and cut 2 slices of ginger. Finely chop the garlic and ginger. Chop the onion.

4 Quarter the chicken, then chop each quarter into 4 pieces.

5 Halve the bell peppers, remove the pith and seeds and slice the flesh finely.

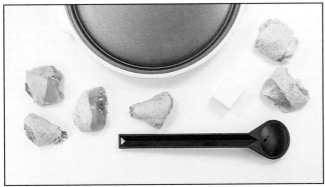

6 Preheat the browning dish on HIGH for 8 minutes. Add 1½ tbsps butter and sauté the chicken pieces. Cook on HIGH for 2 minutes. Set aside.

7 Reheat the browning dish on HIGH for 4 minutes. Sauté the onion, garlic and ginger in 2 tsps butter, and cook on HIGH for 10 minutes.

8 Transfer the vegetables into a casserole and add the chicken, soy sauce, and honey, and season with salt and pepper.

9 Add the drained mushrooms, and bamboo shoots. Add the stock and bell peppers. Cover and cook on HIGH for 15 minutes. Allow to rest for 10 minutes after cooking.

10 Wash and trim the bean sprouts and dry on a kitchen towel.

11 Steam the bean sprouts on HIGH in salted water for 4 minutes. Drain. Reheat the bean sprouts with the remaining butter on HIGH for 2 minutes, stirring once.

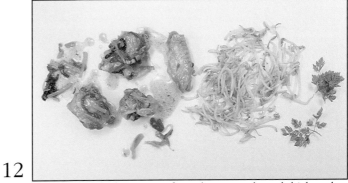

12 Remove the chicken pieces from the casserole and thicken the sauce with the cornstarch dissolved in a little water. Cook on HIGH for 2 minutes. Add the chicken pieces and serve.

STUFFED CHICKEN ROLLS

IN

TOMATO SAUCE

SERVES : 6

PREPARATION TIME : 45 minutes
COOKING TIME : 25 minutes

Boned chicken legs are rolled with garlic and fresh basil, then cooked in a fresh tomato sauce. Accompany with cooked macaroni. If time is short you need not bone the chicken first.

STUFFED CHICKEN ROLLS IN TOMATO SAUCE

INGREDIENTS

- ☐ 6 chicken thighs
- ☐ 3 cloves garlic (central shoot removed)
- ☐ 15 fresh basil leaves
- ☐ 6 tomatoes
- ☐ Bouquet garni (parsley, 5 basil leaves, bay leaf)
- ☐ 1/2 cup white wine
- ☐ 1lb 6oz macaroni or other pasta
- ☐ 4 tbsps butter
- ☐ Fresh basil
- ☐ Salt and pepper

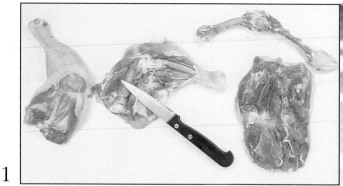

1 Bone the chicken thighs with a small knife, by cutting along the bone. Discard the bones.

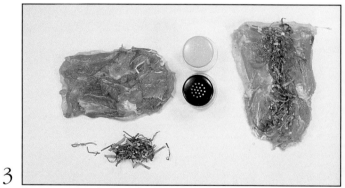

2 Finely chop the garlic and the 15 basil leaves.

3 Cut open the chicken thighs, season with salt and pepper, and dwide half of the garlic/basil mixture evenly between them. Reserve the remaining mixture for the pasta.

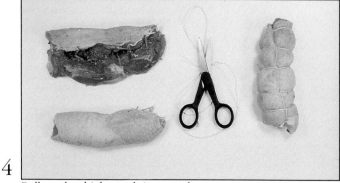

4 Roll up the thighs, and tie securely.

5

Bring to a boil a pot of water and plunge in the tomatoes which have been cored. Cover and allow to rest 1 minute outside the oven.

6

Drain the tomatoes and plunge in cold water. Peel and remove the seeds, then chop the flesh finely to obtain a tomato pulp.

7

Make the bouquet garni, by tying together the parsley, basil and bay leaf.

8

Place the tomato pulp, the white wine, the bouquet garni and the chicken rolls in a dish. Cover and cook on HIGH for 15 minutes. Allow to rest covered 10 minutes, after cooking.

9

Bring to a boil a large pot of salted water, and cook the pasta on HIGH for 5 to 10 minutes.

10

After cooking, drain the pasta, rinse and place in a dish with the remaining garlic/basil mixture, and the butter, salt and pepper. Reheat on HIGH for 3 minutes.

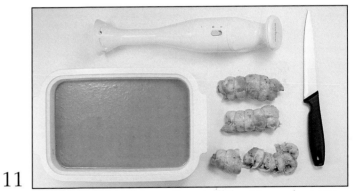

11

After cooking the chicken rolls, cut off the string and cut into even rounds. Blend the tomato sauce with a hand mixer.

12

Serve the chicken rolls with the pasta and the tomato sauce. Garnish with the remaining fresh basil.

STUFFED CHICKEN BREAST

WITH

HERB VINAIGRETTE

SERVES : 4

PREPARATION TIME : 40 minutes
COOKING TIME : 10 minutes
CHILLING : 30 minutes

This is an elegant chicken dish to serve as a cold lunch or supper dish. Chicken breasts are rolled around a ground chicken and herb stuffing. They are baked and chilled, and acompanied with a salad of julienne vegetables flavored with fresh herbs.

INGREDIENTS

☐ 1 clove garlic (central shoot removed)
☐ 15 fresh basil leaves
☐ 5 chicken breasts
☐ 1 egg
☐ 1 tbsp heavy cream
☐ 2 tsps butter
☐ 2 carrots
☐ 2 stalks celery
☐ 1 cooked beet
☐ ¼ bunch fresh chervil
☐ ½ bunch chives
☐ 1 sprig tarragon
☐ 1½ tbsps vinegar
☐ 3 tbsps olive oil
☐ Fresh basil
☐ Salt and pepper

1 Chop the garlic and the 15 basil leaves finely.

2 Finely grind 1 chicken breast with the egg in a food processor.

3 Transfer the ground chicken to a bowl, add the cream, and half the basil and garlic mixture. Mix well and set aside in the refrigerator.

4 Slice the remaining chicken breasts lengthwise, without cutting them in two completely.

5 Using a spatula, spread the ground chicken over the chicken breasts and fold them up.

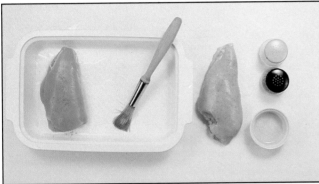

6 Place the stuffed chicken breasts in a large, buttered baking dish, season with salt and pepper and cook covered on HIGH for 10 minutes.

7 Peel the carrots and celery stalks, and cut first into strips, then into fine julienne.

8 Peel the cooked beet, finely slice and cut into julienne.

9 Trim the fresh chervil, chives, and tarragon. Chop finely.

10 Prepare the vinaigrette dressing : combine the vinegar, salt and pepper, and the remaining garlic and chopped basil. Thicken by beating in the olive oil.

11 As soon as the chicken has cooled, cut each breast crosswise into thin slices.

12 Serve the chicken accompanied with the julienne vegetables, and seasoned with the herb vinaigrette. Garnish with the remaining fresh basil.

CHICKEN TORTILLAS

SERVES : 6

PREPARATION TIME : 30 minutes
COOKING TIME : 25 minutes

Boned chicken meat is mixed with chopped tomato, chickpeas and corn, and flavored with garlic and hot chili. This is used to stuff corn tortillas and served with two sour cream sauces, one flavored with chopped chives and the other with ketchup. Serve cold accompanied with a julienne salad for a unique lunch or supper dish

INGREDIENTS

- ☐ 1 carrot
- ☐ ½ leek
- ☐ 1 onion
- ☐ 1 clove
- ☐ 3 chicken thighs
- ☐ 1 small hot pepper
- ☐ 2 tomatoes
- ☐ ½ cup chickpeas, cooked
- ☐ 1 lettuce
- ☐ 1½ cups sour cream
- ☐ 2 tbsps chives, chopped
- ☐ 3 tbsps ketchup
- ☐ 6 tortillas
- ☐ Tabasco
- ☐ Fresh basil
- ☐ Salt and pepper

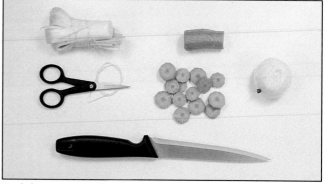

1 Peel the carrot, and cut in rounds. Quarter the leek, wash and tie up. Peel the onion and stud with the clove.

2 Cook the chicken thighs with the carrot, onion and leek in salted water to cover, on HIGH for 15 minutes.

3 Cut the hot pepper in half, and extract the seeds. Cut the tomato in half, squeeze out the seeds and the juice, then finely chop the flesh.

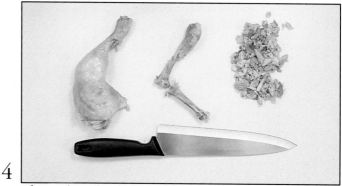

4 After cooking the chicken thighs, drain them and allow to cool. Bone the thighs and shred or chop the meat coarsely. Reserve 4 tbsps of the stock.

5

Rinse and dry the chick peas. Place in a casserole with the chicken and the corn.

6

Add the garlic, hot pepper, and the reserved stock and cook, covered, on HIGH for 10 minutes. Stir after 5 minutes and remove the cover. Season with salt and pepper and allow to cool.

7

Wash and trim the lettuce, and then shred finely.

8

Mix together in a bowl the sour cream, the chives, a few drops tabasco, and salt and pepper, and divide the sauce in half.

9

To the second half of the sour cream mixture, add the ketchup, stir in thouroughly and reserve.

10

Fill each tortilla with the drained cold chicken mixture, and fold the tortilla over into a half-moon shape.

11

Stand the filled tortillas upright in a casserole, and serve promptly, so the tortillas do not become soggy.

12

Serve the chicken tortillas cold, accompanied with the lettuce and the 2 sauces. Garnish with the fresh basil.

GAME HENS

WITH

CARAMELIZED CARROTS

SERVES : 4

PREPARATION TIME : 40 minutes
COOKING TIME : 19 minutes (with resting time)
PREHEATING : 20 minutes

*Boned game hens are glazed with a honey
sauce and accompanied with caramelized
onions and carrots. If time is short, the game
hens need not be boned.*

INGREDIENTS

- [ ] 2 game hens
- [ ] 3 tbsps honey
- [ ] 1 tbsp Worcestershire sauce
- [ ] 1 sprig fresh tarragon
- [ ] 1 onion
- [ ] 1lb 6oz carrots
- [ ] 1 tbsp olive oil
- [ ] 2 tbsps butter + a little for searing
- [ ] Fresh chervil
- [ ] Salt and pepper

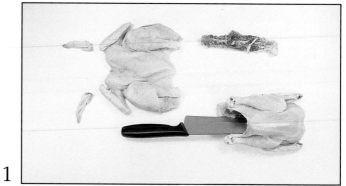

1 Cut the game hens in half.

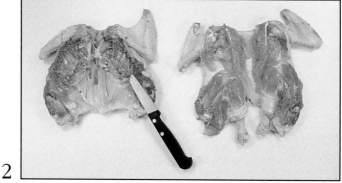

2 Bone completely, if desired.

3 In a bowl, mix together 2 tbsps of the honey, the Worcestershire sauce, and chopped tarragon, and season with salt and pepper.

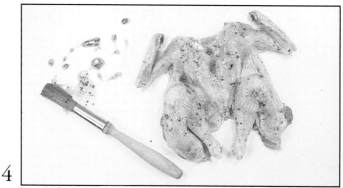

4 Brush the game hens inside and out with this sauce.

GAME HENS WITH CARAMELIZED CARROTS

5
Peel the onion. Cut in half, then chop finely.

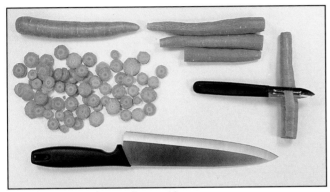

6
Peel the carrots, slice and set aside.

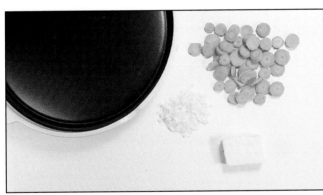

7
Preheat the browning dish on HIGH for 8 minutes. Remove, and sauté half of the carrots and onion in 1 tbsp butter.

8
Return the browning dish to the oven and cook on HIGH for 2 minutes, stirring occasionally. Season. Repeat with the remaining carrots and onion (preheat the browning dish 4 minutes).

9
Transfer the carrots to a casserole. Add the remaining 1 tbsp honey, cover and cook on HIGH for 4 minutes, stirring twice.

10
Reheat the browning dish on HIGH for 8 minutes. Remove and melt a little butter. Sear the game hens, skin side down.

11
Cook the game hens on HIGH for 3 minutes each side. Remove from the oven and allow to rest 5 minutes, covered with aluminium foil, before serving.

12
Serve the game hens quartered, accompanied with the caramelized carrots, and garnished with the fresh chervil.

CHICKEN

IN

THE POT

SERVES : 6

PREPARATION TIME : 25 minutes
COOKING TIME : 40 minutes

≈ ☙ ❧ ≈

This is a traditional French dish for which every family has their own recipe. In this one, the boiled chicken and vegetables are flavored with ginger and clovs to make it original.

INGREDIENTS

- ☐ 1 large stewing chicken
- ☐ 3 carrots
- ☐ 2 stalks celery
- ☐ 1 onion
- ☐ 1 clove garlic (central shoot removed)
- ☐ Bouquet garni (parsley, thyme, bay leaf)
- ☐ 2 slices fresh ginger root
- ☐ 2 large turnips
- ☐ 2 potatoes
- ☐ 1 egg yolk
- ☐ 1 tsp mustard
- ☐ ¾ cup oil
- ☐ Fresh chives and tarragon
- ☐ Salt and pepper

1 Tie up the chicken with kitchen string.

2 Peel the carrots and cut in half. Quarter the leek, wash and tie it up with kitchen string.

3 Peel the celery and cut in several pieces. Peel the onion and stud with the clove. Set aside.

4 Prepare the bouquet garni, by tying together the parsley, thyme and bay leaf. Peel a piece of ginger root and cut two slices.

5 Place the chicken in a large casserole of hot water, add salt and the bouquet garni. Cook, covered, on HIGH for 5 minutes, turning once during cooking.

9 Make a mayonnaise : in a bowl, mix together the egg yolk, mustard, and 2 tbsps each chopped chives and tarragon, and season with salt and pepper.

6 Peel the turnips and quarter. Peel the potatoes and quarter. Cover both with water.

10 Gradually add the oil, beating continuously, until a mayonnaise forms. Set aside.

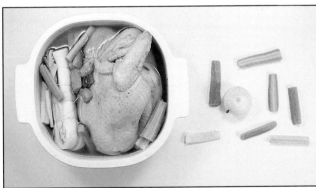

7 Remove the casserole from the oven, skim the surface, if necessary. Add the leek, carrot, celery and onion.

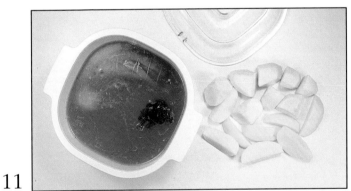

11 After cooking the chicken, remove it and cook the drained potatoes and the turnips in the stock, covered, on HIGH for 15 minutes.

8 Add the 2 ginger slices and pepper. Cover and cook on HIGH for 10 minutes, then on MEDIUM for 10 minutes. After cooking, allow to rest for 5 minutes, still covered.

12 Cut the chicken into serving portions and serve accompanied with the vegetables, the mayonnaise and the stock, if desired. Garnish with additional chopped chives and tarragon.

CHICKEN CURRY

SERVES : 6

PREPARATION TIME : 25 minutes
COOKING TIME : 36 minutes
PREHEATING : 12 minutes

Boned chicken is quickly seared and then cooked with garlic, onion, tomato and curry powder. Pineapple, fresh or canned, is added to give a little sweetness to the dish. Serve over buttered rice for an easy main course.

INGREDIENTS

- ☐ 2 onions
- ☐ 2 cloves garlic (central shoot removed)
- ☐ 3 tomatoes
- ☐ 1 large chicken
- ☐ 6 slices pineapple
- ☐ 2 tbsps oil
- ☐ 1 tbsp flour
- ☐ 3 tsps curry powder
- ☐ Bouquet garni (parsley, thyme, bay leaf)
- ☐ 12oz rice
- ☐ 3½ tbsps butter
- ☐ Fresh chervil
- ☐ Salt and pepper

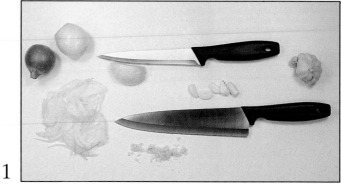

1 Peel the onion and chop finely. Finely chop the garlic.

2 Boil a casserole of water on HIGH, plunge in the cored tomatoes, cover and leave for 1 minute outside the oven.

3 Plunge the tomatoes into cold water, peel and halve. Remove the seeds, then chop the flesh finely.

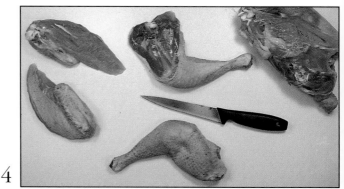

4 Cut up the chicken. Remove the thighs and breasts.

5 Cut the chicken meat into pieces, removing the bones. Peel the pineapple, remove the eyes and cut the 6 slices into even-sized chunks.

6 Preheat the browning dish on HIGH for 8 minutes, and have ready the chicken, butter and oil.

7 Melt 1 tbsp oil and 1 tsp butter on the browning dish, sauté half the chicken pieces, then cook on HIGH for 3 minutes, stirring twice. Repeat with the rest of the chicken. Season.

8 After cooking, combine the chicken and pineapple in a casserole.

9 Add the onions and 1 tbsp flour, mix well and cook on HIGH for 1 minute. Remove from the oven and stir.

10 Add the garlic, curry powder, bouquet garni tomato and 1/2 cup water. Cover and cook on HIGH for 10 minutes, stirring twice. After cooking, allow to rest 5 minutes, still covered.

11 Cook the rice in boiling salted water on HIGH, for 12 to 13 minutes, stirring twice. After cooking, drain the rice, rinse, add the remaining butter and reheat for 1 minute in a serving dish.

12 Serve the chicken curry over the rice, garnished with the fresh chervil.

BREAST OF DUCK

WITH

GRAPEFRUIT

SERVES :

PREPARATION TIME : 40 minutes
COOKING TIME : 20 minutes
MARINADE : 1 hour

*Duck breasts are brushed with a mixture
of grapefruit juice, honey, soy sauce and
cinnamon, then allowed to marinate to absorb
all the fragrant flavors. They are quickly seared,
then baked in the microwave, and served with
boiled potatoes and fresh grapefruit segments.*

INGREDIENTS

- [ ] 2¹/₂ grapefruit
- [ ] 2 tbsps honey
- [ ] 1 tbsp soy sauce
- [ ] ¹/₄ tsp cinnamon
- [ ] 3 duck breasts (1lb 6oz)
- [ ] 1 clove garlic (central shoot removed)
- [ ] 3 sprigs parsley
- [ ] 1lb 6oz boiling potatoes
- [ ] 5oz butter
- [ ] 1 tbsp wine vinegar
- [ ] ¹/₂ chicken stock
- [ ] 1 tsp cornstarch
- [ ] Fresh basil
- [ ] Salt and pepper

1 Peel 2 of the grapefruit down to the flesh, using a small, sharp knife. Separate into segments.

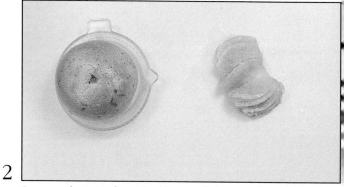

2 Squeeze the juice from the ¹/₂ grapefruit, as well as the peel (since some flesh still adheres to the peel), in order to extract the maximum amount of juice.

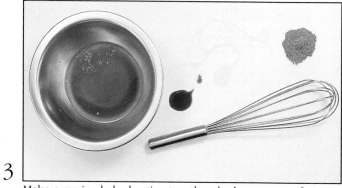

3 Make a marinade by beating together the honey, grapefruit juice, soy sauce and cinnamon.

4 Lightly score the skin of the duck breasts with the point of a small knife. Place above in the marinade and allow to marinate for 1 hour in the refrigerator.

5 Finely chop the garlic. Wash and dry the parsley, then finely chop.

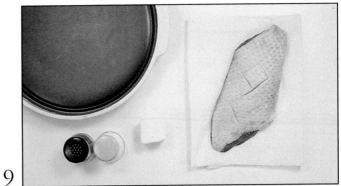

9 Preheat the browning dish on HIGH for 8 minutes. Add 1½ tbsps butter and sauté the duck breasts, season. Cook them on HIGH for 4 to 5 minutes, turning after 2 minutes.

6 Peel the potatoes (if they are new potatoes, this may not be necessary, but prick with a fork). Reserve in water to prevent discoloration.

10 Once the duck is cooked, remove and allow to rest on a sheet of aluminum foil for 5 minutes.

7 Cook the potatoes, covered, in a long baking dish with ½ cup water on HIGH for 5 to 7 minutes (according to the size of the potatoes), and stir once after 3 minutes.

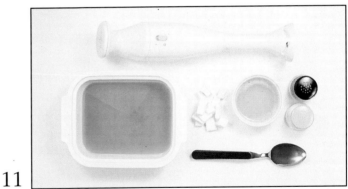

11 In a dish, cook the vinegar, stock, marinade on HIGH 5 minutes. Thicken the sauce with the cornstarch dissolved in a little water. Bring the sauce to a boil, stir, gradually adding the remaining butter, cut into pieces.

8 After cooking, dry the potatoes and place in a dish with the garlic, parsley, 3 tbsps butter, season. Cook on HIGH for 2 minutes. Remove the duck breasts, reserving the marinade.

12 Add the grapefruit segments to the sauce and serve the duck breasts sliced and accompanied with the sauce and the reheated potatoes. Garnish with fresh basil.

ROAST BEEF

WITH

BÉARNAISE SAUCE

SERVES : 4

PREPARATION TIME : 30 minutes
COOKING TIME : 15 minutes
PREHEATING : 8 minutes

There is nothing more popular than succulent roast beef. In this recipe, it is accompanied with a tarragon flavored potato purée and served in a classic Béarnaise sauce prepared entirely in the microwave.

INGREDIENTS

- ☐ 4 large baking potatoes
- ☐ ¼ red bell pepper
- ☐ ¼ green bell pepper
- ☐ 3 sprigs fresh tarragon
- ☐ 2 tbsps heavy cream
- ☐ 1 rib roast, boned (2lbs 8oz)
- ☐ 1 tbsp olive oil
- ☐ 2 tsps butter
- ☐ 5 peppercorns
- ☐ 2 shallots
- ☐ 2 tbsps vinegar
- ☐ 3 egg yolks
- ☐ 5oz butter, melted
- ☐ Salt and pepper

1 Wash the potatoes and pierce in several places with a fork. Cook the potatoes on a turntable on HIGH for 10 minutes.

2 Once the potatoes are cooked, allow to cool. Slice off the top ¹/₃ of the potatoes and hollow out the center.

3 Dice each ¼ bell pepper.

4 Remove the tarragon leaves and chop finely. Reserve one sprig for the garnish.

5 Sieve the potato pulp, add half the tarragon, the diced peppers, and the cream, and season with salt and pepper.

9 Crush the peppercorns with a rolling pin and finely chop the shallot.

6 Mix well and stuff the potato shells with the above mixture.

10 In a casserole, cook the peppercorns, shallot, vinegar and some salt on HIGH for 1 minute. Stir in 1 tbsp cold water and the egg yolks. In another dish, melt the 5oz butter on HIGH for 2 minutes.

7 Preheat the browning dish on HIGH for 8 minutes. Season the beef, and heat the 2 tsps of butter with the oil on the browning dish.

11 Pour the tepid melted butter over the egg yolks, beating constantly. Cook on HIGH for 10 seconds, beat. Cook 15 seconds, beat again. Cook 10 seconds. The mixture should be thick. Add the tarragon.

8 Sear the roast on one side, cook on HIGH for 2 minutes. Turn over cook another 2 minutes. Insert a meat thermometer into the meat and cook until 140°F (for rare meat) approximately 4 minutes.

12 Serve the roast beef after allowing it to rest for 5 minutes, covered with aluminum foil. Accompany with the reheated potatoes and the Béarnaise sauce. Garnish with the reserved tarragon.

PAPRIKA BEEF

SERVES : 4

PREPARATION TIME : 46 minutes
COOKING TIME : 20 minutes
PREHEATING : 16 minutes

*This beef ragout can be prepared ahead and
reheated, so that all the delicious flavors have
time to mellow. Tender sliced, beef is served in a
creamy mushroom sauce, flavored with
paprika, and accompanied with fresh
asparagus.*

INGREDIENTS

- [ ] 1lb asparagus
- [ ] 1lb 8oz tender steak
- [ ] 1 onion
- [ ] 8oz mushrooms
- [ ] 3½ tbsps butter
- [ ] 2 tsps paprika
- [ ] 1 tbsp Cognac
- [ ] ¾ cup heavy cream
- [ ] Fresh chervil
- [ ] 2 sprigs parsley, chopped
- [ ] Salt and pepper

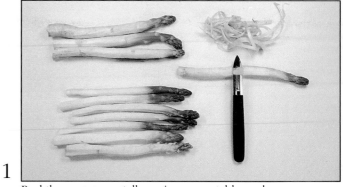

1 Peel the asparagus stalks, using a vegetable peeler.

2 Cook the asparagus, covered with boiling salted water, on HIGH for 8-10 minutes.

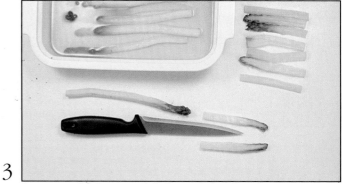

3 Drain on a kitchen towel, halve and slice lengthwise.

4 Cut the steak into thin slices and set aside.

5 Peel the onion and chop finely. Wash the parsley, dry and chop finely.

9 Preheat the browning dish on HIGH for 8 minutes. Sauté the beef strips in 2 tsps butter, season and cook on HIGH for 2 minutes, stirring once.

6 Trim the stalks of the mushrooms, wash briefly, dry and slice them finely.

10 Drain the meat and transfer to the casserole with the onions and mushrooms. Add the paprika and Cognac.

7 Preheat the browning dish on HIGH for 8 minutes. Melt 2 tsps butter and sauté half the onion and the mushrooms. Cook on HIGH for 2 minutes. Repeat for the remaining onion and mushrooms.

11 Stir in the cream, and season with salt and pepper. Cook on HIGH for 3 minutes, stirring twice.

8 Transfer the above to a casserole, without the cooking juices, and cook on HIGH for 4 minutes, stirring once.

12 Serve the paprika beef accompanied with the asparagus reheated with the remaining butter. Garnish with the chopped fresh parsley and chervil.

BEEF STEW

WITH

TAGLIATELLE

SERVES : 6

PREPARATION TIME : 35 minutes
COOKING TIME : 1 hour 20 minutes

*Braising beef is cubed and cooked until tender
with aromatic herbs and vegetables,
accompanied with tagliatelle noodles tossed in
butter and chopped olives. This is always a
popular dish.*

INGREDIENTS

- ☐ 2lbs 8oz braising beef
- ☐ 2 carrots
- ☐ 2 onions
- ☐ 6oz bacon
- ☐ Bouquet garni (parsley, thyme, bay leaf)
- ☐ 1 small stalk celery
- ☐ 2 tbsps olive oil
- ☐ 5 tbsps butter
- ☐ 2 cups beef or chicken stock
- ☐ 8 black olives
- ☐ 12oz tagliatelle
- ☐ 2 tsps butter
- ☐ 2 tsps flour
- ☐ 1 tbsp Worcestershire sauce
- ☐ Fresh chervil
- ☐ Salt and pepper

2 Peel the carrots and onions. Chop finely.

1 Trim any fat or gristle from the meat, and cube evenly.

4 Prepare the bouquet garni, tying together the parsley, thyme and bay leaf. Trim the celery and chop.

3 Remove the bacon rind and slice the flesh into small pieces.

5
Preheat the browning dish on HIGH for 8 minutes. Add ½ tbsp olive oil and 2 tsps butter. Sear the meat and cook on HIGH for 2 minutes, stirring once. If necessary, repeat the operation twice.

6
Remove the meat, and reheat the browning dish. Add 1 tbsp olive oil and 2 tsps butter, and sauté the carrot, onion, and celery on HIGH for 2 minutes, stirring once.

7
Place the meat in a casserole with the above vegetable mixture, and the bacon and season with salt and pepper. Stir well.

8
Add the beef or chicken stock, the bouquet garni, and cook covered at MEDIUM for 1 hour, stirring from time to time.

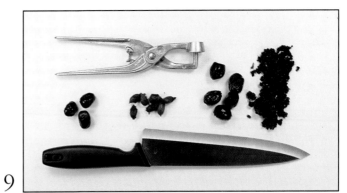

9
Pit the olives, then chop finely.

10
Cook the tagliatelle in salted boiling water on HIGH for 7 to 10 minutes. Drain and rinse. Turn onto a serving plate with 3 tbsps butter and the olives. Season and set aside.

11
Remove and thicken the sauce with a mixture of 2 tsps butter and 2 tsps flour worked together. Beat the sauce well. Cook on HIGH for 1 minute. Add the Worcestershire sauce.

12
Reheat the tagliatelle on HIGH for 2 minutes, stirring once. Serve with the beef stew, garnished with the fresh chervil.

GROUND BEEF CASSEROLE

WITH

FRESH HERBS

SERVES : 6

PREPARATION TIME : 35 minutes
COOKING TIME : 28 minutes
PREHEATING : 8 minutes

Cooked ground meat, flavored with fresh herbs, is layered in a casserole with creamy potato purée, and baked with a topping of Gruyère cheese. Other meat can replace the beef, making this a good dish for using up leftovers.

INGREDIENTS

- ☐ 1lb 12oz beef, for grinding
- ☐ 2 onions
- ☐ 1 clove garlic (central shoot removed)
- ☐ 1lb 12oz potatoes
- ☐ 1¾ cups chicken stock
- ☐ Bouquet garni (parsley, thyme, bay leaf)
- ☐ 2 sprigs fresh tarragon
- ☐ ¼ bunch chervil
- ☐ 4 sprigs fresh basil
- ☐ 12 small pickles
- ☐ 3 tbsps heavy cream
- ☐ 1 tbsp butter
- ☐ 3½oz Gruyère cheese, grated
- ☐ Nutmeg
- ☐ Salad (optional)
- ☐ Vinaigrette dressing (optional)
- ☐ Salt and pepper

1 Cut the meat in pieces, then grind coarsely in a food processor.

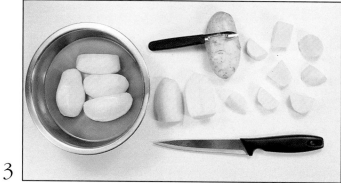

2 Peel the onions and chop finely. Finely chop the garlic.

3 Peel the potatoes and cut in even-sized pieces. Cover with water and set aside.

4 Cook the potato pieces in 1½ cups chicken stock with the bouquet garni, and salt and pepper, on HIGH for 12 minutes.

5
Finely chop the the tarragon, basil and chervil. Set aside. Reserve some basil for the garnish.

9
Preheat the browning dish on HIGH for 8 minutes. Melt 2 tsps butter, sauté the onion, and cook on HIGH for 2 minutes, stirring once.

6
Slice the pickles, then dice finely.

10
Pute the browned beef in a casserole with the onion, pickles, and the remaining stock and cook covered on HIGH for 10 minutes, stirring twice.

7
After cooking the potatoes, press them through a sieve to obtain a potato purée. Reserve the cooking liquid.

11
Butter a baking dish with 1 tsp butter. Arrange in it a layer of meat, then the potato purée and a second layer of meat. Top with the grated Gruyère. Cook on HIGH for 10 minutes.

8
Add the cream, salt, pepper, a little grated nutmeg, the finely chopped herbs and ½ cup of the reserved cooking liquid from the potato.

12
After cooking, allow the casserole to rest for 5 minutes. Serve garnished with the reserved basil, and accompany with a salad tossed in vinaigrette dressing, if desired.

LAMB CHOPS

WITH

MIXED VEGETABLES

SERVES : 8

PREPARATION TIME : 30 minutes
COOKING TIME : 25 minutes
PREHEATING : 12 minutes

Sautéed lamb chops are served with chopped spring vegetables quickly cooked in the microwave. The lamb and vegetables are accompanied with a garlic and parsley flavored butter.

INGREDIENTS

- ☐ 16 small lamb chops
- ☐ 3 carrots
- ☐ 2 turnips
- ☐ 8oz green beans
- ☐ 1lb fresh peas
- ☐ 2 tbsps leaves parsley
- ☐ 1 clove garlic (central shoot removed)
- ☐ 8oz butter, softened to room temperature + extra for searing
- ☐ Juice of ¼ lemon
- ☐ Fresh tarragon
- ☐ Salt and pepper

1 Trim any fat and gristle from the lamb chops. Trim the ends of the bones, if necessary.

2 Peel the carrots, and cut into small thin, sticks. Do the same for the turnips.

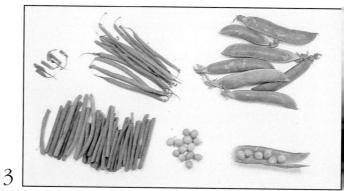

3 String the green beans and shell the peas.

4 Chop the parsley leaves and the garlic.

Cook the carrots in 4 tbsps salted water, covered, on HIGH for 4 minutes, stirring once. After cooking, drain and rinse.

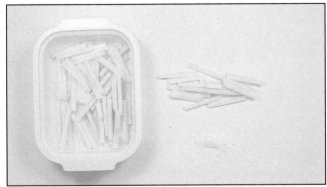

Cook the turnips in the same manner, but only for 3 minutes. Drain and rinse.

Cover the peas with salted water, and cook on HIGH for 10 minutes. Drain and rinse.

Cook the beans in the same manner as the peas, but for 8 minutes only. Drain and rinse.

9

Place the softened butter in a small bowl, mix in the parsley, garlic, and lemon, and season with salt and pepper. Set aside.

10

Preheat the browning dish on HIGH for 8 minutes. Meanwhile, wrap the herb butter in aluminum foil, forming into a sausage shape, and place in the freezer. Season the lamb chops.

11

Melt a little butter on the hot browning dish, sear a few of the lamb chops. Cook each side 1 1/2 minutes on HIGH. Repeat. Reheat the vegetables with a little butter 3 minutes on HIGH.

12

Serve the hot lamb chops accompanied with the reheated vegetables. Accompany with the hardened herb butter, sliced. Garnish with fresh tarragon.

MOUSSAKA

SERVES : 6

PREPARATION TIME : 40 minutes
COOKING TIME : 24 minutes
PREHEATING : 28 minutes

*This is an elaborate casserole of Greek origin.
Layers of ground lamb and sautéed sliced
eggplants and tomatoes are cooked in a light
béchamel sauce, topped with shredded
Swiss cheese.*

INGREDIENTS

- [ ] 3 eggplants (1lb 8oz)
- [ ] Flour for dredging
- [ ] 6 tbsps olive oil
- [ ] 2 tbsps butter
- [ ] 3 tomatoes
- [ ] 2 tbsps butter
- [ ] 2 tbsps flour
- [ ] 2 cups milk
- [ ] Nutmeg
- [ ] 1lb boned lamb shoulder
- [ ] 2 tbsps chopped onion
- [ ] Fresh thyme
- [ ] 4oz Gruyère cheese, grated
- [ ] 4 portions of salad
- [ ] 4 tbsps vinaigrette dressing
- [ ] Salt and pepper

1 Trim off the ends of the eggplants and slice thinly.

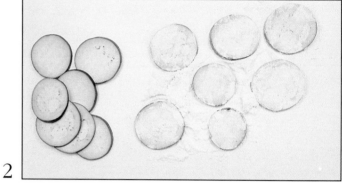

2 Coat each slice with flour, shaking off any excess flour.

3 Preheat the browning dish on HIGH for 8 minutes. Heat ½ tbsp olive oil with 1 tsp butter. Sear several slices of eggplant.

4 Cook on HIGH for 2 minutes, turning once, and drain on paper towels. Repeat 5 times, or until all the eggplant is cooked (reheating the browning dish 4 minutes each time).

5 In a casserole, bring to a boil some water for blanching the tomatoes. Immerse the cored tomatoes . Cover the casserole and allow to rest 1 minute outside the oven.

6 Plunge the tomatoes into cold water, peel, remove the seeds and chop the flesh finely. Dry on paper towels.

7 Make a béchamel sauce : melt the second 2 tbsps butter on HIGH for 30 seconds, stir in 2 tbsps flour, and cook on HIGH for 30 seconds, stir again.

8 Pour the boiling milk onto the butter and flour mixture, stirring rapidly, and cook on HIGH for 1 minute, stirring twice. Season with salt and pepper and a little grated nutmeg.

9 Grind the lamb in a food processor, adding the chopped onion, and seasoning with salt and pepper, then set aside. Do not grind the meat too finely.

10 Mix together the béchamel sauce and the meat.

11 In a small buttered dish, lay : eggplant, tomato, meat. Finish with a layer of eggplant, then sprinkle with the thyme and grated Gruyère.

12 Cook on HIGH for 10 minutes, then allow to rest for another 10 minutes, covered. Serve the moussaka accompanied with a salad tossed in vinaigrette dressing.

LAMB BLANQUETTE

WITH

MUSHROOMS

SERVES : 6

PREPARATION TIME : 35 minutes
COOKING TIME : 48 minutes

A blanquette is a creamy stew that is very popular in France, in which boned lamb is cooked with aromatic herbs and vegetables. The sauce consists of the cooking juices and cream, with the added flavor of morille mushrooms available dried in specialty foodshops. The morilles can be replaced by any variety of wild mushroom.

INGREDIENTS

- [ ] 10g dried morille mushrooms
- [ ] 2lbs 8oz boned lamb shoulder
- [ ] 2 carrots
- [ ] 1 onion
- [ ] 8oz button mushrooms
- [ ] Bouquet garni (parsley, thyme, bay leaf)
- [ ] 1 cup chicken stock
- [ ] ¾ cup heavy cream
- [ ] 1 tsp potato flour
- [ ] Fresh chervil
- [ ] Salt and pepper

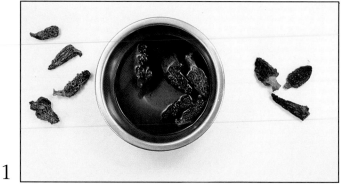

1

Soak the dried morille mushrooms in water for 10 minutes and rinse well to eliminate any sand.

2

Remove the excess fat from the lamb, and chop the meat evenly.

3

Peel the carrot and onion, then slice. Cut the onion slices in half.

4

Cut the stems off the button mushrooms, rinse briefly, and dry on a kitchen towel. Chop finely.

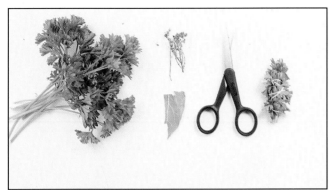

5 Prepare the bouquet garni, by tying together the parsley, thyme and bay leaf. Set aside.

9 After cooking the blanquette, allow to rest for 10 minutes. Remove the pieces of meat, stir in the cream and chopped morille mushrooms. Cook on HIGH for 3 minutes, stirring twice.

6 Blanch the meat in salted water, covered, on HIGH for 6 minutes. Drain and rinse.

10 Dissolve the potato flour in a little water and stir gradually into the sauce. Cook on HIGH for 3 minutes, stirring 3 times with a wire whisk.

7 In a casserole, combine the meat, the chicken stock, the carrots, onions and mushrooms. Cook on HIGH, covered, for 35 minutes.

11 Once the sauce is ready, add the reserved morille mushrooms, halved, and the meat. Remove the bouquet garni and mix the dish well.

8 Squeeze the morille mushrooms to remove excess water and chop finely. Reserve a portion for the garnish.

12 Reheat the dish on HIGH for 1 minute before serving garnished with the fresh chervil.

SPICY ROAST LEG

OF

LAMB

SERVES : 6

PREPARATION TIME : 20 minutes
COOKING TIME : 1 hour 35 minutes
SOAKING : 12 hours

*In France roast leg of lamb is traditionally
served on high days and on holidays. It is
always accompanied with flageolet beans. In
this modern version the lamb roast is flavored
with exotic spices.*

INGREDIENTS

- ☐ 3 cloves garlic (central shoot removed)
- ☐ Bouquet garni (parsley, thyme bay leaf)
- ☐ 1 onion
- ☐ 4 tbsps butter
- ☐ 1lb dried flageolet beans (soaked 2 hours)
- ☐ 4 cups chicken stock
- ☐ 2 tbsps soy sauce
- ☐ 1 tsp turmeric
- ☐ 1 tsp curry powder
- ☐ ½ tsp cinnamon
- ☐ 1 (2lbs) leg of lamb
- ☐ Salt and pepper
- ☐ Fresh chervil

1 Make the bouquet garni, by tying together the parsley, thyme and bay leaf.

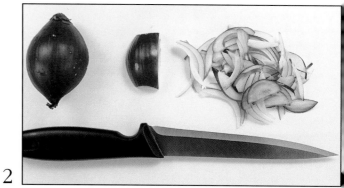

2 Peel, halve and finely chop the onion.

3 In a casserole, melt 2½ tbsps of the butter, and add the chopped onion and one clove garlic cut in half ; cook on HIGH for 2 minutes, stirring twice.

4 Add the soaked and drained beans with the bouquet garni. Mix well.

5

Pour in the stock, season with salt and pepper and allow to cook, covered, on HIGH for 1 hour, stirring every 10 minutes. The beans should be well cooked, almost to a purée.

6

Combine the soy sauce, turmeric, curry powder, cinnamon and a little pepper.

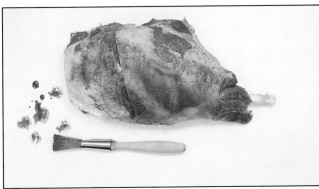

7

Brush this sauce on the leg of lamb. Preheat the browning dish on HIGH for 8 minutes.

8

Make incisions in the lamb, insert the remaining garlic halves. Wrap the bone of the leg in aluminum foil. Brown the leg on the browning dish in the remaining butter on HIGH for 2 minutes.

9

Cook the leg of lamb on a grill over a casserole. Insert the cooking thermometer to the center of the leg. Cook on HIGH for 5 minutes and at MEDIUM for 28 minutes.

10

After removing the leg from the oven, cover with aluminum foil and allow to rest for 10 minutes until the thermometer reaches 70°C (WELL DONE). Reserve the cooking juices.

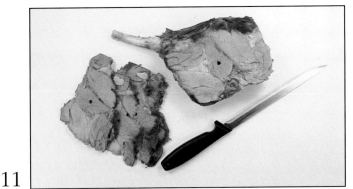

11

Remove the aluminum foil and slice the lamb thinly.

12

Serve the lamb with the reheated beans, and the cooking juices, the whole garnished with the fresh chervil.

VEAL ROLLS

WITH

WILD MUSHROOMS

SERVES : 4

PREPARATION TIME : 35 minutes
COOKING TIME : 20 minutes.
PREHEATING : 8 minutes

Veal scallops are stuffed with ground veal, rolled and baked quickly in chicken stock. They are served in a wild mushroom cream sauce. This recipe calls for girolle mushrooms, available dried or canned in specialty food shops.

INGREDIENTS

- ☐ 4 long, thin scallops of veal
- ☐ 8oz veal, ground
- ☐ 1 tsp Cognac
- ☐ 1 egg
- ☐ 1 tbsp heavy cream
- ☐ 4 tbsps chicken stock
- ☐ 2 cloves garlic (central shoot removed)
- ☐ 3 sprigs parsley
- ☐ 14oz girolle mushrooms (or other wild variety)
- ☐ 2 tbsps butter
- ☐ ½ cup heavy cream
- ☐ 1 tsp cornstarch
- ☐ Fresh tarragon
- ☐ Salt and pepper

1 Flatten the scallops by placing between two sheets of plastic wrap and pounding with the flat of a cleaver.

2 Chill the 8oz veal, then grind in a food processor, adding the Cognac, egg, and heavy cream. Season the stuffing with salt and pepper and reserve.

3 Using a spatula, place a thin layer of stuffing on each scallop.

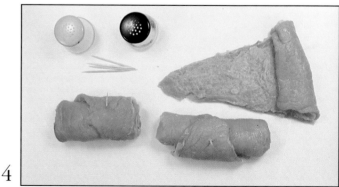

4 Roll up the scallops and secure with toothpicks.

Place the veal rolls in a buttered casserole with the chicken stock, and cook covered on HIGH for 7 minutes. Allow to rest 10 minutes after cooking.

9 After cooking the veal rolls, remove from the oven and add the cream, and the remaining parsley and chopped garlic. Cook on HIGH for 5 minutes.

Chop the garlic finely. Wash and dry the parsley, and finely chop.

10 Dissolve the cornstarch in a little water, add to the sauce, stir and cook on HIGH for 1 minute. Season with salt and pepper. Blend with a hand mixer.

Trim the stalks of the mushrooms, wash briefly, quarter and dry on a kitchen towel.

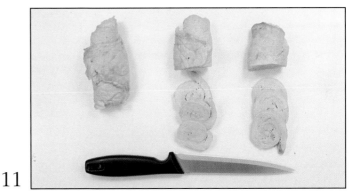

11 Remove the toothpicks, and stice the veal rolls evenly. Reheat the mushrooms.

Preheat the browning dish on HIGH for 8 minutes. Add 1 tbsp butter, sauté half the mushrooms with ¼ of the parsley and chopped garlic. Season, repeat for the rest of the mushrooms.

12 Serve the veal rolls with the sauce and mushrooms, garnished with the fresh tarragon.

SAUERKRAUT CASSEROLE À L'ALSACIENNE

SERVES : 4

PREPARATION TIME : 20 minutes
COOKING TIME : 46 minutes
SOAKING : 4 hours

*Sauerkraut casserole is a traditional
German dish, also popular throughout France.
It is cooked with several cuts of pork and
sausages, and flavored with juniper berries.
Serve accompanied with boiled potatoes and
mustard on the side. This dish is often even
better reheated the next day.*

INGREDIENTS

- ☐ 1lb 6oz raw sauerkraut
- ☐ 3 juniper berries
- ☐ 1 clove
- ☐ 4 peppercorns
- ☐ ½ cup white wine
- ☐ 1 onion
- ☐ 1 carrot
- ☐ 12oz salt pork (soaked 4 hours)
- ☐ 8 medium-sized potatoes
- ☐ 6oz smoked bacon
- ☐ 4 frankfurters
- ☐ 1 smoked sausage (6oz)
- ☐ 1 tbsp chopped chives
- ☐ Salt

1 Soak the raw sauerkraut 1 hour in cold water. Rinse, drain and squeeze out the excess water.

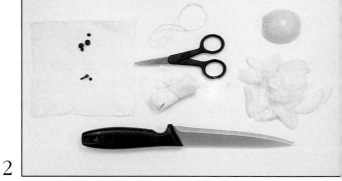

2 Tie up the juniper berries, clove, and peppercorns in a small piece of cheesecloth. Finely chop the onion.

3 Put the sauerkraut into a small casserole, add the white wine, the spices, onion and ½ cup water.

4 Peel the carrot, quarter and add to the sauerkraut, with the salt pork, cut in half. Cover and cook on HIGH for 10 minutes, stirring often.

Peel the potatoes, quarter and trim into oblong shapes. Place in water to prevent discoloration.

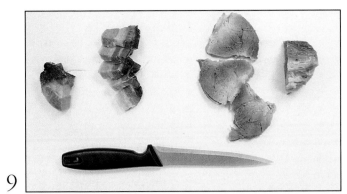

9 Cut the salt pork and bacon into even-sized pieces.

Remove the sauerkraut, take out the pork, mix the sauerkraut with a fork and replace the pork along with the bacon. Cover, and cook on HIGH for 25 minutes, stirring occasionally.

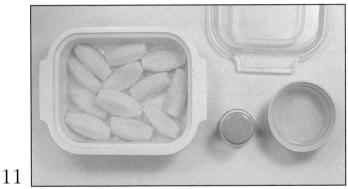

10 Add the smoked sausage, frankfurters and chopped salt pork and bacon to sauerkraut and cook, covered, on HIGH for 8 minutes. Allow to rest 10 minutes, covered, after cooking.

7 Pierce the frankfurters with a fork and slice.

11 Cook the potatoes in boiling salted water, covered, on HIGH for 6 to 7 minutes. Stir after 3 minutes.

8 Remove the sauerkraut from the oven, and take out the meat, spices and carrots, draining well.

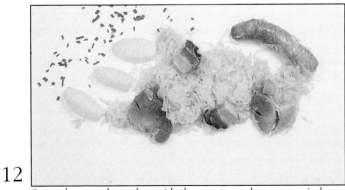

12 Serve the sauerkraut hot with the meats, and accompanied with the potatoes. Garnish with the fresh chives.

PORK AND LENTIL CASSEROLE

SERVES : 4

PREPARATION TIME : 30 minutes
COOKING TIME : 45 minutes
SOAKING : 12 hours

*This is a well known French dish
called "Petit Salé", which refers to the lightly
salted pork cooked with the lentils. The dish is
enhanced with smoked sausage and
frankfurters, and accompanied with a fresh
spinach salad. This dish is often even better
reheated the next day.*

INGREDIENTS

- [ ] 12oz green lentils
- [ ] 1 onion
- [ ] 1 clove
- [ ] Bouquet garni (parsley, thyme, bay leaf)
- [ ] 1lb 12oz salt pork (soaked 2 hours in water)
- [ ] ½ leek
- [ ] 1 carrot
- [ ] 1 smoked sausage
- [ ] 3 cups chicken stock
- [ ] 6 frankfurters
- [ ] 12oz young spinach or watercress
- [ ] 1 tbsp vinegar
- [ ] 3 tbsps oil
- [ ] 2 shallots, chopped
- [ ] ½ bunch chives
- [ ] Fresh chervil
- [ ] Salt and pepper

1 Soak the lentils for about 12 hours. Drain.

2 Peel the onion and stud with the clove. Prepare the bouquet garni by tying together the parsley, thyme and bay leaf.

3 Blanch the salt pork, by placing in a casserole, and covering with water. Bring to a boil and cook, covered, on HIGH for 10 minutes.

4 Quarter the leek, wash well and make a large bouquet garni by tying together the leek and sliced carrot.

5

Drain the blanched salt pork, rinse and slice.

6

In a casserole, combine the lentils with the leek, onion, and salt and pepper to taste.

7

Add the stock, bouquets garnis, and sliced pork and cover. Cook on HIGH for 30 minutes, stirring occasionally.

8

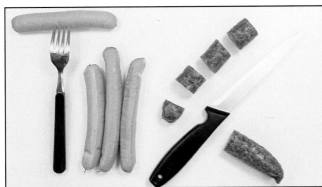

Slice the smoked sausage and pierce the frankfurters with a fork.

9

Trim the stalks from the spinach. Wash, dry and shred the leaves coarsely.

10

Prepare a vinaigrette dressing : combine salt, pepper and vinegar in a bowl ; beat in the oil gradually. Add the shallots and chopped chives.

11

After cooking the lentils, add the frankfurters and the smoked sausage. Cook, covered, on HIGH for 5 minutes. Allow to rest 10 minutes after cooking.

12

Serve the pork and lentil casserole with the spinach salad tossed in the vinaigrette dressing. Garnish with the chopped chervil.

ROAST PORK

WITH

MUSTARD

SERVES : 6

PREPARATION TIME : 30 minutes
COOKING TIME : 22 minutes
PREHEATING : 8 minutes

A joint of pork is seasoned with fresh basil, thyme and parsley, rolled and roasted in the microwave, then served in a sauce made from the cooking juices, cream and mustard. It is accompanied with an unusual vegetable side dish of cooked sliced lettuce.

INGREDIENTS

- [ ] 2lbs pork roast
- [ ] Fresh herbs (basil, thyme, parsley)
- [ ] 2 tbsps olive oil
- [ ] 4 tbsps butter
- [ ] 3 heads lettuce
- [ ] $\frac{1}{2}$ cup chicken stock
- [ ] 2 tbsps heavy cream
- [ ] 2 tbsps mustard
- [ ] Fresh basil
- [ ] Salt and pepper

1 Trim any excess fat from the meat. Slice open the roast without cutting it in half.

2 Chop the parsley and basil. Season the roast with salt and pepper. Sprinkle with fresh thyme leaves and the chopped parsley and basil.

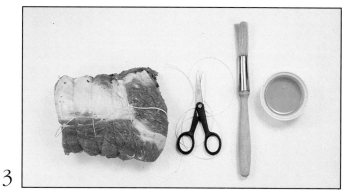

3 Reassemble the roast, tie with kitchen string and brush with olive oil.

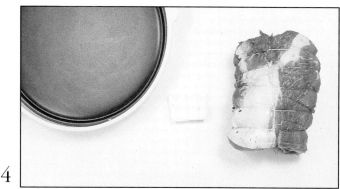

4 Preheat the browning dish on HIGH for 8 minutes. Remove from the oven, add 2 tsps butter and sear the roast on all sides. Cook on HIGH for 2 minutes, turning once.

5 Place the roast on a cooking grill over a casserole to catch the cooking juices. Insert a meat thermometer. Cook on HIGH for 10 minutes, or until the temperature reaches (150°F).

6 Separate the lettuce leaves. Wash and drain.

7 Place the lettuce leaves in a casserole ; cover and cook on HIGH for 2 minutes, stirring twice. Cook the lettuce in three batches.

8 Drain the lettuce, rinse and squeeze out any excess water. Cut the lettuce into strips.

9 After cooking the roast, wrap with aluminum foil. Add the chicken stock to the cooking juices, allow to reduce on HIGH for 6 minutes, then add the cream, salt and pepper. Set aside.

10 Reheat the lettuce with the remaining butter on HIGH for 2 minutes. Season to taste.

11 Remove the pork and slice for serving. Add the mustard to the sauce and reheat on HIGH for 1 minute. Mix with a hand mixer before serving.

12 Serve the slices of roast pork with the lettuce and the sauce. Garnish with fresh the basil.

PORK SPARERIBS

WITH

PEANUT BARBECUE SAUCE

SERVES : 6

PREPARATION TIME : 30 minutes
COOKING TIME : 20 minutes

This is an original variation of barbecued spareribs. The barbecue sauce contains crushed peanuts, maple syrup and ketchup. If you like, spice it up with a little tabasco. The spareribs are served with pineapple slices and onion sautéed in butter, and accompanied with a salad tossed in vinaigrette dressing.

INGREDIENTS

- ☐ 3lbs pork spareribs
- ☐ 1 carrot
- ☐ 3 onions
- ☐ Bouquet garni (parsley, thyme, bay leaf)
- ☐ 2 tbsps peanuts

Barbecue sauce :
- ☐ 3 tbsps soy sauce
- ☐ 1 tbsp vinegar
- ☐ 3 tbsps maple syrup or honey
- ☐ 3 tbsps ketchup
- ☐ 1 lettuce
- ☐ 2 tbsps butter
- ☐ 4 slices pineapple
- ☐ 4 tbsps vinaigrette dressing
- ☐ Fresh chervil
- ☐ Salt

1 Separate the spareribs.

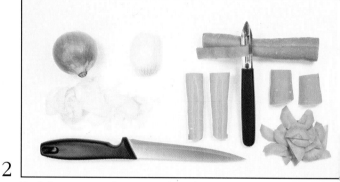

2 Peel the carrot and onions. Chop the carrot and 1 onion finely.

3 Make the bouquet garni, tying together the parsley, thyme and bay leaf. Set aside.

4 Blanch the spareribs in salted water with the bouquet garni, the chopped carrot and onion on HIGH for 8 minutes, stirring twice.

5

Remove the spareribs and drain.

6

Crush the peanuts with a rolling pin or in a food processor. Separate the chervil leaves.

7

Prepare the barbecue sauce by mixing together the soy sauce, vinegar, maple syrup or honey, and the ketchup. Add the chopped peanuts.

8

Arrange the spareribs in a baking dish, cover with the barbecue sauce and stir well to coat the ribs.

9

Cook on HIGH for 10 minutes, stirring often so they caramelize evenly.

10

Finely chop the remaining 2 onions. Prepare the lettuce and set aside.

11

Preheat the browning dish on HIGH for 8 minutes. Add the butter and sauté the pineapple and the onions on HIGH for 2 minutes, stirring twice.

12

Mix the sautéed onions and pineapple with the pork spareribs. Serve with the lettuce dressed with the vinaigrette dressing, and garnished with the fresh chervil.

PEAR CAKE

SERVES : 6

PREPARATION TIME : 30 minutes
COOKING TIME : 20 minutes

*Fresh chopped pears go into the batter of this
cake to add interesting texture and flavor,
complemented by an accompanying
fresh pear purée.*

INGREDIENTS

- ☐ 4 pears
- ☐ 1 tbsp butter
- ☐ 2 eggs
- ☐ ²/₃ cup sugar
- ☐ 1½ cups flour
- ☐ Pinch of salt
- ☐ 3 tbsps oil
- ☐ 1 clove
- ☐ ¼ cup ground hazelnuts
- ☐ 1 tbsp pear liqueur
- ☐ Fresh mint

1 Peel and core the pears. Cut into pieces.

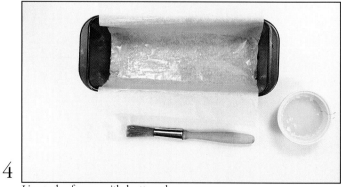

2 Cook the pear pieces in a casserole for 8 minutes on HIGH.

3 Drain the pears, and purée with a hand mixer or food processor.

4 Line a loaf pan with buttered wax paper.

5 Make the cake batter : mix together the eggs, ²/₃ cup sugar, flour, some salt and ¹/₂ the pear purée.

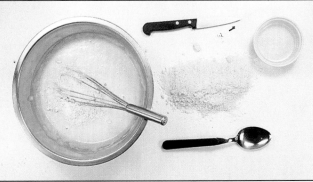

6 Add the oil, a little grated clove and the ground hazelnuts. Mix together well.

7 Turn the batter into the loaf pan.

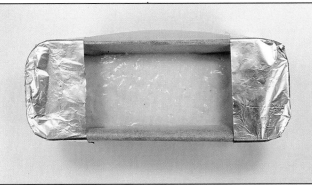

8 Cover the ends of the loaf pan with aluminum foil and cook MEDIUM for 10 minutes

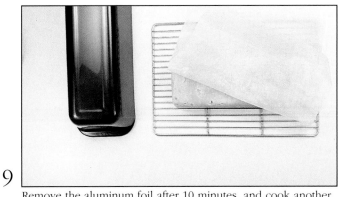

9 Remove the aluminum foil after 10 minutes, and cook another 2 minutes on HIGH. Allow the cake to rest for 5 minutes, covered with a kitchen towel. Unmold the cake.

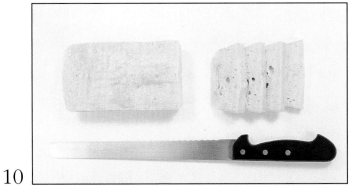

10 Cut the cake into slices with a serrated knife.

11 Flavor the remaining pear purée with the liqueur. Mix in well.

12 Serve the cake slices with the pear purée, and garnished with a few mint leaves.

NUT

AND

RAISIN PUDDING

SERVES : 6

PREPARATION TIME : 20 minutes
COOKING TIME : 20 minutes

Here is a delicious and simple recipe. The ingredients are always available and on hand. Brioche, a sweet breakfast bread, is soaked in a custard preparation and mixed with raisins and nuts, then baked. Serve warm or cold.

INGREDIENTS

- [ ] 1 cup milk
- [ ] 1 cup heavy cream
- [ ] 6oz brioche, or other sweet bread
- [ ] 4 tbsps raisins
- [ ] 4 tbsps walnuts
- [ ] 4 eggs
- [ ] $^2/_3$ cup sugar
- [ ] 2 tsps butter
- [ ] 1 cup cane sugar syrup
- [ ] 12oz raspberries
- [ ] Scant 1 cup heavy cream
- [ ] 3 tbsps confectioners' sugar
- [ ] Fresh mint

1 Cut up the brioche and soak in the milk and the 1 cup heavy cream, with the raisins.

2 Finely grind the nuts in a food processor.

3 Beat the eggs, ground nuts and sugar with a whisk.

4 Heat the soaked brioche on HIGH for 4 minutes. Beat in the egg mixture.

5

Melt the butter to grease a baking pan. Pour in the pudding and cook on HIGH for 10 minutes, folding the edges in towards the center after 2 minutes.

6

Bring to a boil the cane sugar syrup and cook on HIGH for 3 minutes. Add the raspberries. Cook on HIGH for 2 minutes.

7

Purée the raspberry mixture.

8

Press the raspberry purée through a sieve to obtain a smooth "coulis." Set aside in the refrigerator.

9

Pour the scant 1 cup heavy cream into a bowl, and place in the freezer for 5 minutes. Add the confectioners' sugar and whip until stiff.

10

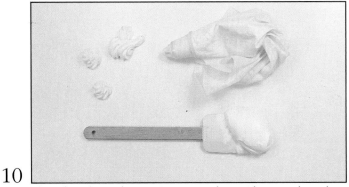

Place the whipped cream in a pastry bag with a star-shaped nozzle.

11

Unmold the warm pudding and allow to cool before slicing.

12

Serve the pudding with the chilled raspberry coulis, decorated with the whipped cream and garnished with mint leaves.

MANGO SPONGE ROLL

SERVES : 6

PREPARATION TIME : 40 minutes
COOKING TIME : 14 minutes

A wonderful filling of fresh chopped mango is rolled up in a classic sponge cake. Slices are served with a freshly made sweet strawberry purée called a "coulis". You may use frozen strawberries if fresh are not in season.

INGREDIENTS

- ☐ 3 eggs
- ☐ ¼ cup sugar
- ☐ 1 cup flour
- ☐ 2 tsps butter
- ☐ 2 egg yolks
- ☐ ¼ cup sugar
- ☐ 2 tbsps flour
- ☐ 1 cup milk
- ☐ 12oz strawberries
- ☐ 1 mango
- ☐ 1 cup cane sugar syrup
- ☐ Fresh mint

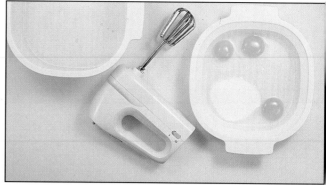

1 In a double boiler over boiled water, mix the eggs and sugar with an electric mixer for approximately 10 minutes (reheat the water once during the operation).

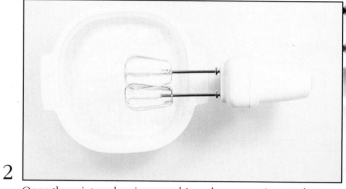

2 Once the mixture has increased in volume, continue to beat until cooled.

3 Gradually add the sifted flour, folding in with a rubber spatula.

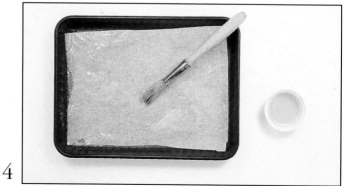

4 Butter a sheet of wax paper and place in a flat baking pan.

5 Add the cake mixture, spreading it out evenly, and cook on HIGH for 8 minutes, turning the pan every minute, to cook the cake evenly.

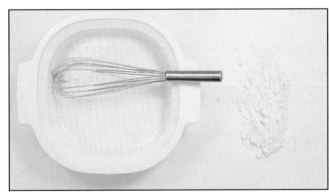

6 After cooking the cake, allow to rest for 3 minutes, covered with a kitchen towel. Turn out onto a damp kitchen towel, remove the wax paper and roll up. Allow to cool.

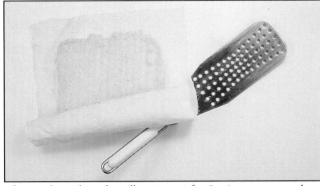

7 Prepare the pastry cream : whisk together 2 egg yolks and the second ¼ cup sugar. When light and lemon-colored, add 2 tbsps flour. Mix in well.

8 Bring the milk to a boil and add to the egg/sugar mixture, stirring rapidly. Cook on HIGH for 1½ minutes, stirring once. Set aside.

9 Wash the strawberries, trim and quarter. Halve the mango, remove the pit, and make criss-cross slashes in the flesh. Turn the skin inside-out and remove the pieces of mango.

10 Bring to a boil the cane sugar syrup (2 minutes), add the strawberries, cook on HIGH for 2 minutes. Purée with a hand mixer, allow to cool. Coarsely chop the mango, add to the pastry cream.

11 Carrefully unroll the sponge cake, spread with a fine layer of mango pastry cream, roll up and refrigerate for at least 1 hour.

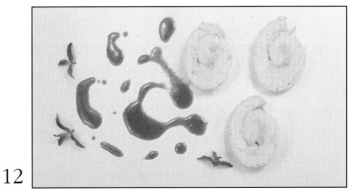

12 Slice the cake for serving, decorate with the mint leaves and serve with the strawberry purée and any remaining pastry cream.

FRUIT FLAN

SERVES : 6

PREPARATION TIME : 25 minutes
COOKING TIME : 14 minutes

A lovely combination of fresh cherries, mango and red currants is cooked in a light egg custard. Serve garnished with sliced grapefruit and mint leaves. You may vary the fruits according to personal taste and seasonal availability.

INGREDIENTS

- ☐ 6oz cherries
- ☐ 6oz strawberries
- ☐ ½ mango
- ☐ 4 tbsps red currants
- ☐ Fresh mint
- ☐ ½ cup sugar
- ☐ 7 eggs
- ☐ 1 tbsp kirsch
- ☐ 1¾ cups milk
- ☐ 4 tbsps raisins
- ☐ ½ cup flour
- ☐ 2 grapefruit
- ☐ Salt

1 Pit the cherries, then cut in half.

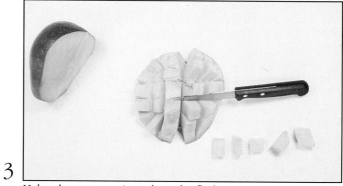

2 Wash and hull the strawberries, then quarter them.

3 Halve the mango, pit, and cut the flesh in a criss-cross pattern. Turn the peel inside-out and remove the flesh.

4 Wash and stem the red currants. Separate the mint leaves.

5 In a bowl, beat together the sugar, eggs, kirsch and a pinch of salt.

6 Bring the milk to a boil with the raisins, covered, on HIGH.

7 Add the flour to the egg and sugar mixture, mixing well.

8 Pour the hot milk over the mixture, stirring rapidly. Turn into a deep baking pan, cook the flan MEDIUM for 4 minutes. After 2 minutes, remove from the oven, fold the edges in towards the center.

9 After 4 minutes, add the red currants, and mix well with a whisk, stirring the edges in towards the center.

10 Add the cherries, strawberries and mango. Mix with a spatula and cook MEDIUM for 10 minutes. Allow to rest, covered, for 10 minutes.

11 Peel the grapefruit, removing the white membrane. Separate the grapefruit segments.

12 Allow the flan to cool, chill in the refrigerator, then serve with the grapefruit segments, and garnished with the mint leaves. The flan can be served warm.

CARROT

AND

ALMOND CAKE

SERVES : 6

PREPARATION TIME : 15 minutes
COOKING TIME : 17 minutes

*Freshly grated carrots and ground almonds
create a moist and flavorful cake. It is served
with a simple cinnamon custard sauce.*

INGREDIENTS

- ☐ ½lb carrots
- ☐ 2 eggs
- ☐ ¾ cup sugar
- ☐ 3 tbsps ground almonds
- ☐ ¾ cup flour
- ☐ 1 tsp baking powder
- ☐ 2 drops almond extract
- ☐ 3 tbsps oil
- ☐ 1 tbsp butter, melted
- ☐ 3 egg yolks
- ☐ ⅓ cup sugar
- ☐ 1 cup milk
- ☐ 1 tsp orange flower water
- ☐ Fresh mint

1 Peel the carrots and grate.

2 In a mixing bowl, whisk together the eggs, ¾ cup sugar and the ground almonds.

3 Add the flour, baking powder, almond extract and the oil, and mix together well.

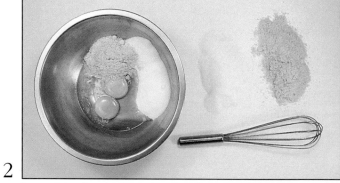

4 Stir in the grated carrots with a spatula.

5

Butter a piece of wax paper and use to line a loaf pan. Pour the cake batter into the lined pan.

6

Cover the ends of the pan with aluminum foil and cook for 10 minutes on MEDIUM. Remove the aluminum foil, then cook another 2 minutes.

7

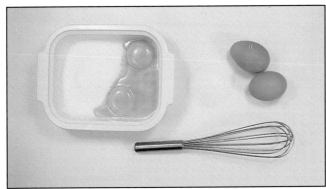

Prepare the custard sauce. Mix together the egg yolks and the sugar, and in another dish bring the milk to a boil.

8

Pour the boiling milk over the egg yolks and sugar mixture, stirring continuously. Cook on HIGH for 30 seconds. Stir with a whisk.

9

Cook 30 seconds more. Whip again and cook another 20 seconds. Allow to cool. The custard should be thick enough to cover the back of a metal spoon. Stir in the orange flower water.

10

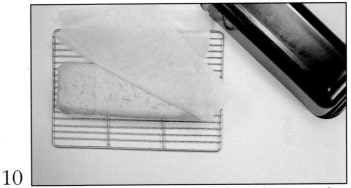

Allow the cake to rest for 10 minutes after cooking, covered with a kitchen towel, then turn out.

11

Cut the cake into even-sized pieces with a serrated knife.

12

Serve the cake with the custard sauce, garnished with mint leaves.

RASPBERRY TART

SERVES : 6

PREPARATION TIME : 40 minutes
COOKING TIME : 11 minutes

This is a classic French dessert adapted for the microwave. A pie shell is part baked, then cooked again with a buttery almond and kirsch filling. After cooking, it is topped with fresh raspberries and covered with a raspberry jelly glaze.

INGREDIENTS

- ☐ 2½ cups flour
- ☐ 4 tbsps water
- ☐ 1 egg yolk
- ☐ ⅔ cup butter
- ☐ 4 tbsps butter, softened to room temperature
- ☐ 4 tbsps sugar
- ☐ 4 tbsps ground almonds
- ☐ 1 egg
- ☐ 2 tsps flour
- ☐ 1 tsp kirsch
- ☐ 2 tsps butter
- ☐ 1lb raspberries
- ☐ 5oz raspberry jelly
- ☐ Fresh mint
- ☐ 6 tbsps whipped cream (optional)
- ☐ Salt

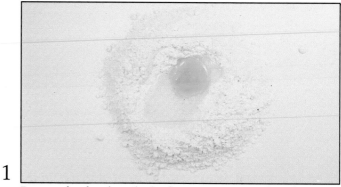

1 Prepare the dough : pile the flour onto your work surface, make a well in the center and add the water, salt and egg yolk.

2 Add the butter in pieces. Incorporate all the ingredients, using your fingers.

3 Work into a dough and shape into a ball ; refrigerate for 30 minutes.

4 Prepare the almond cream : whip together the 4 tbsps softened butter with the equal amount of sugar.

5 Add the ground almonds and the egg, stirring constantly.

6 Sift in the flour, add the kirsch and blend well. Set aside in the refrigerator.

7 Rapidly wash the raspberries (if necessary), and dry. Remove the tart pastry dough from the refrigerator and roll out.

8 Butter a pie pan and line with the dough. Prick the bottom with a fork. Place a sheet of wax paper on the dough and a small plate on top. Cook on HIGH for 4 minutes.

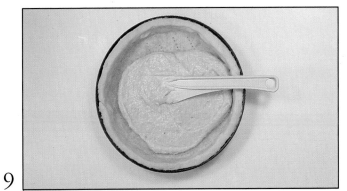

9 Remove the plate and wax paper, allow the pie shell to cool. Spread the almond cream over the with a spatula, cook on HIGH for 6 minutes. Allow to rest, covered, for 5 minutes.

10 After cooking, allow the tart to cool, and arrange the raspberries over the top.

11 Heat the raspberry jelly on HIGH for 1 minute, and lightly brush the jelly over the raspberries in the tart.

12 Serve the raspberry tart cut into slices, garnished with the fresh mint leaves and the whipped cream.

CARAMEL CUSTARD

WITH

ORANGE FLOWER WATER

SERVES : 6

PREPARATION TIME : 20 minutes
COOKING TIME : 18 minutes

Every country has a variation on this classic dessert. In this recipe, egg and milk custard is flavored with orange flower water and served with a fresh orange syrup, orange slices and mint leaves.

INGREDIENTS

Caramel :
- ☐ ½ cup sugar
- ☐ 1 tsp water

Custard :
- ☐ 4 eggs
- ☐ ½ cup sugar
- ☐ ½ vanilla pod
- ☐ 2 cups milk
- ☐ 1 tbsp orange flower water
- ☐ 2 sprigs fresh mint
- ☐ 4 oranges
- ☐ 3-4 tbsps sugar

1 Make the caramel : combine the sugar and water in a heavy bowl. Cook on HIGH for 4 to 5 minutes. The caramel continues to brown outside the oven.

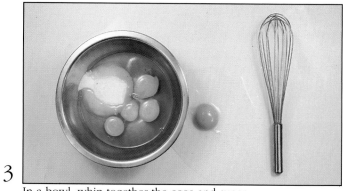

2 Have ready 6 ramekins. When the caramel is ready, divide it between the ramekins.

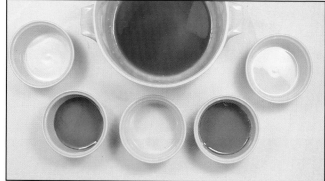

3 In a bowl, whip together the eggs and sugar.

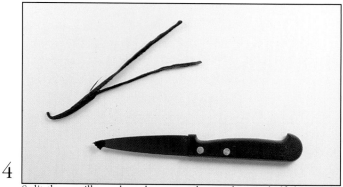

4 Split the vanilla pod, and remove the seeds. Mix half the seeds with the milk and bring it to a boil, covered, on HIGH.

5 Pour the boiling milk over the egg and sugar mixture, whipping continuously.

6 Add the orange flower water, and allow to rest for 10 minutes.

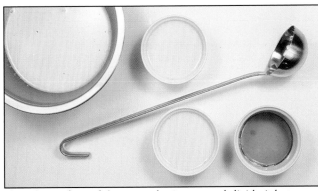

7 Skim the surface of the custard mixture, and divide it between the 6 ramekins. Cook on HIGH for 5 minutes, and MEDIUM for 2 minutes.

8 Separate the mint leaves and slice finely.

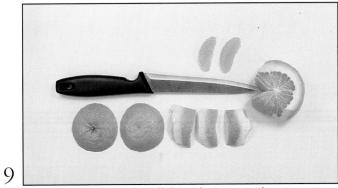

9 Peel 2 oranges, removing all the pith. Separate the segments and chill in the refrigerator.

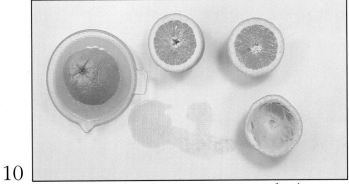

10 Squeeze the juice from the remaining oranges. After the custards are cooked, allow them to cool. Refrigerate.

11 Mix together the orange juice and 3-4 tbsps sugar in a casserole, and cook on HIGH for 5 minutes to obtain a light syrup.

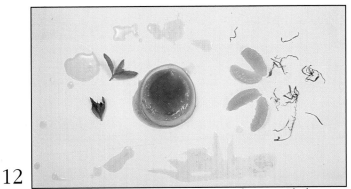

12 Once the custards are chilled, turn out and serve with the orange syrup, the chilled oranges segments, and garnished the chopped fresh mint.

PINEAPPLE

AND

RED FRUIT CRUMBLE

SERVES : 6

PREPARATION TIME : 40 minutes
COOKING TIME : 18 minutes

A wonderful combination of pineapple, cherries, raspberries, strawberries and raisins makes a flavorful crumble quickly cooked in the microwave. If any of the fruits are not available fresh, use canned or frozen. Serve the crumble warm, or cold with cream.

INGREDIENTS

- ☐ 1 pineapple
- ☐ 12oz cherries
- ☐ 8oz strawberries
- ☐ 4oz raspberries
- ☐ 2 tsps butter
- ☐ 3 tbsps sugar
- ☐ 4 tbsps raisins
- ☐ 1 tbsp rum
- ☐ 2 cups flour
- ☐ 4oz butter
- ☐ 4 tbsps sugar
- ☐ Fresh mint
- ☐ 6 tbsps heavy cream (optional)

1 Trim and peel the pineapple.

2 Remove the eyes of the pineapple.

3 Quarter the pineapple, cut away the core and cube the flesh.

4 Pit the cherries.

5

Wash, trim and quarter the strawberries. Wash the raspberries if necessary.

9

Make a crumble topping : cut the remaining butter into the flour.

6

Arrange the red fruits in a baking pan with 1½ tbsps sugar and the 2 tsps butter. Cook on HIGH for 4 minutes, stirring once. Allow to cool and strain off half the juices to serve with the crumble.

10

Add the 4 tbsps sugar and mix in with your fingers.

7

In another casserole, cook the pineapple with 1½ tbsps sugar, the rum and raisins on HIGH for 4 minutes.

11

Cover the fruit with this mixture and cook on HIGH for 10 minutes.

8

Add the pineapple to the red fruit (reserving the pineapple juice).

12

Serve the crumble warm or cold with the heavy cream, fresh mint and a mixture of the fruit juices.

FLOATING ISLANDS

SERVES : 6

PREPARATION TIME : 20 minutes
COOKING TIME : 10 minutes

*A classic dessert that is always sure to please.
Light, microwaved meringues are served in a
vanilla custard sauce and topped with
caramelized sugar and sugared almonds.*

INGREDIENTS

☐ 6 eggs, separated
☐ ²/₃ cup sugar
☐ ¹/₂ vanilla pod
☐ 2 cups milk
☐ 2 tbsps confectioners' sugar
☐ 4 tbsps candied almonds
   (for decoration)
☐ 4 tbsps sugar (for the caramel)
☐ 4oz strawberries
☐ Fresh mint
☐ Salt

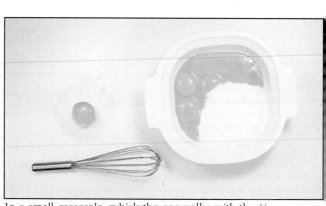

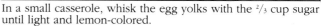

1 In a small casserole, whisk the egg yolks with the ²/₃ cup sugar until light and lemon-colored.

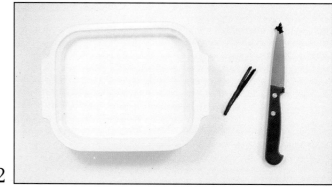

2 Slit the vanilla pod in half and remove the seeds. Bring the milk to a boil with the vanilla seeds, covered, on HIGH for 4 minutes.

3 Pour the boiling milk over the egg yolks and sugar. Mix well. Cook on HIGH for 1¹/₂ minutes, whipping every 30 seconds. Then cook for another 15 to 20 seconds, and allow to cool.

4 Beat the egg whites with a pinch of salt until thick and foamy.

5 Gradually add the confectioners' sugar and continue beating until stiff.

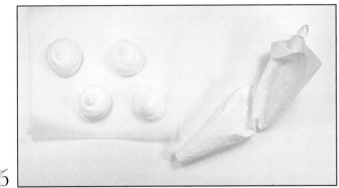

6 Put the meringue mixture in a pastry bag with a large nozzle. On wax pipe press out small mounds of mixture. Cook 30 seconds MEDIUM.

7 Coarsely chop the candied almonds.

8 In a casserole make the caramel stirring together the 4 tbsps sugar and 2 tbsps water. Cook on HIGH for 4 to 5 minutes.

9 Once the caramel has browned sufficiently, drizzle it over the meringues, using a fork.

10 Remove the meringues from the wax paper, and arrange them on a serving plate.

11 Wash and trim the strawberries. Slice thickly, then dice.

12 Serve the meringues with the custard sauce, the chopped candied almonds, and the diced strawberries, the whole garnished with fresh mint leaves.

CHOCOLATE CAKE

WITH

FRESH PEACH SAUCE

SERVES : 6

PREPARATION TIME : 15 minutes
COOKING TIME : 20 minutes
CHILLING : 4 hours

This is an interesting chocolate pudding, which is good for using up leftover croissants. The croissants are soaked in a cream and egg mixture, blended with melted chocolate and baked like a cake. It is served cold with a fresh peach purée flavored with almonds and kirsch.

INGREDIENTS

- ☐ 4 croissants
- ☐ 8oz unsweetened chocolate
- ☐ 4 tbsps butter
- ☐ 5 tbsps sugar
- ☐ ³/₄ cup heavy cream
- ☐ ²/₃ cup milk
- ☐ 2 eggs
- ☐ 4 peaches
- ☐ 2¹/₂ tbsps sugar
- ☐ 1 tbsp kirsch
- ☐ 1¹/₂ tbsps chopped almonds
- ☐ Fresh mint

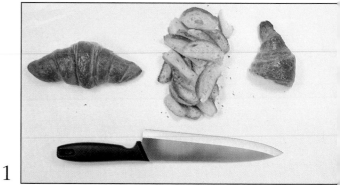

1 Cut the croissants into small pieces.

2 Coarsely chop the chocolate and melt in a dish with the butter and the 5 tbsps sugar on HIGH for 2¹/₂ minutes. When cooked, whip for 1 minute.

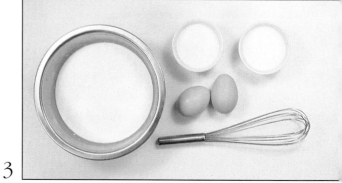

3 In a bowl whip together the heavy cream, milk and eggs.

4 Add the croissant pieces and allow to rest 2 minutes.

5 Add the cream/croissant mixture gradually to the chocolate, stirring continuously.

6 Butter a round baking dish and pour in the pudding mixture. Cook MEDIUM for 8 minutes.

7 After 2 minutes, remove the cake from the oven and stir the outer edges toward the center. Replace in the oven and cook another 6 minutes MEDIUM.

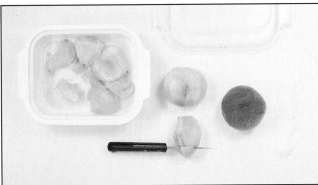

8 Peel and pit the peaches. Chop the flesh coarsely and place in a dish with the 2½ tbsps sugar. Cover and cook on HIGH for 4 minutes, stirring once.

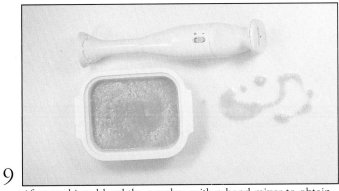

9 After cooking, blend the peaches with a hand mixer to obtain a purée.

10 Add the kirsch and the chopped almonds to the peach purée. Mix thoroughly and refrigerate.

11 After cooking, allow the cake to rest 10 minutes, covered. Chill in the refrigerator 4 hours before serving.

12 Serve the cake sliced, with the peach purée, and garnished with a few fresh mint leaves.

CAKE

WITH

PORT AND MELON SAUCE

SERVES : 6

PREPARATION TIME : 20 minutes
COOKING TIME : 10 minutes

A buttery cake is cooked in the microwave and then soaked in a port syrup. It is served with a sweet melon purée and garnished with sliced fresh melon and mint leaves.

INGREDIENTS

- ☐ 6oz butter
- ☐ ²/₃ cup sugar
- ☐ 3 eggs
- ☐ 1³/₄ cups flour
- ☐ 1 tsp baking powder
- ☐ 1 melon
- ☐ ¹/₂ cup cane sugar syrup
- ☐ 3¹/₂ tbsps port
- ☐ Fresh mint

1 Work the butter with a spatula until softened.

2 Add the sugar and whip until light and flutly.

3 Add the eggs, flour and baking powder. Whip in well and set aside.

4 Line a loaf pan with buttered wax paper.

5

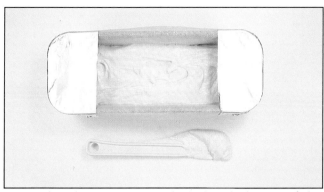

Pour in the cake mixture. Cover the ends with aluminum foil. Cook MEDIUM for 8 minutes. Remove the aluminum foil and cook on HIGH for 2 minutes.

9

Unmold the cake after allowing it to rest for 10 minutes. Slice thickly.

6

Halve the melon. Discard the seeds and cut the flesh of half the melon into pieces.

10

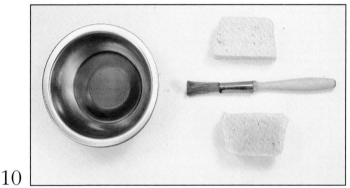

Soak each slice of tepid cake in the port syrup.

7

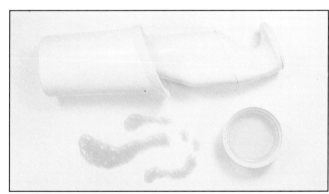

In a casserole, combine the chopped melon with 1¹/₂ tbsps cane sugar syrup. Purée, using a hand mixer.

11

Finely slice the second half of the melon and set aside.

8

Mix together the remaining cane sugar syrup with the port and 4 tbsps water.

12

Serve the sliced cake with the puréed melon and the melon slices, garnished with fresh mint leaves.

FRUIT COMPOTE

WITH

ALMOND BUTTER COOKIES

SERVES : 4

PREPARATION TIME : 30 minutes
COOKING TIME : 11 minutes

*For a refreshing summer dessert, bake this
tantalizing array of fruits in the microwave,
then chill and serve accompanied with crisp
almond flavored cookies.*

FRUIT COMPOTE WITH ALMOND BUTTER COOKIES

INGREDIENTS

- [ ] 1⅓ cups flour
- [ ] ½ egg, beaten
- [ ] ½ cup sugar
- [ ] ⅓ cup butter, softened to room temperature
- [ ] ¼ cup candied almonds
- [ ] 2 pears (not too ripe)
- [ ] 2 peaches
- [ ] 6oz plums
- [ ] 6oz seedless grapes
- [ ] 1 banana
- [ ] 2 oranges
- [ ] Salt
- [ ] Fresh mint

1 Prepare the cookie dough : mix together the flour and a little salt with the ½ beaten egg and ¼ cup sugar.

2 Incorporate the butter in pieces and the candied almonds, until you can form a ball of dough. Leave in the refrigerator for 30 minutes.

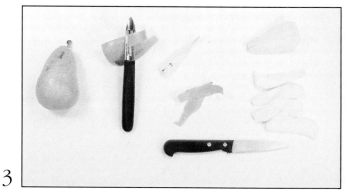

3 Quarter the pears, peel and core them. Cut in small pieces.

4 Arrange the pears on a small plate, and mix with 2 tbsps water and 1½ tbsps sugar. Cook, covered, on HIGH for 3 minutes.

5

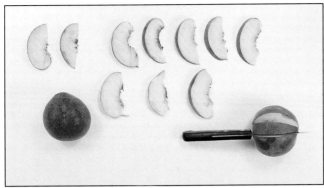

Quarter the peaches.

6

Arrange the peaches on a small plate, and mix with 2 tbsps water and the remaining sugar. Cook, covered, on HIGH for 3 minutes.

7

Pit the plums. Cut the grapes in half. Slice the banana.

8

Cook the fruits, covered, on a small plate, on HIGH for 3 minutes, stirring once.

9

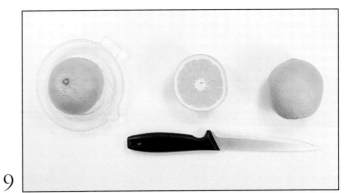

Halve the oranges and extract the juice.

10

Mix together all the fruits with the cooking juices and the orange juice. Leave in the refrigerator for at least 2 hours.

11

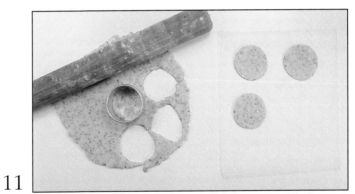

Roll out the cookie dough, flouring lightly as you roll. Cut out the cookies with a cutter and arrange the cookies on wax paper. Cook on HIGH for 2 minutes.

12

Allow the cookies to cool. Serve the fruit compote garnished with fresh mint, and accompanied with the almond butter cookies.

APPETIZERS

BAKED EGGS WITH RED WINE
SAUCE 50 - 52
BELL PEPPER SAUTE WITH
EGGS 46 - 49
CAULIFLOWER AND HAM AU
GRATIN 74 - 76
CHINESE NOODLE SOUP 22 - 24
CREAM OF ASPARAGUS
SOUP 26 - 28
CREAM OF CHICKEN
SOUP 30 - 33
ONION SOUP 18 - 20
PIQUANT CHORIZO
OMELETTE 54 - 56
ROQUEFORT-NUT
QUICHE 62 - 65
SPINACH FLAN WITH
NUTMEG 58 - 60
SPRING ROLLS 34 - 36
SQUID AND VEGETABLE
RAGOUT WITH CHORIZO 66 - 68
VEGETABLE MOLDS 42 - 44
VEGETABLE QUICHE 38 - 40
VEGETABLE SOUP 14 - 17
VEGETABLE-STUFFED FENNEL
BULBS 70 - 72

RICE, PASTA and POTATOES

BEEF MACARONI AU
GRATIN 82 - 84
CHINESE NOODLES WITH
DUCK 86 - 88
FRESH PASTA WITH HAM, CREAM
AND BASIL 78 - 81
SPAGHETTI BOLOGNESE 90 - 92
VEGETABLE RISOTTO 94 - 97

FISH and SEAFOOD

COD WITH WATERCRESS
SAUCE 126 - 129
FILLET OF SOLE WITH
ASPARAGUS 134 - 136
HADDOCK WITH GREEN
PEPPERCORNS 98 - 100
LOBSTER A LA NAGE 122 - 124
SALMON A LA BASQUAISE
118 - 120
SALMON TERRINE WITH
SHELLFISH 106 - 108
SALT COD FRITTERS WITH
PIQUANT SAUCE 102 - 104
SEA TROUT WITH LEEKS AND
SHRIMP 110 - 113
TURBOT WITH TOMATO
HOLLANDAISE 114 - 116
VEGETABLE AND SHRIMP
GALETTES 130 - 132

POULTRY and GAME

BREAST OF DUCK WITH
GRAPEFRUIT 166 - 168

CHICKEN CURRY 162 - 164

CHICKEN IN THE POT 158 - 161

CHICKEN TORTILLAS 150 - 152

GAME HENS WITH CARAMELIZED
CARROTS 154 - 156

GLAZED CHICKEN WITH
CHINESE VEGETABLES 138 - 140

STUFFED CHICKEN BREAST WITH
HERB VINAIGRETTE 146 - 148

STUFFED CHICKEN ROLLS IN
TOMATO SAUCE 142 - 145

MEAT

BEEF STEW WITH
TAGLIATELLE 178 - 180

GROUND BEEF CASSEROLE WITH
FRESH HERBS 182 - 184

LAMB BLANQUETTE WITH
MUSHROOMS 194 -196

LAMB CHOPS WITH MIXED
VEGETABLES 186 - 188

MOUSSAKA 190 - 193

PAPRIKA BEEF 174 - 177

PORK AND LENTIL
CASSEROLE 210 - 212

PORK SPARERIBS WITH PEANUT
BARBECUE SAUCE 218 - 220

ROAST BEEF WITH BEARNAISE
SAUCE 170 - 172

ROAST PORK WITH
MUSTARD 214 - 216

SAUERKRAUT CASSEROLE A
L'ALSACIENNE 206 - 209

SPICY ROAST LEG OF
LAMB 198 - 200

VEAL ROLLS WITH WILD
MUSHROOMS 202 - 204

DESSERTS

CAKE WITH PORT AND MELON
SAUCE 262 - 264

CARAMEL CUSTARD WITH
ORANGE FLOWER
WATER 246 - 248

CARROT AND ALMOND
CAKE 238 - 241

CHOCOLATE CAKE WITH FRESH
PEACH SAUCE 258 - 260

FLOATING ISLANDS 254 - 257

FRUIT COMPOTE WITH ALMOND
BUTTER COOKIES 266 - 268

FRUIT FLAN 234 - 236

MANGO SPONGE ROLL 230 - 232

NUT AND RAISIN
PUDDING 226 - 228

PEAR CAKE 222 - 225

PINEAPPLE AND RED FRUIT
CRUMBLE 250 - 252

RASPBERRY TART 242 - 244

ACKNOWLEDGEMENTS

Mr. Bonnat of Villeroy and Boch, glasses.
Mr. Krief of Daniel Hechter, chinaware.
Mr. Lochon of Rubbermaid, microwave utensils
Mr. Larturière of Guy Degrenne, cutlery.

THE LOOKS OF LOVE

50 Moments in Fashion
That Inspired Romance

Hal Rubenstein

HARPER
DESIGN

An Imprint of HarperCollinsPublishers

For David.
His is my favorite look of love, ever.
Lucky me.

CONTENTS

Introduction   9

50 Moments in Fashion
That Inspired Romance   12

Acknowledgments   246

Select Bibliography   248

Photography Credits   254

INTRODUCTION

Years ago, my parents and I were together at a family wedding. I hadn't seen my father in a few weeks and though we talked every day, he wanted to hear about everything I was doing, face-to-face. It didn't matter that my sideburns had already turned partially silver. To him, I would always be that kid on the tricycle, and to be honest, I kind of liked it that way. Plus, his ever-fervent interest never failed to make me happy and feel loved. As we were speaking, my mother walked by, wearing an organza gown with an impressive neckline for a woman in her early sixties, and a bell skirt that attracted attention in a lush, vintage gold, blue, and brown floral print. She looked lovely, and I wasn't the only one who thought so. My father gazed at her the way he continuously had for more than fifty years, as if he couldn't believe how he had wound up the luckiest guy on earth. He remained staring, straining his neck for one last glimpse, as if she were leaving on an extended trip, until finally she disappeared into a gathering of guests. When he turned back toward me, his smile was shy and his eyes were both glittering and searching, because in looking at her he'd completely lost his train of thought. "What the hell were we talking about?" he asked as he blushed in embarrassment. I was delighted, and I was used to it. Because it happened all the time.

I am my father's son, and that makes me a fool for love in all its forms and guises—whether directed toward a person, a city, a movement, or even an ideal—because of the unmatchable power romance possesses to engage us, to make us go to extremes, and to alter our reality.

The Looks of Love: 50 Moments in Fashion That Inspired Romance is a cavalcade of grand passions that opened our eyes; jump-started our senses; threw us way off the rails; shocked, teased, titillated, amused, horrified, or dazzled us enough to generate shifts in our social interactions; irrevocably modified our dating habits, even influenced how and whom we chose to marry. The book delves into films that offer embraces and entrances we won't ever forget, highlights others that remind us how ardor can be one heartbreak away from insanity, and celebrates those that surprised us with bold approaches toward sex, the power of women, the vulnerability of men, and other fresh stances for each gender to try on for size. Of course, some movies are here simply because they're meant to be swooned over, since at some point, everyone has dreamed of falling in love "the way they do in the movies."

Television may now have an even greater influence on affecting morals and behavior in everyday life, so in this book there are some of the shows and series that became appointment television, either because the relationships portrayed operated at a level of such heightened reality and mercurial lust that we could relish them as primers of inappropriate conduct, or because they were as enlightening as they were entertaining in revealing an acute awareness of the challenges and expectations we now encounter in facing marriage, friendship, separation, or loss.

Naturally, how can you thrill to a first date, a first kiss, a wedding, a midnight tryst, or a hot seduction on a dance floor if you don't dress the part? The clothes actors wore to cast their spells on and off the screen, the garments advertisers chose to outfit models in so we'd crave their products, the dresses veiled brides donned to walk down the aisle, and best of all, the looks brilliantly inspired designers sent down runways to offer us new visions of beauty are literally the uncommon threads that are woven through *The Looks of Love.* Here are the women who were courted wearing smart berets paired with maxi skirts or the soigné swirl of a bias-cut dress. Others unleashed tempestuous emotions accented by piles of teased tresses atop buttress-padded shoulders or to the syncopated rhythm of beaded, blond cornrows. There are men we adored who were oh-so-preppy, and some of the sharpest were natty, thanks to Savile Row. One man only selected suits from a Milanese designer who changed menswear forever, and then there's a singular star who wore a leather jacket men and women just keep right on buying because no one has ever looked cooler than he did.

I know how ridiculously blessed I am to have had the parents I did, to witness and learn firsthand how much richer life becomes when feelings aren't suppressed, when humor and intelligence are sources of sexual attraction, if constant agreement isn't a requirement for happiness, and when you know looking your best for someone else isn't superficial at all—it's a total rush. But my folks were just one couple. Recognizing the rarity of their relationship is what's always stoked my curiosity to seek other sources and discover whom, what, and where people have turned to become activated, elevated, or decimated by their emotions and urges. Evidently I'm not alone, because it's remarkable how intimately so many of us have been affected by the moments chronicled and remembered in this book.

My hope is that *The Looks of Love* educates and excites you, makes you smile as you recall the past, and allows you to go forward just a wee bit more aware of why we love, how we love, and whom we love. I'd be proud if you find something in these pages that will nudge you, whether it's today or sometime in the near future, into gazing upon the person with whom you've chosen to share a life with a look something akin to the way my father used to look at my mother. Life offers many choices, but when in doubt, I'll take romance every time. —H.R.

WHERE DO YOU BEGIN?

Love Story, 1970

Cheaply produced, poorly shot, and badly edited, *Love Story*'s plot stumbles along so devoid of pace or grace you can't help suspecting that Yale classics professor-turned-screenwriter Erich Segal pitched his novel of doomed young love to Paramount Pictures executives using flash cards written in Magic Marker. Compared to the sparkling banter between the magnetic screen couplings of Katharine Hepburn and Spencer Tracy or Doris Day and Rock Hudson, the initial flirtations between trust-fund hockey jock Oliver Barrett IV and poor but headstrong Jenny Cavilleri are so hampered by chips on every shoulder and defensive sarcasm masquerading as wit you can't imagine these two kids taking a stroll across campus, let alone giving up everything to be together.

Then why and how did *Love Story* leave millions of moviegoers eagerly sobbing hysterically into a puddle of soaked tissues? Made for a mere two million dollars, the film earned fifty times that to become the highest-grossing film of 1971, its tear-stained success due to the rare alignment of brilliant marketing, fortuitous timing, savvy casting, a reassuring return to overlooked attire, a single rhapsodic production element, and one rapturous plug from a famous fan.

Though first conceived as a screenplay, Segal's agent suggested he publish a novelization of an actual romance he had heard about as an undergrad at Harvard. The slender 132-page book with its eye-catching red, green, and blue cover graphic proclaiming its all-capitalized title, *LOVE STORY* (a riff on pop artist Robert Indiana's LOVE sculpture) was published on Valentine's Day 1970. That morning, on television's most popular rise-and-shine program, *Today,* cohost Barbara Walters announced, "I was up most of the night reading a book I couldn't put down, and when I finished it, I was sobbing. I cried and cried." Later, she introduced the unknown author by anointing his "tender, romantic, and lovely" novel as the book of the year. Segal, who had earned a reputation at Yale for his effusively theatrical lectures, responded with a charming balance of blushing self-satisfaction and "this is my best side" showmanship. By day's end, heart-shaped boxes of candy were the fallback gift if you couldn't procure one of the first printing's seventy-five hundred now-sold-out copies. Within several months, the personable author had appeared on every

noteworthy national radio and talk show (Johnny Carson had him on *The Tonight Show* four times in one month); the novel that Kurt Vonnegut called "as hard to put down as a chocolate éclair" was cemented onto the bestseller list, where it remained for forty-one weeks; and on a trajectory to sell nearly twenty-one million copies in hardcover and paperback in more than twenty languages. According to a Gallup poll, one in five Americans had read *Love Story.* The movie was released that same year, one week before Christmas.

Love Story begins with a piano gently plinking out the movie's now immediately recognizable theme. In fact, Francis Lai's Oscar-winning score may have been the film's single most successful marketing tool. The constant ramping of its inescapable melody from plaintive to full orchestral anguish was so effective in generating tears, whether you heard it in the theater, your car, the elevator, or every- where else it seemed to play in 1970 that film footage seemed almost unnecessary.

That is, until you saw *them.* Heralded by harpsichords and violins and initially framed against snow-blanketed backdrops, it is physiologically impossible not to marvel at the frosty-cheeked, genetically blessed loveliness of Ali MacGraw and Ryan O'Neal. MacGraw's striking looks had already been confirmed by both her career as a successful teen cover girl and her notable screen debut as the shiksa goddess in the film version of Philip Roth's *Goodbye, Columbus*. She had recently married Paramount's executive vice president Robert Evans. Friends with Segal for more than a decade, MacGraw championed the script, and Evans wanted to make his new wife happy.

O'Neal also came with preordained golden-boy status thanks to six years of playing Rodney Harrington, the tousle-haired heartthrob on television's first primetime soap opera, *Peyton Place*, adapted from Grace Metalious's once scandalous novel. O'Neal's tumbling golden locks, crooked smile, woefully earnest gaze, and varsity-jock gait made his handsomeness appear accessible to women yet unthreatening to men. To be honest, both actors give performances that offer less depth than an angora sweater. However, it didn't matter. Audiences had already committed Segal's clunky dialogue to memory. You couldn't find two more perfectly realized vessels to deliver the words.

Another reason for its popular embrace is *Love Story*'s release during the ascendency of the collective consciousness known as Woodstock Nation. Its headbanded participants regarded their bleached bell-bottoms, Indian-inspired embroidered tunics, Moroccan-inspired flowing djellabas, Jamaican-inspired beaded necklaces, and Asian-inspired water buffalo sandals as standard daywear, whether attending class or antiwar rallies. In addition, fashion was still riding the final waves of the British Invasion and its reliance on the neon hues and angular silhouettes of pop and op art. After all, Jenny loved the Beatles almost as much as she loved Ollie.

For the millions unseduced by and uncomfortable with such obvious flamboyance, there was cozy reassurance in gazing at MacGraw walking on a protest-free campus in a black turtleneck with a yellow tartan plaid skirt and matching scarf, going to a hockey game in a navy peacoat, and walking arm in arm with Ollie in her camel-hair wrap coat with red turtleneck or a smashing white wool trench—not bad for a girl on financial aid. As for Ollie, he was as unequivocally "preppy" as Jenny claimed, wearing Harris Tweed blazers over Shetland sweaters, blue oxford cloth shirts with the collars out, and a shearling coat. If his odious father didn't keep bringing up his family's

wealth, you might surmise that Oliver had been raised by the sales staff at Brooks Brothers. Looking at Ollie and Jenny together you can't help but come to the conclusion that as long as there are private schools, the New England coastline, Palm Beach, and people who want unassailable assurance of the appropriateness of their wardrobe, preppiness is now and forever. Abercrombie & Fitch, Tommy Hilfiger, J.Crew, and Ralph Lauren may serve as the shrines of this perpetually appropriate style, but its patron saints should be Mr. and Mrs. Oliver Barrett IV.

In the movie, we never learn what actual disease was killing Jenny, which could be why MacGraw looks no worse at her demise than someone who has just tolerated an overly aggressive cleanse. But did we really want to see MacGraw wasting away from leukemia? *Love Story*'s enduring success is the promise that love lost can be remembered as gloriously as love in bloom, and if you believe in this reality, you will never really be alone.

But as for love meaning never having to say you're sorry, that's pure fantasy. . . .

GRUNGE'S ROYAL COUPLE

Kurt Cobain and
Courtney Love, 1992

Marc Jacobs would be the first to admit he didn't create the "grunge" trend or claim his clothes were the real thing. As he stated in my book *100 Unforgettable Dresses*, "I was adjusting these beautiful silk plaids I had woven in factories in Lake Como whose patterns were copied from shirts I had bought for three dollars on Saint Mark's Place." It was the fashion press that stamped Jacobs's formative spring/summer 1992 ready-to-wear collection for Perry Ellis "grunge," both prodding its influence and ensuring his failure at the company. With most innovative fashion concepts, it takes several seasons for its signature elements to start bobbing into the retail mainstream, which is when the mall-shopping public either embraces or rejects it.

But the grunge staples of knit hats, plaid flannels, shapeless cardigans, dark striped T-shirts, and torn denim defied the natural order of merchandising. Casually adopted as the unofficial uniform of bands like Pearl Jam, Sonic Youth, and the Stone Temple Pilots, whose raw vocals, dissonant harmonies, jagged guitar riffs, and joy-free lyrics defined alternative music in the early 1990s, its source of origin were the clothing racks at Walmart, K-Mart, army-navy stores, and thrift shops. Jacobs was fired despite the reams of press—good and bad—that his collection generated. From a corporate point of view, the label couldn't make any money on their collection when Generation Xers were well aware of how to put together the look at a fraction of the runway version's price. "I know I was asking for it," said Jacobs. "But the attitude was so awkward and imperfect and available. And I loved it."

The sound had its own kingdom, the Pacific Northwest, and the look its own fashion capital—Seattle, Washington. And for the too-brief time they were a couple, the realm's reigning monarchs were Courtney Love, lead singer for the band Hole, and her husband, Kurt Cobain, front man of Nirvana and cowriter of what came to be Generation X's anthem, "Smells Like Teen Spirit," a title taken from the name of a deodorant Cobain wore.

Though their union turned out to be similarly star-crossed and, depending on your musical tastes, nearly as memorable, Cobain and Love's courtship played out a little differently than that of Romeo and Juliet. "We were peers on the same festival circuit before Nirvana clicked," recalls Love. "And we enjoyed a sense of competition, you know, that my band will kick your band's ass." Though Love was dating another alternative rocker (Billy Corgan of the Smashing Pumpkins), she "had a crush on Kurt right away. He was so damn pretty, except he didn't know it because he was small and thin and raised in a town [Grays Harbor, Washington] where the burly look of a longshoreman is what passed for handsome. So he was tentative around me for months. With us, it was more like me chasing him around the office, except our desks were stages in Amsterdam, London, and Seattle."

Initially, Love's tepid response to Nirvana's music made it easier for her to handle Cobain's reticence. "At first, I thought they sucked," says Love. "That was until I listened to their song 'Sliver' and then thought, 'Wow, this guy knows how to write a hook. I'm going to get him.'" So she walked up to Cobain and told him to "dump all those other bitches" hanging out in the back of the Nirvana van. He didn't argue. "Yeah, I was pretty aggressive," she says, "but I had the stuff to back it up."

Love also had a hell of a look that was hard to miss amid mosh pits filled with plaid shapelessness. In the early 1980s, Love had worked in the wardrobe department of Paramount Pictures under the tutelage of Bernadene C. Mann, who had supervised the clothes worn in such conspicuously style-savvy films as *American Gigolo, Eyes of Laura Mars,* and *Mommie Dearest.* "Because of Bernadene, I knew about fabric, the cut of clothes, and how they could help you make a statement," recalls Love. "I wasn't making any money as an actress, but I wanted to be noticed, so I hit

the thrift shops and bought all these nighties, especially ones made of crepe because they would hang the best and not shrink when washed. Then I cut them down and had someone on the staff sew them into baby-doll dresses. And that's what I wore 24/7." Even Love's wedding dress was a variation on the baby-doll theme. (Kurt wore pajamas.)

But as for the male side of grunge, it was nowhere near as calculated or aimed at starting trends. The garb was cheap and utilitarian, because in 1992, Seattle, like the rest of the United States, was in the midst of a severe economic recession that grunge bands had yet to cash in on. Love adds, "The idea was dress with no dependency on fashion or the outside world's opinion." Kurt often piled on the layers and hid his face behind his long blond hair "because he had a certain naïveté about his physicality," says Love. "Dysmorphia really."

The *New York Times* in its just-launched Styles section acknowledged the growing influence of the music but dismissed the requisite attire with hostile sarcasm. "This generation of greasy Caucasian youths in ripped jeans, untucked flannel, and stomping boots spent their formative years watching television, inhaling beer or pot, listening to old Black Sabbath albums, and dreaming of the day they would trade in their air guitars for the real thing so that they, too, could become famous rock-and-roll heroes." Not surprisingly, author Rick Marin missed the point of grunge. As fashion editor James Truman observed, "Punk was anti-fashion. Grunge is not about making a statement, which is why it's crazy for it to become a fashion statement."

By 1993, Nirvana's second album, *Nevermind,* was on its way to selling thirty million copies, while the *New York Times* dubbed Jacobs "the guru of grunge," even though he'd never set foot in Seattle. But the words *success* and *alternative* was not the kind of dissonance Cobain, now a rock idol whose look was being copied head to toe by fans world wide, felt was music to his ears. "When they started calling Kurt 'beautiful,' he did whatever he could do make himself look even more unattractive," recalls Love. "That's when he started dyeing his hair red and green. He didn't understand that people were dressing like him because they wanted to be like him. And because they liked *him.*"

Love didn't react the same way. Upon walking into Patricia Field's boutique in New York City (Field, who

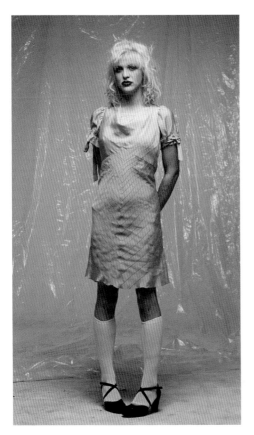

was also the costume designer for HBO's *Sex and the City*, owns the most reasonably priced, irreverently choose-it-or-lose-it clothing store in town), and seeing rows upon rows of baby-doll dresses, Love thought to herself, "Shit! I am the center of the universe. This won't go on forever, but right now I feel amazing."

Unfortunately, Love's delight wasn't contagious. The combination of drug addiction, chronic stomach pain, and overbearing guilt that fame was synonymous with selling out was too much for Cobain. After several unsuccessful attempts, during which Love saved his life, the singer committed suicide on April 5, 1994. In the letter he left behind, Cobain called his wife "a goddess . . . who sweats ambition and empathy" and feared that their daughter, Frances, would become "the miserable self-destructive death rocker I've become. . . . It's better to burn out than fade away."

Live Through This, Love's album with her band Hole, released the same week as Cobain's death, quickly went platinum and became the bestselling record of her career. In 1997, she was nominated for a Golden Globe for

her role in *The People vs. Larry Flynt* and continues to act (playing a troubled singer modeled after her former self on *Empire)* and record, although she's given up her baby-dolls for designer dresses, even appearing in advertisements for Versace and Saint Laurent. As for grunge, it's never really left, because the inexpensive sources of those clothes that caused Jacobs to be fired still exist and are thriving. Every few years, some style pundit will look at a couple of utility-themed collections that feature plaids and corduroys and cry that grunge is back, but since when are plaids, cords, and knit hats anything new? Go to any college campus today and they're part of the student body's standard-issue uniform. And that's the unfortunate irony of Cobain's demise.

"Kurt and I bought a Lexus (to replace Cobain's cherished old Volvo) when we started making money, and the night we brought it home someone keyed it because they must have thought we were selling out," says Love. "I have to say I agree with Bono who said that selling out means there are no more tickets left at Madison Square Garden, so everyone who's jealous should just shut the fuck up."

VERSACE
SIGNATURE

NEW YORK   BEVERLY HILLS   SAN FRANCISCO   WASHINGTON   HOUSTON   SAN DIEGO
CHICAGO   LAS VEGAS   BAL HARBOUR   HONOLULU   NEW YORK CITY   VANCOUVER   TORONTO

WHAT TO WEAR IN PARADISE

Gianni Versace's
Miami Collection, 1992

In 1992, my oh-so wonderful friend, designer Gianni Versace, and his lover, Antonio D'Amico, were on their way to Cuba. Since there were no direct flights from Milan to Havana, they landed in Miami for a ten-hour layover until their chartered departure to Castroland. Forever impatient and unapologetically addicted to visual stimulation, Versace told his chauffeur to "take [him] some place that isn't boring." The driver dropped him off at the News Cafe on Ocean Drive in South Beach. Five minutes later, an elated and thoroughly smitten Versace canceled his flight to Cuba and stayed in Miami Beach for two weeks in a constant state of euphoria. Everywhere Versace looked he saw what he liked best. As he said to me, "My God, Halino. There is beauty everywhere! These boys and girls are heaven. ¡Questo e il paradiso! (This is paradise!)"

Thanks to its titillating depiction as a nonstop sun-baking, love-making, booty-shaking, and drug-taking candy-colored playground on the 1980s television series *Miami Vice* (plus some savvy if somewhat shifty rapid urban redevelopment), South Beach swiftly transformed itself in the late 1980s from being known as "God's Waiting Room" (due to flocks of northeastern-based senior citizens, aka "snowbirds," who occupied its small hotels to escape winter) to "the American Riviera." Credit for South Beach's population makeover needs to be shared with the dozens of fashion magazine editors and photographers, led by Bruce Weber, who targeted this southernmost stretch of Miami

Beach from the marina to Lincoln Road as an incredibly affordable, location-rich, and climate-friendly place to produce photo shoots. And where there are lots of fashion shoots, there are lots and lots of real and would-be models. By the time Versace arrived, if you had been sitting at a nearby table at News Cafe, playing a drinking game whereby every time a torso sporting less than 10 percent body fat Rollerbladed by you had to take a shot of tequila, within fifteen minutes Versace would have had to step over you.

So infatuated was the designer with the city's "sights"; its infectious, Latin-infused sensuality; its collective state of flirtatiousness; and its incessantly invigorating sunlight, that he wasted little time buying the only private residence on Ocean Drive as well as the hotel and land adjacent to it. He invested nearly $40 million in creating his gated and gilded villa, Casa Casuarina, and began returning almost monthly, often to design his collections. He once said to me, "What is there to look at in Milan? Please! In Miami, I imagine my clothes everywhere, on everyone. We belong here." Versace was not alone in this thought: even prior to his encampment, the sands of South Beach were already studded with printed bikinis and Speedo-size bathing suits sporting his trademark Medusa. The designer's slim fit and peekaboo perforated cotton pants were nearly as common as denim in local clubs and bars.

Perpetually tan, Versace had already expressed his enthusiasm for being seaside with his 1992 women's spring ready-to-wear featuring prints that combined red and gold starfish, seashells, and coral against stark black-and-white geometrics. But he no longer needed to conjure a fantasy beach. Now he could celebrate his home away from home.

Introduced halfway into the presentation of his samba-ready women's 1993 spring/summer ready-to-wear collection, exploding into a full phantasmagoria of glorious optic overkill with his pulchritudinous 1993 men's spring show, and then photographed in its entirety for blatant can't-catch-your-breath sexual intensity by Bruce Weber for the Versace Jeans Couture campaign, Versace's Miami collection is riotous, dazzling, luxurious, ridiculous, almost unimaginable, cheekily laughable, and tongue-in-every-cheek erotic.

Exhausting possibly all available silk worms on the planet Versace created shirts, dresses, bandeaus, and jackets that combined his already identifiable Palladian architectural embellishments, animal prints, and signature Greek key design, with neon-bright art deco curves and arches, bejeweled starfish, conch shells, tiger lilies, hibiscus blooms, seahorses, palm trees, birds of paradise, boating flags, and endless ways to enshrine the letters *M-I-A-M-I* and *F-L-O-R-I-D-A* against backgrounds that gleefully color-clashed: sunset orange with lime green, blush pink and royal blue, or lipstick red with black and four shades of gold. He paired these deliberately failed exercises in subtlety with either white cotton or black leather pieces lavishly embellished in gold studs, Western-style.

It was the era of the supermodel, and since Versace is primarily responsible for promoting the term and elevating these women into modern-day goddesses, he employed every one of them on the runway and in advertising, including Cindy Crawford, Linda Evangelista, Christy Turlington, and most prominently, his favorite, Naomi Campbell. The male models were on at least equal par for beauty, although most people wouldn't know their names today. At the time, you just wished you did—as well as their phone numbers. Together, the clothes and the cast were staggering.

So were the price tags on the collection. A weightless silk shirt was $1,500. It didn't matter. In the summer of 1993, if you thought that you were sexy and you were anywhere that cast a shadow, you were wearing something by Versace. In Miami, even at that price, the silk shirts became second skin, and Versace became the beloved unofficial patron saint—and sinner—of South Beach.

Despite their prohibitive cost, Versace actually thought his Miami collection was very "casual." "My dear, I will show you the best way to wear these shirts," he told me as he walked to his closet (though I was much taller, we were almost the same size). "First, you tie one around your waist. Then you take another and slip it on but don't button it. Then pull on your bathing suit, lace up your Rollerblades, and glide down Ocean Drive with your shirts flying behind you like a beautiful bird. That's why you are here, my darling. Miami is no place to be shy. You won't be sorry, I promise, you." All the while he was dressing me, his eyes were twinkling.

BUYING INTO HER REALITY

Newlyweds, 2003

Admit it. You giggled when she couldn't understand how tuna from a can could be called Chicken of the Sea or when she treated her Louis Vuitton Murakami bag like it was a prized Yorkie. You probably felt very superior when she didn't know exactly what to do with a mop or almost any kitchen appliance. Well, now Jessica Simpson doesn't have to bother to figure it out.

The Jessica Simpson Collection is the retail industry's most successful celebrity-based clothing company. Founded in 2005 in partnership with the late shoe magnate Vince Camuto, it supplies more than thirty product lines, from its bestselling "you can dance all night in them" shoes to a complete array of womenswear and accessories as well as maternity and children's clothes. Sales from the collection, sold in thirty countries around the world, have topped $1 billion. Simpson launched a home collection in early 2015 too. All this from the woman who couldn't make a bed.

How did this blond power balladeer with a four-octave range, who dropped out of school at sixteen to sign with Mariah Carey's former husband-manager Tommy Mottola, who intended to mold her into a more talented alternative to Britney Spears, come to spearhead such a trusted mass-market brand? Why, when she makes personal appearances at Macy's and Dillard's, where her brand is a top seller, do the stores have to cordon off the street to accommodate her fans even though she is touting fragrance and not singing a note?

Simpson's success in the fashion industry is not a result of her album sales, though she has records that have gone gold and platinum. Nor can it be tied to her highly attended concerts, where the rush of seeing a big voice come out of such a little Texas girl with folksy charm was often compromised by her scattered patter and occasionally wavering pitch. Television is ultimately what made Simpson so successful, more specifically, it was the first reality TV show ever to feature a young couple straight from their wedding, trying to coordinate their happily-ever-after in a hurry that positioned her to soar to the top. Both as cute as they were guileless and just a little bit clueless, Jessica Simpson and her then husband, 98 Degrees singer Nick Lachey, soon become known everywhere as the "Newlyweds."

Watching their show, *Newlyweds,* ten years later is rough: it's plagued by crude, overlit visuals; every shot lingers three beats too long; and scenes extend until they're running on fumes. The premise follows Nick and his bride, four months into their marriage, as they rattle around a barely furnished, utterly beige McMansion groping for answers as to how to furnish it or fill a day when they're not performing. Their affection for each other is obvious, yet their conversations lack awareness of the world outside their lavish if generic love nest. They tend to accept each other's statements at face value without seeking insight, and exhibit only intermittent curiosity about getting to know each other any better than they did on their wedding day. It's as if the two had tied one on together after being crowned king and queen of the prom, then woke up the next morning to discover a jointly signed marriage license on the nightstand.

But *Newlyweds* had an irresistible hook that dumbfounded men and fascinated women. In an effort to

differentiate Simpson from her equally blond but overtly sexier pop competition, Britney Spears and Christina Aguilera, Simpson declared to the press that she was a virgin and would remain so until her wedding night. If she had unearthed Jimmy Hoffa's remains word wouldn't have spread as fast. Prior to the show's premiere on MTV, the pretty Southern belle and her testosterone-riddled consort dated for nearly four years without consummating their relationship. *Newlyweds* began on their wedding day. Simpson, attired in a strapless Vera Wang lace gown was a true picture-book bride, lovely and blushing for all the right reasons. Lachey looked happy too—and about to explode. MTV was suddenly very glad Michael Jackson and Lisa Marie Presley had turned them down, as Nick and Jessica were an instant hit. The show debuted with 1.3 million viewers, the highest ratings ever posted for a reality series opening on the network. By the premiere of the second season, *Newlyweds* had amassed an audience of nearly five million. More astonishing was that the show was besting its network primetime television competition in attracting the coveted target demographic audience of viewers aged twelve to thirty-four that advertisers crave.

Today, we are approaching bold-faced name overkill, but in 2003, audiences were still voyeurs-in-training. The 1971 PBS cinema verité series *An American Family* that followed the drama and dissolution of the Loud Family was the first to go this route, but the genre didn't really catch on until 1992, when MTV scored big with *The Real World*, which brought together unrelated youths to live under one roof. But *Newlyweds* focused on something entirely new: famous folks.

With a camera trailing almost every move, celebrity reality TV couldn't help but be snoopier, juicier, and more intrusive than *Photoplay*, *People*, *InStyle*, or even

Entertainment Tonight. Newlyweds quickly spread the word that most of the world was composed of closeted peeping Toms and Tinas. Luckily, lots of celebrities turned out to be latent exhibitionists. In no time at all, there was too much information from Tori Spelling and Dean McDermott, Beyoncé and Jay Z, Whitney Houston and Bobby Brown, and Kimora Lee and Russell Simmons. *Newlyweds* also hinted at the viability of *Celebrity Apprentice* and *Dancing with the Stars*, and ultimately gave license to demonically manufactured subspecies of humanity famous for being famous; flotsam like the Gosselins, at least a hundred heavily painted housewives, and the clan we watch with equal parts hate and resolute envy, the Kardashians.

Notoriety is one way reality "stars" choose to capitalize on their fleeting fame. But Jessica Simpson didn't do that. Despite her obvious domestic and intellectual challenges, there was something about this pretty, incredibly insecure, always slightly overwhelmed girl that struck a chord—and projected an endearing innocence. It turned out the prom queen with everything—looks, talent, money, success—constantly yearned to be someone's one and only, and sank low when her husband neglected to confirm it. To its millions of fans, *Newlyweds* proved Jessica was one of them. And so began a love story that has now lasted a lot longer than her marriage to Nick.

Newlyweds ran for four seasons. In 2006, a year after the show ended and her divorce from Lachey became final, Simpson took her first steps into retail with a shoe collection; Lachey is now a well-liked emcee and host on television competition shows like *The Sing-Off*. But like any celebrity stepping into unfamiliar territory, Simpson became an easy target. Yet when the press mocked her for masking her extra weight in "mom jeans," Jessica went on *Oprah* and insisted they were cute and comfortable and, that she, like a lot of women, sometimes had to make the best of it, even if she wasn't always at her best. Hearing a kindred soul, women rallied to her side. She parlayed this affinity into a documentary series for VH1 entitled *The Price of Beauty*, in which she traveled the world, looking at other cultures' beauty standards, rather than at herself. Not long after, she signed on as a spokesperson for Weight Watchers. Clearly, her fans trusted her.

Meanwhile, her shoes, which provided the look of coveted Louboutins for under $100, were an immediate success. At Camuto's urging, she chose to enter the fashion arena. Success was hardly guaranteed. After all, Jennifer Lopez, Lindsay Lohan, Queen Latifah, Rihanna, Justin Timberlake, even Sarah Jessica Parker, had tried and failed. But maybe if one of them had said to their potential customers what Simpson did, their results might have been more like hers. "I have been every size on the planet and I understand women," Simpson said. "And I just know how to dress them. I know there are all different kinds. There's life in the whole world beyond LA and New York. I understand Middle America and their mind-set."

Simpson is espousing more than mere empathy. Instead, what she has come up with is a singularly fresh approach for a celebrity line. For once, it's not about looking like a Jennifer, a Rihanna, or a Jessica. Rather than cajole girls and women into dressing so they can pretend they are rock and movie stars, Simpson turned to the lives of her potential customers for her inspiration while simultaneously proving that she was also one of them. Those millions of women now believe in her, sharing Simpson's hope "that a girl [can] go to the shopping mall with her mother and she'd [find] a great new outfit and still have some money left over for lunch at McDonald's." So who needs tuna fish?

LOVE IN DEATH

Bonnie and Clyde's
Last Looks, 1967

I was so excited. *Two for the Road* (1967) was finally at a theater near my university. You couldn't produce a movie more up my alley. Stanley Donen, the director of *Singin' in the Rain* (1952), the best musical ever, had collaborated with Frederic Raphael, screenwriter of the caustic and hip *Darling* (1965) on this new film that leap-frogged back and forth in time highlighting five pivotal stages in the marriage of a couple played by Albert Finney at his post–*Tom Jones* (1963) swarthiest and a never-more-bewitching Givenchy– and Paco Rabanne– clad Audrey Hepburn.

My friends and I went to see the film on a Saturday night, when theaters often advertised a "sneak preview" in addition to the regularly scheduled film. Since the sneak was always a mystery, we decided to catch it first and save the obvious best for last.

Two for the Road ranks as one of my five favorite romances. But I didn't make that judgment until I saw the film again two weeks later, because after exiting the theater that night I could barely remember any of it. The second half of my evening was a disoriented blur, so emotionally shattered and physically shaken was I by the film that ran first: *Bonnie and Clyde.*

It begins with a close-up of Faye Dunaway's cherry red lips. Then the camera pulls back to introduce her guiche-curled character, Bonnie Parker, getting herself ready for something or someone to rescue her from the mundane life she fears destined for. Her savior is right beneath her window, fixing on stealing her mama's car. Most girls would scream out the window for help at first sight of a thief. But when the thief, Clyde Barrow, happens to be Warren Beatty at the height of his beauty, you can't blame a girl for racing out of the house—furiously buttoning her only

decent dress—to confront him face-to-face. Their conversation is all tease and taunts, a meet cute infused with danger. But sparks are flying everywhere. By the time she slides in next to him and they're driving away in Mama's car, they're well on their way to becoming America's first love-struck pair of notorious media stars, and we're delighted, convinced they belong together.

Had *Bonnie and Clyde* followed the familiar structure of a gangster picture, Warner Brothers might have known how to market the film. But no shoot-'em-up had ever initiated a nonstop crime spree just twenty minutes after a scene of flirtation and slapstick humor punctuated by a sprightly banjo-picking sound track. Genre films weren't supposed to shift gears so abruptly. After a comically bungled robbery, an ambitious teller jumps on the getaway car's running board. In a panic, Clyde shoots him in the face at close range. Suddenly, the film abandons its Walker Evans palette of prairie serenity, and we're eye-to-eye with the teller as blood splatters from behind his cracked glasses all over the car's shattered window. Clyde is stunned, Bonnie is hysterical, and we are paralyzed.

Like a diabolical hypnotist, director Arthur Penn has us spellbound, rooting for the lovers regardless, which we do against our better judgment, right up to the film's end, one of the most violent ambushes ever staged in an American film—a heart-stopping fusillade of bullets shot in balletic slow motion so the audience can savor the impact of each shot. Adding to the agony, the film crosscuts twice between Bonnie and Clyde, who are separated when surrounded. The first shot reveals each one's awareness of their doom; the second shows each looking at the other with all the passion, pain, ache, excitement, and gratitude they've found in each other. They couldn't be closer if they'd died in each other's arms.

Warner Brothers premiered the film at a Texas drive-in and then dumped it in second-run theaters. Critics were merciless. *Time* hated it, *Newsweek* hated it. The *New York Times*'s moralizing Bosley Crowther went on a rampage condemning it as "a cheap piece of bald-faced slapstick comedy that treats the hideous depredations of that sleazy, moronic pair as though they were as full of fun and frolic as the jazz-age cutups in *Thoroughly Modern Millie*."

Three events saved *Bonnie and Clyde* from obscurity. Beatty, who had produced the film, took it to the Montreal Film Festival, where it was cheered with a standing ovation. Then *The New Yorker* published a seven-thousand-word rhapsody by Pauline Kael, a rising critic with a contrary nature who would eventually achieve cultlike devotion, claiming the film "restored [her] faith in Hollywood's audacity. . . . It puts the sting back in death." Following Kael, *Time*'s film critic Stefan Kanfer reversed his initial assessment, running a second essay on *Bonnie and Clyde* as a cover story. Finally, there was a new audience of young baby boomers. The spirit of rebellion was in their clothes and music. The Vietnam War and race riots were brought into their living room, courtesy of the evening news. With disillusion all around them, they identified with the romanticism of the film's lawlessness. Despite being children of the Depression, Bonnie and Clyde made perfect folk heroes for the 1960s. Responding to such pressure, *Bonnie and Clyde* was not only in rerelease by year's end, it was a smash hit, earning ten times its initial run.

In addition to responding to the film's antiheroism, audiences also went crazy for how Bonnie and Clyde looked and what they wore. Though this was Theadora Van Runkle's first film as a costume designer, the former fashion illustrator wisely surmised that an unconventional period film needed a new approach, so she ruled out "dull colors and marcelled hair. . . . The styles had to be palatable by Hollywood standards. The stars were, after all, two very good-looking people." After reading that whenever the real Bonnie and Clyde came into money they would order clothes from the Marshall Field catalog, Van Runkle envisioned the characters as burgeoning junior executives. She patterned Clyde's wardrobe of three-piece chalk-stripe suits and vests after studying photographs of the dapper gangster Pretty Boy Floyd—the polar opposite of the flower-power guise of the guys in the audience.

But the miniskirted girls with waist-length hair and a curtain of bangs sitting next to them were in for a bigger surprise. Van Runkle saw Bonnie as "a career girl who discovers her own niche with bank robbery, adopt[ing] the masculine image of power with midi skirts, jackets, and berets." To complete the wardrobe, she added long cardigans, deep V-neck white silk blouses, and A-line skirts to reflect Bonnie's need for easy movement and constant travel.

Van Runkle's finishing touch was hats. Believing they imparted the inept yet daring thieves an air of much needed

confidence, she gave Clyde straw fedoras and poor-boy caps, while Bonnie was almost never without a beret, which according to Van Runkle was "the final culmination of the silhouette . . . combining all the visual elements of elegance and chic. Without the beret [her outfits] would have been charming but not the same." Beret production in the French town of Nay, outside Lourdes (site of the world's only beret museum) went from five thousand to twelve thousand a week. And women, who had rejected midi skirts initially, suddenly craved them, and runway shows in 1968 reflected that. By the end of the decade, midis were far more acceptable work attire.

The film's seismic effect on style is due to a bit of cheating, however. Despite their wardrobe, both stars looked contemporary because they rejected the hair and makeup of the period. Beatty refused to chop his hair in a bowl cut or part it in the middle as Clyde Barrow had done. Dunaway's golden skin, near nude lip, and black-winged eyeliner were as current as her long bob (which became the 1960s version of the Rachel, the oft copied hairstyle worn by Jennifer Aniston on *Friends*). Dunaway's 1968 *Vogue* cover looks as if it could have been shot on the set between takes—and her look is still relevant now.

The American Film Institute rates *Bonnie and Clyde* number twenty-seven on the list of 100 Greatest Films of All Time. As immune as our culture has become to on-screen violence, the lovers' last looks before death still tear a hole in your heart. Should you need your faith restored in the power of love, then download *Two for the Road*. Just wait a few days.

AN INTIMATE DINNER FOR FIVE HUNDRED

Dries Van Noten's
Fiftieth Collection Presentation,
2004

It never fails. Just as the Paris Fashion Week schedule ramps up at the end of the monthlong, four-city sojourn of ready-to-wear collection viewing—editors, journalists, buyers, and bloggers all hit their version of the marathon runner's "wall." Their conversation runs dry. They are sick of wearing everything they've packed and, most grating of all, have had it with sitting in a limo for six hours a day, schlepping from one end of town to another in order to accommodate designers who insist on presenting another runway presentation in yet another newly discovered obscure location sure to do their new strokes of sartorial genius justice.

Lesser-loved designers who opt for staging in obscurity run the risk of no-shows. However, Dries Van Noten's ravishing, unpredictable, brilliantly detailed, yet undeniably pragmatic clothes are such a joy to behold, the fashion crowd will follow him anywhere. "But this is halfway to Belgium!" griped one editor when she saw the address in the twenty-third arrondissement on the invitation for the Antwerp-based designer's spring/summer 2005 presentation.

The aviation factory where Van Noten chose to present and celebrate his fiftieth ready-to-wear collection for spring/summer 2005 is in an area called La Courneuve, which is about a forty-minute drive outside Paris if there is no traffic. But show time was set at 8:00 P.M., which meant attendees would have to travel in rush hour. It seemed little consolation that the invitation stated that dinner would be served. In fact, the combined effect of distance, traffic, appointed time, memories of too many languidly served, never-ending mass-industry dinners, and the weird seating assignments (the invitations gave no indication of section or row; mine featured merely the number *251*) didn't deter many, but everyone on their way was in a collective pout.

Fashion and punctuality are rarely on speaking terms, so by 9:00 P.M., those already in attendance had had their fill of the odd specialty cocktails and the intense, disorienting scarlet and indigo lighting in a makeshift anteroom surrounded by heavy velvet curtains. Even Dries's most ardent fans were beginning to lament not having played hooky for an early dinner at the usual Paris Fashion Week hangouts of L'Avenue or Caviar Kaspia.

And then the curtains parted.

In a vast hangar, large enough to accommodate several planes, all attention was focused on one table—463 feet long, covered by a single white tablecloth, lit by the glow of 125 Murano glass chandeliers and, in a display of jaw-dropping splendor and almost obsessive-compulsive precision, appointed with five hundred place settings of Lenox Hamilton china, Colbert silver, and hand-carved crystal stemware.

Each of the Napoleon III dining chairs were marked by a number that corresponded to the one printed on each invite. Music from two grand pianos accompanied the short search for one's seat at the table. The overwhelming visual rivaled the banquet scene in Stanley Kubrick's *Barry Lyndon*. Still, the immediate conversation at the table alternated between "Where are the clothes?" and "How long is it going to take to feed all these people?"

The latter question was answered when 250 waiters, each holding two plates of coquille St. Jacques, emerged from out of the darkness to form two uniform lines behind both long sides of the table. At a signal evidently only dogs and waiters could hear, five hundred guests were served simultaneously. Clearing and the arrival of the main course, cod en papillote, repeated the same staging.

As glorious as the meal, setting, and direction was, there was still one issue: When and where would the collection appear? Only a few observant guests remarked that the table was abnormally wide—eight feet instead of the usual three or four. The reason soon became clear as the Murano chandeliers rose and models wearing Van Noten's collection came strutting down the middle of the dining table. Far from being anticlimactic, each look was the perfect picture of what to wear on a day to walk hand in hand with someone under cherry blossoms in April—voluminous, full-skirted white cotton dresses, old tapestry prints screen-printed onto washed linen skirts, bands of bold stripes alternating with elaborate Indian beading, and hand-painted silk coats. The wine wasn't making his dinner guests giddy, but Van Noten's singular "I couldn't care less what is trending, because this is what I like" bravado was at its most lighthearted and flirtatious. As the show ended, the chandeliers lowered, surrounded by a shelf containing five hundred bound books covered in gold foil jackets featuring all of Van Noten's previous collections, with a Polaroid of the dinner table taken from exactly the seat it faced affixed to the inside front flap.

Before leaving, I ran backstage to thank Van Noten for the most unexpectedly marvelous evening I'd ever experienced during any fashion week. With an odd mix of blushing modesty and knowing nonchalance he replied, "Please. That's very kind. But I did it for me." We were so ardently gushing during the ride back to Paris it seemed to take minutes. The next day, there was nothing but pity for the shows being presented. All anyone could focus on was memories of the night before, with an occasional break to gloat over those who had chosen to skip the evening for a free night in Paris. As for the show, fashion editor Cindy Weber-Cleary admitted that it wasn't until she saw the runway photos of it that she realized, "I had seen maybe forty of Dries's fifty shows and this may have been my favorite show of his ever. But last night, my mind was so completely blown, that I couldn't even process the clothes. I just wanted the recipe for the cod."

OBSESSION

Calvin Klein

PERFUME

AH...
THE
SMELL
OF IT

Calvin Klein's
Obsession, 1985

"In the 1980s, everyone was just insane about sex," recalls Calvin Klein. "It's all my friends and I thought about. Not falling in love. Sex." Then again, if you were in Klein's circle, how could you *not* think about it? It was the driving force of his success.

While Klein was resolute in his devotion to a cerebral, austere minimalism in his ready-to-wear collections, when it came to merchandising his diffusion lines, the designer never wavered from erogenous thinking. To launch Calvin Klein jeans in 1980, Richard Avedon's camera panned an unnervingly alluring fifteen-year-old Brooke Shields as she asked, "You want to know what comes between me and my Calvins? Nothing." To introduce Calvin Klein underwear in 1982, the designer hired photographer Bruce Weber to capture a heroically chiseled Olympic pole-vaulter named Tom Hintnaus—clad only in a pair of the designer's eponymous waist-banded white briefs featuring a noticeable bulge and the faint but unmistakable outline of his penis—framed against the whitewashed walls and Aegean blue sky of Santorini, Greece. When the ad appeared on a huge billboard over Times Square, it snarled traffic, every poster version installed in a New York City bus shelter was stolen within a week, and it was voted one of the ten pictures that changed America by *American Photographer* magazine. One of the few designers as handsome as his models, Klein even featured himself in a menswear campaign. "Men, women, *everyone* was in love with Calvin," says Diane von Furstenberg. "He was the most seductive man."

So when it came time to publicize Obsession, the new scent in his growing fragrance line, with its sensual top notes of mandarin orange, vanilla, peach, and basil, Klein "couldn't bring myself to think about young couples holding hands or some virgin picking flowers in a field. I wanted sweat. I wanted lust. I wanted the scent of someone driven mad with desire."

The ads for Obsession shattered convention. Nearly stripped of color, Bruce Weber's sepia-toned and slate-blue–washed ads were dense with oiled and muscled male and female nudes, sometimes posed as austerely as statuary positioned by Leni Riefenstahl, or in ensemble shots with limbs so tangled it was hard to tell what belonged to whom. Klein frankly admits, "These were my fantasies, some of them realized. And I enjoyed them." In the center of the first print ad, Klein focused on model Josie Borain. "I was mad about her," says Klein. "She was so androgynous, and not obviously sexy, but her eyes were yearning and her lips captivating." Borain's face was riveting, to be sure, but fully lacking in expressing a sense of connection or satisfaction. In fact, the only eye contact in an Obsession ad occurred when a model in a television spot would look directly at the viewer and spout some portentous lines of unrequited passion cribbed from F. Scott Fitzgerald or Ernest Hemingway and then vanish in pursuit of his or her distraction. The screen would then cut to a shot of the curvy, ergonomic bottle as a voice intoned, "Calvin Klein's Obsession . . . Ah, the smell of it."

"I really did think it smelled like sex," says Klein. He was hardly alone. Domestic sales of Obsession were $30 million in its first year and more than $100 million by 1987.

OBSESSION FOR MEN

OBSESSION FOR MEN Calvin Klein

Calvin Klein

To Order Call Toll Free 1-800-645-6789. Credit Card Orders Only.

STUCK
IN THE
GARDEN

Woodstock, 1969

Woodstock's powerful aftermath cannot be denied, as it was both the catalyst and the calling card for a generation. The 450,000 people (including me) who attended thought they were going to "An Aquarian Exposition in White Lake, N.Y.—3 Days of Peace and Music." After all, that's what the weekend of August 15–17, 1969, was called on the original poster. But when we came home, all anybody would ask us was: "Really?! You went to Woodstock?!"

Watch the movie or listen to the album and it's inarguable. The artists and their music ranged from major to mind-blowing. From Richie Havens's feverishly passionate performance of his anthem "Freedom" to climax his opening set on late Friday afternoon, through the explosive career blastoff of Santana on Saturday afternoon, the ecstatic response of this instant city when spotlights revealed a dense marijuana cloud overhead as Sly and the Family Stone sang "I Want to Take You Higher" at three on Sunday morning, the unexpected power of a new talent like Joe Cocker opening your eyes wide by midday, the collective rush of witnessing Neil Young blend his harmonies as the new addition to Crosby, Stills & Nash late Sunday night, to finally, the truly legendary experience of Jimi Hendrix's electric guitar version of "The Star-Spangled Banner" to send us home on Monday morning it was a *you are there* moment that, while not all of it can be recalled with equal clarity, remains unforgettable all the same.

But what happened in Bethel, New York, forty miles from the town whose name bears the touchstone, was more than a mere music festival: it was the defining cultural movement of the second half of the American twentieth century. The Woodstock generation was a term used to define anyone, living anywhere in our nation, who participated in the

anti-Vietnam war movement, free love, folk rock, communes, "magic" buses, racial equality, smoking pot, ungraded tutorial college programs, and organic farming. It applied to those who grew their hair long or left it natural or wore a headband. It applied to those who favored the peace symbol as a sartorial motif, be it a belt buckle, a collection of buttons, an iron-patch, or a T-shirt in a wardrobe that housed bell-bottoms, dashikis, Mykonian tunics, peasant blouses, Indian prints, Birkenstocks and leather sandals, handmade jewelry and love beads, granny glasses, and something with fringe.

Though she didn't perform at the event, Joni Mitchell wrote that the goal of the Woodstock generation was "to get ourselves back to the garden." A lovely thought. But in reality, the goal of most of the hundreds of thousands who attended Woodstock was to get themselves back to New York City, except they couldn't because their cars were stuck in the mud. While images from the *Woodstock* film were skillfully chosen to create a feeling of commonality and universality, "the greatest peaceful event in history," as *Time* called it, was mainly populated by one specific demographic from only one geographic region. That's because there was no Ticketron or StubHub in 1969. The only places you could buy tickets for the festival were New York City record stores. Some were available by mail order—a much slower and not very popular process.

In addition, tickets for the whole weekend cost twenty-four dollars, a considerable sum at a time when the average price of a movie ticket was $1.50, a subway token cost twenty cents, and you could have seen the Beatles at Shea Stadium in 1964 (*see page 181*) for $4.50. So, in fact, the vast majority of those who bought the initial 186,000 tickets sold for Woodstock were middle-class white kids from New York City who drove up with a suitcase full of "outfits" from hip clothing stores in Manhattan like the Different Drummer in the trunk of their cars, expecting to change when they got to the local motel or B&B to wash and change for each day's events.

But that didn't happen. Instead, another quarter million people showed up, clogging the local roads and the New York State Thruway. Everyone parked their cars wherever they could, as close as they could, and then walked. For miles. And once the skies opened up late Friday night while Joan Baez was singing and dumped a relentless thunderstorm on this instant city sitting on blankets in a natural amphitheater, there was no going anywhere. It is amazing that despite overflowing Port-O-Sans, four hundred bad acid trips, three thousand medical emergencies, eight miscarriages, one death, a severe lack of food and water, and epic lines for less than a

half dozen telephones to call Mom and Dad to tell them you were okay, no incidents of violence or theft were reported. It helped that we were stuck, that everywhere you went looked just like where you were, so why bother, and that the crowd heeded both promoters and performers who repeatedly stressed community and sharing. It also helped that an unofficial report claimed that nine out of ten people at Woodstock were high. I think the figure is low.

Savvy local farmers charged as much as twenty dollars to tow your car out of the mud. Most attendees had so much of it caked on their feet, shoes, and bodies, they looked like tribesmen in a *National Geographic* spread.

But it was only when we came back to the city that the mythology began. The press marveled at hundreds of thousands celebrating in harmony, and a nation held on, however briefly, to the notion that this was the true dawning of the Age of Aquarius. What were the most obvious symbols of this soon-to-be-hallowed, highly evolved throng of pioneers? The clothes. Consequently, it didn't take long for everyone who didn't get to attend Woodstock to want to look like they had—or pretend that they had. No wonder the Different Drummer soon expanded. And more than four decades later, in a world far more cynical and riddled with disharmony, there is ample evidence that the notion of Woodstock Nation lingers as a desirable utopia. Because while most past seismic fashion movements—like disco and 1980s glitz—are now relegated to theme or Halloween costume party getups, the trappings of this accidental, mystical congress keep reappearing on retail shelves and racks.

For spring 2015, *Vogue* cited among the trends they were most eager to see return: flared pants, bohemian evening, suede, gladiator sandals, and mismatched earrings. *Elle* cited knee-grazing sweaters, fringe, the tent top, and mismatched layering. Every one of these options was on prominent display at Woodstock. Their constant reappearance brings us back to a time when we felt freer and easier about ourselves, when expressing one's individuality seemed effortless and unlikely to be judged. There were no "it bags" at Woodstock. No "to die for" $1,600 shoes you needed to have for the weekend. A half million people wore what they liked (or what they were stuck wearing), and no one judged them on the *Fashion Police* the next morning. And with Joni Mitchell's face recently adorning an ad campaign for Saint Laurent, perhaps it's a reminder that we would still like to get back to the garden. Not a bad idea. Now if I could only find those extra unworn outfits that were left packed in the trunk.

LOVE FLIRTS

The Tantric Tease of
Pillow Talk, 1959

Attention women of the world who celebrate those who led the way for equal rights, equal pay, and the shattering of the glass ceiling: you have egregiously overlooked one of your earliest, most influential pioneers. Before *Ms.* magazine launched in 1972, before Gloria Steinem gave her seminal "After Black Power, Women's Liberation" speech in 1969, before Marlo Thomas launched *That Girl* on television in 1966, even before Betty Friedan published *The Feminine Mystique* in 1963, there was a woman who used her position as America's number one box-office star to portray a successful, self-employed working woman—with a smashing wardrobe and an apartment to match—who lived alone and liked it. Her name? Doris Day. Yes, lovely, funny, "Que Sera, Sera"–singing Doris Day starred as a woman in charge during the same era when others of the fair sex were employed as secretaries by Mad Men. If you don't recall her groundbreaking role as Jan Morrow in *Pillow Talk*, maybe that's because the film is best remembered as the first smash hit "sex comedy," not as a feminist tract. However, for this fresh film genre to work, it had to be a tale of two equals.

It's odd that *Pillow Talk* remains the most winning example of the sex comedy because no one in the movie is getting any. In fact, there's not one moment in the movie when any two people are resting their heads on pillows in the same bed.

But what made the genre so immensely popular wasn't watching folks have sex: audiences got off on the chemistry between its stars. In *Pillow Talk,* Doris Day and Rock Hudson cast a spell on each other that utterly changed their careers and our perceptions of how to play at and win the battle of the sexes.

Day first garnered attention singing with Les Brown's band in the 1940s, then established her film career as the sweet-yet-never-sticky ingenue in a series of pleasant enough musicals. But after standing with toe-to-toe toughness opposite James Cagney as singer Ruth Etting in *Love Me or Leave Me* (1955) and handling Alfred Hitchcock's twist on her good-girl persona with perverse effectiveness in *The Man Who Knew Too Much* (1956), audiences began to suspect the pretty blonde had grit as well as a voice that always sounded like music.

It was immediately apparent that Rock Hudson had the perfect *everything*. With a name coined by his Svengali-esque agent Henry Wilson (Hudson was born Roy Fitzgerald) and the word *beefcake* invented by gossip columnist Sidney Skolsky to describe him, Rock was six foot five inches of superhero-comics handsomeness, with a voice that could have made him millions in the phone-sex industry. He became certifiably worthy of worship as the hunk in the tissue-grabbing *Magnificent Obsession*, then respectable as the scion in the epic saga *Giant*.

It was producer Ross Hunter's idea to cast Hudson in the comedy as Brad Allen, a marriage-phobic playboy songwriter so horndoggishly cliché that Hudson could make fun of his hunkalicious image. For Day, Hunter had a bolder mission. He was determined to expose the actress's latent sex appeal in her role as Jan Morrow, an interior decorator and Brad's telephone-party-line-sharing adversary. Despite Day's assertion that she was "the peanut butter girl next door" both offscreen as well as on, Hunter was set on taking advantage of "one of the wildest asses in Hollywood" by giving her a makeover to "chic her up" so that "every secretary and housewife will say, 'Look at that—look what Doris has done to herself. Maybe I can do the same thing.'"

Though the plot of *Pillow Talk* is based on the hoary notion that New Yorkers still contended with party lines in the late 1950s (by 1959, multiple parties sharing one phone line was mainly confined to rural areas), it allowed for the classic setup employed in romantic comedies since Shakespeare:

mistaken identity. An exasperated Jan can't get through to her clients because Brad is constantly enticing his conquests on the phone. Interrupting his wooing, she calls him a slimy pervert. He accuses her of being a priggish old maid. They have never laid eyes on each other. Through a plot contrivance, they finally come face-to-face, or rather Brad first marvels at Jan's swaying "fanny" when he spies her dancing in a club. Overhearing her subsequent conversation at an adjoining table he realizes the knockout he just eyed is his phone nemesis and probably out of his league. Thinking quickly when he's able to come to her timely aid in dealing with her inebriated escort, he pretends to be exactly whom one might wish Rock Hudson to be in your fantasy daydream—an aw-shucks-ma'am, mountain-owning Texas cowboy, new to the big city, with a best-ever porn-star name: Rex Stetson. Falling for his refreshing guileless honesty, Jan is hooked. Rex even takes her home and won't come in for coffee. Date after date avoids the bedroom. Innocence reigns and then strains.

Because the roles have been reversed, girl-next-door Doris winds up in a revolutionary position for a female romantic lead in a 1950s film—the sexual aggressor. Though there's the ever tipsy, always salty maid (played by the great Thelma Ritter) spouting age-old adages like, "If there's anything worse than a woman living alone, it's a woman saying she likes it," Jan doesn't look either unhappy or undatable. On the contrary, she is ravishing. Producer Hunter kept to his word. Bill Thomas is credited with devising the costumes, but Hunter brought in designer Jean Louis—famous for the black strapless gown Rita Hayworth wore to sing "Put the Blame on Mame" in *Gilda* to create the key looks for Day's sensational wardrobe. In reality, her ensembles are somewhat extravagant for an interior designer, even a successful one—she wears Balenciaga-inspired swing coats and mink hats to go on daily appointments—but Hunter's goal was to show off the actress in a way that was more urbane than bombshell. He was so successful in achieving this, one could imagine every look as part of the wardrobe of the incoming president's wife, Jacqueline Kennedy.

Jan's clothing choices also serve as a barometer measuring her increasing frustration to heat up her relationship with supposed virginal "Rex." When Brad first spies that "fanny," it's covered in an off-white silk sheath gown with a demure draped boatneck. Jan's also sporting an updo that seemingly transforms her blond hair into a halo. On their

first date, her Dior-like emerald silk cloak has a closure as high as the blouses under her daywear suits. But it's not long before Rex's charm has her choosing sexier stuff: a deep jade-green spaghetti-strapped sheath with trapunto pleating on the bodice and a flirtier, more feathery hairstyle. A red velvet scoop-neck dress gets her invited away for the weekend. When Jan realizes she's been duped by Brad, she's back in fitted black suits with a buttoned-up white blouse tied way too tightly with a bow. Of course, at the end, when Brad ultimately carries Jan off to bed, she's in silk pajamas. Why waste any more time?

Of course, the plot's predictable, but what makes *Pillow Talk* a movie you can't help watching with a stupid grin on your face is that Day and Hudson are simply delicious together, like Astaire and Rogers, except no one has to lead, or Tracy and Hepburn, with less banter but much cuter and better dressed. Though the furthest the pair ever gets to physical contact during *Pillow Talk* is playing footsies from separate bathtubs that position the actors side by side

with the aid of split-screen technique and one "Finally, at last!" kiss, somehow that's enough because we've been basking in nonstop starlight for an hour and a half in a relationship between equals. Day gives as good as she gets in *Pillow Talk*—and eventually gets what she wants on her terms.

On-screen, Day and Hudson made two more hit films together (*Lover Come Back* [1961] and *Send Me No Flowers* [1964]). Offscreen, Day and Hudson became lifelong friends. Two months before Hudson became the first public figure to die of AIDS in 1985, his last on-camera appearance was as Day's first guest on her new cable show *Doris Day's Best Friends,* on which she promoted the Doris Day Animal Fund. "I had to have Rock Hudson as my first guest," she said. "So I called him and he said, 'I'll be there. You can count on me.' And that was the truth." On the show, Day told Hudson that her favorite movie was *Pillow Talk.* "I miss those laughs we used to have. We really had fun making movies. We should do it again." That would have been real nice.

STAIRWAY TO HEAVEN

John Galliano Transforms
the Palais Garnier, 1998

Dior's spring/summer 1998 haute couture collection at the garishly ornate Palais Garnier opera house in Paris was an astonishing, phantasmagorical experience, conceived with a buoyant enchantment that delighted in ignoring any reference to reality. It was a presentation that will go down in fashion history as one of its most memorable, undoubtedly vividly imprinted forever in the memory of all who attended. Fashion editor Tim Blanks described the event as "every single drug experience everyone had ever had in their lives concentrated into ten minutes."

The presentation was an authentic spectacle, a fashion show every sartorial client, industry professional, and fashion enthusiast dreams of witnessing, though we could never have imagined exactly what that mind-blowing experience could be. But one man saw it all so clearly, an extraordinary, once-in-a-generation talent with a vision so revelatory that within a mere five years at the helm of the House of Dior, he revitalized the storied yet stolid atelier, redirected the way celebrities dressed for the red carpet, and jolted an industry into remembering that without fantasy, fashion is just merchandise.

In the ten minutes that comprised the presentation, John Galliano instantly assumed the role of haute couture's preeminently joyous romanticist. His inspiration for this unparalleled evening of persistent indulgence were the more than 130 floridly rendered portraits that Marchesa Luisa Casati, the eccentric Italian heiress and patron of the arts, had commissioned of herself from artists such as Giovanni Boldini, Augustus John, and Kees van Dongen during the early twentieth century. A self-proclaimed muse of seemingly unlimited means, Casati declared her life's ambition was, as Oscar Wilde once said, "to be a living work of art," and she worked at it with relentless gusto. A flagrant exhibitionist who would walk the streets of Paris naked under billowing furs with two cheetahs on jeweled leashes, she was photographed by Man Ray and Cecil Beaton; dressed by Fortuny, Erté, Vionnet, and Poiret; claimed to be the catalyst for Cartier's now signature jeweled panther; and was a devoted patron of Sergei Diaghilev's Ballets Russes, whose wildly theatrical productions staged at the Opera Garnier she declared her style primer.

But all of the above is incidental to Casati's notoriety. Her scandalous reputation blossomed to legendary status with jaw-dropping parties, balls, and masques staged at her residences in Paris, Rome, Capri, and Venice (her Palazzo Venier dei Leoni now houses the Peggy Guggenheim art collection), where Nijinsky and Isadora Duncan might perform; dinner would be served by nude waiters covered in gold leaf, and Elsa Schiaparelli, Coco Chanel, and Colette could witness the flame-haired, chalk-white-skinned marchesa dressed as living sculpture by Dalí or wearing live snakes as jewelry.

Galliano marveled at "this woman's determination to spend every penny she had to celebrate extravagance and outrageous imagination." In 1998, he had been at Dior for only two years, though his rise and renown had been swift, initiated by having sold his entire graduation collection from Central Saint Martins in London to Browns, the city's most fearless independent retailer. After school and a few years where financial struggles cramped his creativity, he was hired by Europe's most powerful luxury conglomerate Louis Vuitton Möet Hennessy (LVMH) to design for Givenchy in 1995. After only one rapturously extolled season, LVMH moved him over to the more prominent House of Dior, a once revolutionary brand that now resonated with a bourgeois, meticulously crafted elegance. "I don't know if it was naïveté or arrogance, or perhaps both," says Galliano, "but I had been invited on this magical trip called haute couture and I wanted to push the limits of what was possible, to transform make-believe into something real and to test the *petites mains* [the indispensable white-coated seamstresses in ateliers whose "little hands" routinely outstitch Cinderella's fairy godmother with their unmatched artisanship]. I thought why not re-create Casati's lust for opulence with fresh eyes."

As if the flamboyant grandiosity of Charles Garnier's design for the opera house was not quite enough, Galliano draped yards of fabric from its pillars, installed shutters to intensify the mystery of viewing angles, brought in tables, massive candelabras, and created floral arrangements that must have emptied greenhouses throughout Paris. "Well, isn't that what you would want to see if you get to go to the ball?" Galliano asked with customary cheekiness.

Having turned back time, Galliano then sent down the opera's grandest of all grand marble staircases a parade that incited as much woozy frivolity as wondrous bedazzlement. The collection was more like a pageant: it wasn't driven by one specific motif or consistent aesthetic. One dress had nothing to do with the next. A 1920s-style blush chiffon tea dress with densely embroidered massive silk roses crossed paths with a plum hoop-skirted ball gown with a bustle that Scarlett O'Hara would have envied. A fluid white crepe gown that recalled the sculpted curves of Cristóbal Balenciaga shared a landing with a featherweight short guipure lace dress with bell sleeves. A model in a backless black-and-gold brocade gown that appeared to be held intact by one jeweled strap languished against a pedestal, only to be upstaged by another in a gold lamé gown with a neckline slit to the navel and a leg slit up to a huge bow at the hip, exposing calf-high bejeweled gold lace-up boots. Models dressed in Edwardian gowns, worn with appropriately enormous brimmed hats by Galliano's friend and milliner Stephen Jones, were colorized versions of Cecil Beaton's stark black-and-white costumes that he created for the Ascot race scene in *My Fair Lady* and walked pairs of white Russian wolfhounds. But nothing could outshine the funnel-neck, dolman-sleeved cloak encrusted in dizzying patterns of gold, coral, yellow, tangerine, and cobalt-blue crystals—an Erté lithograph brought to life. The models, gliding down the staircase despite their high-wire Manolo Blahniks, seemed hypnotized with happiness, their hair marcelled in vibrant shades of lemon, cerise, midnight blue, and a deep shade of red Casati favored.

But for all the exuberant theatricality on display, what was unmistakable was Galliano's goal of capturing and celebrating each woman's singular beauty. "Couture can be dominating, because the temptation to let the clothes take over is so powerful," says the designer. "But even in couture, the woman should not be in service of the dress.

The key to glorifying women is in the thrill of understanding how each fabric works against the body, and then crafting it not just with precision but also with emotion. The first skill is admirable. But it's the passion that will make it memorable."

To ensure the women never vanished amid such sorcery, Galliano chose to cut most of the clothes on the bias (cutting fabric on an angle to give it more stretch and suppleness). "The magic of the bias is how it molds itself around the female form," Galliano says. "I find this technique far more erotic than simply exposing skin. What was so thrilling was the constant discovery that each fabric reacted to a bias cut differently. Some taffetas would shrink, others would change texture with dye, and then there was satin-backed crepe—my favorite—that was so mercurial it would become like liquid second skin once it absorbed body heat. This show was the start of my never-ending education with fabric."

There was hardly a single dress a woman could wear to go to real life's more mundane celebrations like weddings and Christmas parties, but that was never the point for either the brand or the designer. In an instant, the House of Dior became a flashpoint once again; a can't-miss stop on the fashion train that lasted throughout Galliano's tenure and now continues thanks to the deft and daring silhouettes of Raf Simons.

Though the delirious audience was blinded at the finale by a shower of hand-cut paper butterflies, Galliano clearly saw pragmatism beaming through the evening's eccentricities. To him, "haute couture is the place to create an atelier's parfum, so that you can distill its essence into the more accessible eau de toilette that is the ready-to-wear, and then the cologne that pervades those must-have accessories." From Galliano's couture explosion came his bias-cut day dresses, the nip-waisted suits, and the gossamer gowns that became the bread and butter of Dior's subsequent ready-to-wear and pre- collections, and the most obvious proof that romance had returned to a house that had lost that loving feeling. Galliano still blushes when he is reminded how precisely those who attended can recall that evening. "I thought I did good." He asks, "I guess I did, didn't I?"

Tim Blanks says, "When you look up the words *fashion show* in the dictionary, this is the show that should be there." With all respect to Tim, when you look up the word *unforgettable*, that's where a picture from this show should be.

DESIGNER CLOTHES MAKE THE MAN

The One True Love in
American Gigolo, 1980

For a movie that's all about sex, *American Gigolo* isn't much of a turn-on. It's a film steeped in loneliness, driven by acts of emotional distancing, and for all the supposed pleasure being provided by the love god at its center, you can count the unforced smiles on one hand.

Julian Kaye (Richard Gere) is a much-in-demand stud, a hooker with a heart of cold, but a man you have to admire, even envy, for the precision he exercises in crafting a guise so thorough and compelling he communicates everything he cares to reveal about himself long before he caresses you, because it's in his walk. Director Paul Schrader shoots Richard Gere gliding down the street, never looking left or right, since he already knows what's happening around him. A peacock secure in the allure of his plumage, Julian is a parade without a band. Take John Travolta's cocky Tony Manero strut in *Saturday Night Fever*, reduce speed slightly and mute the Bee Gees sound track: the result is Julian, a man who covets attention not because he offers anything worth celebrating but because he just wants you to want him.

Travolta was originally set to play Julian, but Gere proved the better man, because Travolta rarely hides his glee at his own good fortune. Gere's studied self-absorption is in harmony with someone who offers momentary ecstasy but never wants to be touched. And though *Gigolo*'s plot, which has Julian being framed for the murder of a one-time client, is resolved by the selfless love for a woman, it's an unmoving happy ending, because, for Julian, the true object of his erection is right there in the mirror. The only believable, enduring romance in *American Gigolo* is between Julian and his Giorgio Armani wardrobe.

Luckily for both, Mr. Armani turns out to be a great lover. Schrader's camera may be unnerving as it stealthily traverses the actor's face and body with stalker-like adoration, including a frontal nude shot as gratuitous as it is appreciated, but the only time Gere's face brightens with unforced delight is when he gets his arms around the clothes in his closet. After swiping a line of coke and putting on Smokey Robinson, this moody poseur is suddenly singing and springing in place as he lays one suit option after the other onto his bed: First a greige one, then gray, then russet brown, then a pale taupe; each more appealing then the next. Then Julian bends and pulls the drawers closer to him. Each reveals one more "sex toy"—silk ties, dress shirts, sport shirts. He is completely in the moment, putting his looks together with the surety of a painter tapping the magic of his muse. In his case, it's Giorgio Armani for whom he is hopelessly smitten. And once the rest of America got a look at what the handsome, silver-haired Italian designer had to offer, so were they.

At the end of the 1970s, menswear had created a chasm between the extremes of body-hugging disco shirts tucked into kick-pleated gabardine and man-in-the-gray-flannel-suit boredom. Meanwhile, American business had started to boom again. The titans of Reaganomics and its mutant race of yuppies had been unleashed onto the landscape, and both craved an image that telegraphed their lust for conquest and sexual energy, not unlike Julian's, except their ardor was more often toward money.

When Schrader called Mr. Armani and asked him to provide the wardrobe for Julian, he sent him pictures of the little-known actor. Armani, who had started his business five years earlier, was impressed with Gere, believing the actor could "reveal all the sensuality of [his] style and its new relationship between clothes and body." Working directly with Schrader, Armani stressed that Julian "expose his need for

fitness, and a certain amount of vanity." He said, "I wanted his narcissim to show through without apology. This meant abandoning the stereotypic dress code of what it is to look a man in favor of softer and looser clothes, like unstructured jackets, which fit naturally and move more gracefully with the body. It was no longer just women who had the right to exude carnality and charm."

Amplifying Armani's impact was the great Italian production designer Ferdinando Scarfiotti, who tempered the harsh, glaring terrain of Los Angeles with shaded settings of muted gold, dusty blues, dune tones, and hints of burnt umber, in other words, he used the same palette Armani did. Richard Gere's apartment predates the launch of Armani Casa, the designer's home collection, by two decades, but Scarfiotti's decor is prescient.

The combination of the film's titillating subject matter, its confidently preening aesthetic, and its rock score featuring Blondie's signature hit "Call Me" proved to be a better ad campaign than Armani could have devised alone. He said, "I never imagined that my clothes would become a symbol for the 1980s, but *American Gigolo* became the vehicle for the style revolution Americans claim I created. I do find it funny how my style transferred so easily from Julian's profession to other business, but I think that's because the clothes looked modern and comfortable, and when you enjoy what you wear, as the handsome Mr. Gere's character did, you feel good and you feel strong. I guess that's why Americans started calling it 'power dressing.'" Julian is damn lucky, not only because sex workers rarely find love while "on duty," but because no matter how covetable his wardrobe, a gigolo's prime is short. As for Julian's first passion, Giorgio Armani remains Italy's most successful designer, maintaining his position as day-to-day creator of his brand's ready-to-wear, underwear, haute couture, furniture, watches, shoes, eyewear, cosmetics, perfume, and hotels. In his eighties, with a net worth of more than $8 billion, he's still got the power.

DONNA KARAN'S BIG LOVE

The DKNY Wall, 1992

For sixteen years, the "painting" dominated the New York City intersection where Broadway crosses into SoHo. Taking full advantage of its canvas—the side of a building six stories high and a half a block wide—the massive black-and-white composition was impossible to ignore. In fact, savvy cabbies would deliberately steer clear of cars racing down Broadway to Houston Street with out-of-town license plates because first-time drive-byers were almost destined to become distracted liabilities. It's not that a fashion label producing traffic-stopping commercial art was anything out of the ordinary. Campaigns for Calvin Klein, Gianni Versace, and Dolce & Gabbana routinely reveled in the extreme beauty to be found in one or both sexes. But not only was this riveting, brand-defining image devoid of any fantasy male or female, it didn't even show clothes!

Instead, the in-your-face billboard featured a north-to-south rendering of the Manhattan skyline viewed through the stencil of four block letters: D-K-N-Y. For Queens-born clothing designer Donna Karan, "New York is the center of the world, the gateway to everything, because it's the one city where life isn't divided into neat categories." Driven by this urban energy she defines as "chaos by design," Karan decided to create a lower-priced streetwise clothing line separate from her ready-to-wear collection, one geared specifically "for grown women who work, for young women who go to school with my daughter Gabby, for people who start the day uptown and, going nonstop, end the day downtown." However, Karan had no clue what to call it until she took out at a pair of shoes to put on and read the label inside the heel: MAUD FRIZON PARIS. At the time, Frizon was the essence of Parisian footwear.

DKNY
THE FRAGRANCE

Since Karan's inspiration was "the city that grounds [her]," she decided to call it Donna Karan New York. But that was too many words to put onto a label, and DKNY was born.

While her marketing department was less than thrilled with Karan going public with her urban love affair ("What are people in LA going to think?" asked one nervous executive), Peter Arnell, the influential advertising authority who handled the brand's campaigns, got so turned on by the image of fusing these initials that he proposed doing away with models, clothes, taglines, retail locations, even explaining what the ad was actually about. "New Yorkers want to be the first to know everything. Peter wanted to see how withholding information would drive people's imagination," recalls Karan. He proposed depicting the New York skyline in black and white and seen through the stencil of the four letters. Karan was delighted: for like Woody Allen, Karan believes that New York is a city that appears at its most romantic and powerful in black and white.

Karan and Arnell found the perfect canvas: fifteen thousand square feet on the side of the building at 600 Broadway. The billboard was hand-painted, which was first rendered on an eight-by-eleven-inch grid and then scaled up one section at a time. The project took six weeks to complete. However, in the original working photograph, the Statue of Liberty appeared insignificant in the upper right corner. Realizing that was no place for this city's most towering and powerful symbol of womanhood, Arnell shifted the image so that he could install her in the vertical showcase of the letter *K*.

The billboard was finished before any clothing with the DKNY label was shown to the press. First year's sales of DKNY topped $40 million, a record sum for a start-up diffusion line. But placement of the billboard was also key to the brand's identity. In the 1980s, SoHo had developed into a city within a city, with new magazines like *Details* and *Paper* chronicling this "downtown" culture that was redefining art and design, reshaping nightlife and dining, and devising a new mode of dress to suit the scene. Karan and her then husband, Stephen Weiss, a sculptor, recognized and identified with this new, cool center of urban energy. The billboard's entryway-to-SoHo positioning was not merely Karan's way of saying "I want a piece of that," it singled out DKNY as the first Seventh Avenue ready-to-wear brand offering the promise of looking "downtown" to all who would wear the brand, whether they lived uptown, in Queens, or points beyond. Karan made good on that promise, designing DKNY by shrewdly blending just enough rough-edged elements like work boots, fused leather jackets, and raw-edged seaming with her signature Seven Easy Pieces—a pulled-together philosophy of dressing that featured jersey dresses, suits with stretch, and leather trenches to make the clothes work no matter where in the city you were headed, day or night. Proof of DKNY's success was not just in the brand's earnings: a younger generation of shoppers was suddenly no longer as skeptical of Seventh Avenue's ability to acknowledge and appeal to them and their buying power.

But just as trees have a life span, signposts of great passion rarely last. In 2009, the building's new tenant wanted to make SoHo fall in love with them too. And so the mural was replaced by a drab wall of taupe exterior flat paint framing just two words: HOLLISTER—CALIFORNIA. Traffic now flows smoothly down Broadway.

SIMPLY IRRESISTIBLE

On the Soundstage in
Singin' in the Rain, 1952

Ask people who favor film as much as they savor fashion to name the most stylish actress in screen history and you can bet your weight in Birkin bags the overwhelming majority would unhesitantly reply, "Audrey Hepburn." And they'd be right.

Now ask the same folk which male star has had the greatest influence on the way men dress and get ready for a lot of forehead scratching. The few willing to take a stab at the answer are likely to cite from the following list of candidates, but as well-appointed and occasionally trendsetting as their wardrobes may be, Cary Grant, Gary Cooper, Gregory Peck, Fred Astaire, Clark Gable, James Dean, Steve McQueen, Marcello Mastroianni, Sean Connery, Warren Beatty, Jean-Paul Belmondo, Johnny Depp, and George Clooney are all the wrong answer.

Gene Kelly exuded a quality none of these men possessed as naturally—a virile nonchalance. This seemingly breezy way of dressing allowed him to move with finesse that never seemed either feminine or androgynous. In 1958, a highbrow television program called *Omnibus* broadcast an hour with Kelly called "Dancing: A Man's Game" that not only featured him in a smashing tap duet with boxing great Sugar Ray Robinson (whose footwork more than holds its own), but in an astonishing series of split-screen images, contrasts Kelly's solo dance moves with similar positions used by legendary athletes as diverse as Mickey Mantle, Johnny Unitas, Dick Button, and the equally virile ballet dancer, Edward Villella.

Watching Fred Astaire, you can't help but ask yourself, "How does he do that?" But when a man watches Kelly dance, he's more likely to think, "I *want* to do that!"

Kelly's superb athleticism infused his work so effectively that his dances were more than just great "numbers." They were soulful expressions of yearning, hope, and joy. He could effortlessly turn dance into courtship because not only did he look like he wanted the girl and would know what to do with her when he got her, but you could also never really tell when he was about to start dancing. That's what makes the title number in *Singin' in the Rain* so glorious to watch. Kelly looks like he's strolling on an emotional high. And then suddenly his happiness gets the best of him and he begins to sing, "Doo-dloo-doo-doo-doo . . ." There's another reason why his dancing seems so organic: his clothes never telegraph that he's a hoofer.

Gene Kelly never looked sexier than when he was wearing some variation of a V-neck sweater over a white shirt with the sleeves rolled up paired with flat front chinos, white socks, and low-slung loafers. In fact, a man could take virtually every single off-screen outfit Kelly sports in *Singin' in the Rain*—the greatest musical of all time, and the most delightful movie about the making of movies—wear it today, and look like he'd put on his Sunday best. Men of his era were secure in a suit and fine in their jeans. It was that wardrobe in the middle where they needed direction. Kelly's look became the touchstone. Via film, he almost single-handedly defined American sportswear for men.

In *Singin' in the Rain*, chorus girl Kathy Selden (Debbie Reynolds) and silent-film star Don Lockwood (Kelly) meet cute at a movie premiere, but it's a meeting that goes horribly wrong. After spending weeks searching for her, Don finds her, but Kathy won't have anything to do with him.

But Don is smitten. When he finally gets her to soften, he tries to express himself in words, except he stumbles, confessing, "I'm such a ham. I guess I'm not able to without the proper setting." He then takes Kathy to what looks like a bare soundstage, until Don creates movie magic: the white cyclorama becomes a limitless pastel sky at sunset. A fog machine sends "mist from the distant mountains." He turns on colored lights, surrounding Kathy in a garden whose blooms are dyed to match her lavender chiffon dress. He positions her on a ladder as if she is a lady "standing on her balcony in a rose-trellised garden." Then, with a soft summer breeze from a wind machine and five thousand kilowatts lighting her best side, Don tells her, "You sure look lovely in the moonlight, Kathy." He begins singing "You Were Meant for Me" in that famous voice with a slight rasp that sounds like corduroy, and then offers his hand in dance. Kelly is wearing a classic tennis vest, a white oxford shirt with rolled-up sleeves, matching tennis white flat front pants, white socks, and white-and-brown loafers. Their dance is part tap, polka, fox-trot, and all flirtation. And when the number is over, with the pair holding each other, we know they will be together forever. How could she refuse him? Kelly moves, looks, and is, simply irresistible.

A year before his death in 1996, I experienced the remember-forever pleasure of dining with Kelly and his wife in his Beverly Hills home. When I praised him for his influential style, he brushed it off, claiming it was less an aesthetic than a desire for "simplicity. I can't deal with fuss. You know, when I travel, regardless of where I am going, I always pack the same suitcase. I put in a pair of black pants, a pair of chinos, a white shirt, a black V-neck sweater, a black turtleneck, a black sport jacket, a long black tie, a black bow tie, plus [a] pair of sneakers. I wear loafers on the plane. And with that, I can dress for any occasion."

If you think about it, he's right. He'd be ready for anything. Even a dance or two.

PAY ATTENTION TO THE GIRLS BEHIND THE CURTAIN!

Isaac Mizrahi's
Fall 1994 Collection

As the wizard of Oz bellows and berates Dorothy and her trio of hopeful misfits, her trusty dog, Toto, scampers to an arc of draped green velvet and toothily tugs it all the way to the right, revealing a snow-white-maned old gent furiously working a light and soundboard. "Pay no attention to that man behind the curtain," he pleads into his microphone. But it's too late. The magic's been exposed. The wizard's a fake.

Even its most ardent and knowing fans often ignore the effort that goes into the creation of art, because it's more fun to believe its existence approaches the miraculous. Beethoven devoted six years to composing the Ninth Symphony, but the last notes of its climactic "Ode to Joy" soar skyward after only sixty-nine minutes. While less crafted for the ages, the preparation of a fashion show starts months in advance, tears through reams of sketch paper and endless yards of muslin, and often requires multiple transatlantic flights in pursuit of inspiration, fabric, and buttons. Each season's presentation employs a battalion of sewers, patternmakers, knitters, tailors, and embroiderers and enlists an army of enviably beautiful women to stand still for hours, then strut, twirl, flirt, pose,

ISAAC MIZRAHI

exit, quickly change, and repeat. But before models set foot on a runway, troops arrive who can create dramatic sets, negotiate the diplomacy of seating charts, edit pretty music, paint one-of-a-kind makeup, and turn hair into an accessory. And after this beat-the-clock timed effort is invested, it's over in fifteen are-you-gonna-love-it-in-an-instant minutes.

After seven years of submitting to this labyrinthine process, Isaac Mizrahi had had enough of letting people assume this whole process was a breeze. "Everything is frustrating except for designing clothes," he said. "That's the easy part." Stung by what he felt was the press's blithe dismissal of his spring 1994 collection and a snarky

questioning of his future relevance, Mizrahi set out to create a fall collection and a production that would recapture his buoyant originality.

For the clothes, the designer dared to incorporate four disparate fixations: eighteenth-century French corsetry, 1950s kitsch, 1970s disco flash, and Inuit-inspired outerwear rendered in outrageously fake fur. In Douglas Keeve's award-winning documentary *Unzipped,* which stalks Mizrahi and friends as he prepares for this "comeback"—and is still the most insightful, personal, and ultimately positive filmed exploration of fashion's triumphs and travails—Mizrahi beams at the vibrant pastel Chewbacca-like faux pelts as if they were dyed Russian sable. A movie junkie, he claims

What Ever Happened to Baby Jane?, *The Flintstones*, *The Red Shoes*, and *Nanook of the North* have initiated as much creative thought for him as would a trip to an exotic place. He believes Jacqueline Kennedy Onassis and Mary Tyler Moore are the two women responsible for shaping the taste level of the American woman. Nevertheless, the designer says he cannot turn away from the 1935 film *The Call of the Wild*, particularly the scene in which Clark Gable discovers a frostbitten Loretta Young "in a skunk coat, all dewy-eyed with perfect makeup and a key light." Young became the unofficial muse of Mizrahi's fall show.

Because Mizrahi is consistently effervescent—which would have made him either a sensational male cheerleader or cruise director in another life—the best models were always eager to walk his runway. And this was in the supermodel era, when the top women exhibited such individuality that the general public recognized many solely by their first names. Mizrahi decided that the public was going to know them by their exposed bodies as well. Instead of erecting the usual canvas flats as both a back wall for the runway and a separation from the dress/hair/makeup areas for the presentation, the designer insisted that he wanted a scrim, a backdrop common in the theater and dance, that when lit from behind, becomes transparent.

Mizrahi wanted the audience to see the energy: the frenzy, the population, the effort, the focus, the dedication, and the timing it took to put together a fluid show. Few on his staff loved the idea. When he first approached his favorite girls about the prospect of being seen by thousands in their bras and panties, the suggestion was greeted with wary, blank stares and the immediate need to go out for a smoke. Mizrahi's response was: "I don't give a shit. I'm doing it."

It's tough to throw the fashion crowd off guard. They prize their undercurrent of world-weariness even more than their Céline bags and Lanvin ballet flats. So when they walked into New York City's stately but shopworn former opera house renamed the Hammerstein Ballroom, the massive front white set gave no indication as to why Mizrahi had chosen the location.

But as the theme from *That Girl* began to reverberate, the spotlights came up both in front and in back of the stage, the audience, which included Liza Minnelli, Roseanne Barr, Sandra Bernhard, and Richard Gere, went wild and schoolboyishly giddy at the sight of Cindy, Naomi, Christy, Carla, Amber, Niki, Yasmeen, and Kristen in their underwear as dressers, hairstylists, and makeup artists tried to catch them on the fly. The models, now too caught up in the rush of the moment to care about an audience of voyeurs, were

a collective study in focused frenzy. But as soon as each girl emerged from behind the scrim, their individual runway personas kicked into high gear to introduce another look from Mizrahi's riotously colorful and harmonious integration of his contrasting references. Instead of giving away all the secrets and destroying the mystique of the runway show, the effect of the scrim to reveal what a thin veneer and a scant few seconds separated studied chaos from the effortlessly graceful was frankly wizardly.

Because the show occurred before cell phones recorded fashion's every passing fad or gas, hundreds in the audience were pointing nearly everywhere at once and remained standing at the show's end to honor this literal and luminous coup de théâtre. Mizrahi received his best reviews since his 1987 debut and immediate orders for his vivid sequin minis and neon-bright flokati-type coats. But his luck was not to last.

In a dispute with Chanel, who had bought a controlling interest in his company, Isaac Mizrahi closed his ready-to-wear business in 1998. He has since designed clothing and home collections for Target and QVC, and costumes for Broadway and the Metropolitan Opera. While continuing to design, he's been amassing a numerous array of television appearances, including hosting two cable talk shows and being the first designer judge on *Project Runway* ahead of Michael Kors. It's a shame Isaac Mizrahi doesn't take up his obvious second calling: magic. He's a natural.

LOVE'S NOT WASTED ON THE YOUNG

Franco Zeffirelli's
Romeo and Juliet, 1968

William Shakespeare's tale of a first love doomed by the squabbling of elders has always been one of the Bard's more frequently staged works despite its being one of his earliest, less substantial plays. *Othello, King Lear*, and *The Tempest* may be more dramatically complex and revelatory tragedies, displaying the more mature Shakespeare's unrivaled genius in conveying man's search for purpose in an existence that insistently challenges and mystifies him, but it's *Romeo and Juliet*'s unbridled exultations of passion and total immersion in the wonder of this-is-it love—life's most thrilling, often unexplainable emotion—that has proven everlastingly alluring to audiences as well as any actor who fancies him- or herself a potential matinee idol.

Unfortunately, too many of the latter felt prone to take on the roles of the ill-fated lovers a little late in the day. The renowned stage actress Katharine Cornell was thirty-six when her Juliet first pressed palms with Maurice Evans's thirty-two-year-old Romeo on Broadway in 1933. Three years later, Irving Thalberg, the wunderkind producer of Metro-Goldwyn-Mayer, mounted a lavish production, directed by George Cukor and starring two of the studio's brightest stars, Norma Shearer (Thalberg's wife) and Leslie Howard. Shearer was thirty-four at the time; Howard, forty-three. Legend has it that Sarah Bernhardt played scenes from the play well into her seventies, even after one of her legs had been amputated. Yet, Shakespeare clearly states that Juliet is not yet fourteen, and though he never nails down Romeo's exact age, references in the text indicate he has yet to reach eighteen.

Romeo and Juliet plays out the downside of the axiom that timing is everything, but when it came to casting the

pair for his film version, director Franco Zeffirelli couldn't have chosen a better moment to ask the world to take Shakespeare at his word. Inspired by an Old Vic production starring a vivacious twenty-six-year-old Judi Dench and twenty-four-year-old John Stride, Zeffirelli tested hundreds of teenagers for the part before selecting two from the London stage: fifteen-year-old Argentinian-born Olivia Hussey and seventeen-year-old Leonard Whiting.

Choosing such young actors for the parts was unprecedented, but Zeffirelli believed his risk was considerably reduced by the tectonic shifts in demographics that were dividing our global culture, economics, politics, and sexual appetites. In 1966, *Time* magazine broke with tradition and proclaimed the entire segment of the population "Twenty-five and Under," which then made up 50 percent of the population in America, as their Man of the Year (the publication hadn't yet evolved to using to word *person*). In 1968, well-organized protests against college administration policies in enrollment, endowment, tenure—the list was

endless—resulted in the high-profile student-led shutdown of Columbia University and the University of California, Berkeley, triggering similar actions at numerous college and university campuses across the United States. There were also highly publicized state-government-led drug raids, particularly at universities in the northeast. The shocking and disastrous Tet Offensive was the catalyst for the SDS (Students for Democratic Society) to ramp up even greater opposition to the Vietnam War. There were major marches on Washington, student-led demands for the boycotting of the Dow Chemical Company for the manufacture of napalm, protests against the impending 1969 draft lottery, and rioting at the 1968 Democratic Convention.

Nor was unrest confined to the United States. University students and sympathetic striking workers shut down Paris for weeks. There were protests in Stockholm, Tokyo, and Belgrade. Pour all this tension into the deep divide in tastes in music and dress, and attitudes regarding premarital sex and women's rights, factor in the assassinations of

Martin Luther King Jr. and Robert F. Kennedy, and there seemed little reason for anyone still fighting acne to argue with Jack Weinberg, the head of the Congress of Racial Equality (CORE) when he declared, "Don't trust anyone over the age of thirty."

With so much dissension and obvious "us against the establishment" sentiment, Zeffirelli could have easily opted for a resonant modern-dress version of *Romeo and Juliet*. His masterstroke was that he did exactly the opposite. Instead, he presented Shakespeare's lovers in a sumptuous and sweeping costume drama, more splendid in period detail and setting than anyone previously had ever envisioned. While the dialogue may be classical, Zeffirelli infused the film with such rambunctious energy and adolescent spontaneity, it rivals and occasionally overshadows the tale's celebrated cinematic predecessor, Robert Wise's and Jerome Robbins's *West Side Story* (1961).

In most productions of *Romeo and Juliet,* the young Capulets and Montagues are virtually interchangeable, benign in their discord, divided merely by call-and-response dialogue, and basically bearers of story exposition so the audience knows the lay of the land. But Zeffirelli uses the fraternities brilliantly to connect with young viewers, who normally would think Shakespeare comes from a world too refined of speech and intent to be relatable. He had Academy Award–winning costume designer Danilo Donati establish the young Veronese as two distinct gangs, making them easy to tell apart by attiring the Capulets in brilliant reds, yellows, and oranges accented with black, while the Montagues are in lavender, gray, and purple accented with navy. Each are an enviably handsome bunch, but both are agitated and easy to provoke. The rules of Verona are strict, and each side is chafing. These bands of young brothers resent their need to play nice but hesitate testing the limits of authority. Quick to anger and eager to claim turf, they strike back by engaging in a verbal scrimmage. The one trait they share is a hatred of being ignored, which they obviously are, because they hardly interact with adults. Despite doublets and codpieces, their frustration and confusion so harmoniously echoed the social discord of the 1960s it resonated with youthful audiences worldwide.

Zeffirelli places his immortal lovers amid the tension that both divides and binds these two factions. What's so exciting is that despite their single-minded focus that comes with love at first sight, the lovers are not mirror images of passion. Leonard Whiting's Romeo responds differently to the world than Olivia Hussey's Juliet. Whiting, who is simply beautiful, an angel with a Beatle-like mop top with a lustrous tenor lilt to his voice, is consistently dressed by Donati in deeply padded channel-quilted doublets in a muted palette to set his softness apart and shield him from his fellow Montagues. Yet when his best friend and ally, Mercutio, is accidentally killed by Tybalt, the leader of the young Capulets, in a swordplay sparring that goes awry, Romeo's response is impulsive and dangerous. His reaction is visceral and adrenaline-fueled. Wearing the blinders of youth, he chooses immediate action, seeking revenge without considering the consequences, thereby dooming his chance at happiness.

The girl he loves, however, only seeks out the good in all. Headstrong but compassionate, effusive yet wary, eager to gush sweetly about the power of her love but emboldened by anyone who would dare try to stop her, Hussey's Juliet is the driving force of Zeffirelli's film. She's the audience's designated touchstone because she embodies all of the uncompromising faith the young have in themselves to change the world. Hussey's performance excites us not just because of her precocious talent in deftly handling the material, but because she and Zeffirelli have conspired to present Juliet as a flower child who believes in her own power. Her cousins in the square may be content to strike macho poses, but this mere teen comes up with her own plan of action. That it's thwarted is due to the failure of conviction by others. Had they had half her resolve, the play might have had a lucrative sequel, since Whiting and Hussey became international idols.

Donati's costumes for Juliet are as cleverly editorial as they are luxurious, an enviable amalgam of period brocades and damask set against saturated jewel-toned velvets and highlighted by seed pearls and leather inserts, whipped up into silhouettes with just enough modernity that they would be at home on the rack of a hip West Village vintage

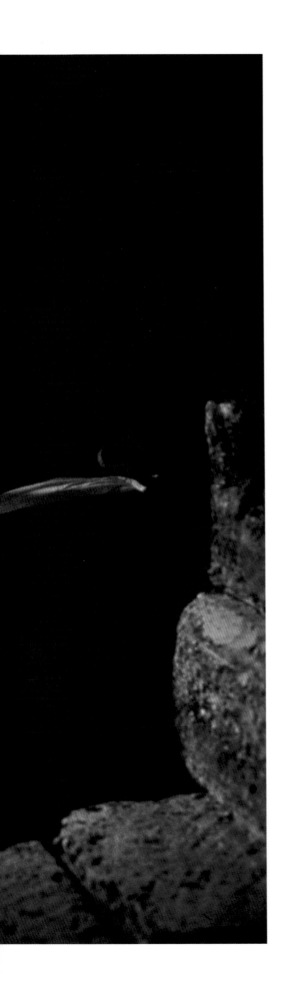

shop like O Mistress Mine. A folk goddess like Judy Collins could have borrowed that red velvet cassock gown with the inserts that Juliet wore to the Capulet ball. The bosom-lifting brocaded Empire gown she dons to guide her newfound lover up the balcony should have been willed to Jane Birkin, while her expansive, multifold white dressing gown with deep bell sleeves would have been exactly right on Laura Nyro. The high-neck, body-hugging, stunningly embroidered striped umber gown with gold thread that she wears to commit suicide has Buffy Sainte-Marie's name written all over it—and it wouldn't look half bad on any red carpet today. If Donato and Zeffirelli had really been enterprising, they could have opened a pop-up store at Woodstock the following year and cleaned up.

In 1996, nearly thirty years after Zeffirelli's film, director Baz Luhrmann, that unrepentant maximalist, created a modern-dress version of *Romeo and Juliet* with a vibrant Leonardo DiCaprio and Claire Danes forced to shout Shakespeare's dialogue—usually on the run thanks to its MTV pacing—and a rock musical soundtrack still worthy of an iPod playlist. When the lovers died, you still felt bad, but that's because you had a headache. In 2013, a very young and attractive Hailee Steinfeld and Douglas Booth were paired in yet another version, directed by Carlo Carlei, but this time the exuberance of youth was replaced by a weird off-putting aura of mystery, as if the cast of *Twilight* were waiting in the wings to turn the lovers to vampires and save them from their mortal fate.

More than forty years after its release, Zeffirelli's version remains the most compelling and relevant screen transfer of them all, not merely because it is a feast for the eye but because the director trusted the Bard's words centuries after they were written to affect an audience that wanted to be heard and understood. Not only did the film address a new generation's angst, but it also reminded them of the wonder, the power, and the fearlessness of true love. "Sin from thy lips?" says Romeo. "O trespass sweetly urged! Give me my sin again." For any generation, it's faith in love that can sustain hope, and we are all "fortune's fool" if we forget its strength.

BABY, DON'T GO

The Sonny & Cher Comedy Hour, 1971

They stand onstage, dressed alike, like hip Hummel salt and pepper shakers. They size each other up. He says, "People say we look like a storybook couple." She says, "Yeah. Beauty and the Beast." They grin as the audience roars and applauds. It's what they came for. Still, though you'd never ask a girl to choose between Warren Beatty and Sonny Bono, and maybe Cher's tongue was way back into her cheek when she said it, but still—that comeback's a little harsh. Sonny was more funny-looking than "Quasimodian," but then what guy wearing 1960s fashion wasn't? And just to be fair, striking as Cher was, is, and always will be, she would have never made finalist—despite easily winning the talent competition—in the Miss California pageant of 1965.

That was the year Sonny and Cher sweetly ambushed Top 40 radio with their soon-to-be anthem "I Got You, Babe," instantly followed by "Baby, Don't Go," charting as the year's best selling duet and promptly crowned rock and roll's favorite and most unlikely lovebirds. The British Invasion, Motown, and the California Sound dominated the Top 40 in the mid-1960s. This married couple didn't fall into any of those musical categories, and sartorially, they were in a league all their own.

Sonny was short, sung from the heart and through his adenoids, usually wore a floral version of what Jerry Seinfeld used to call a "puffy shirt" under what became a signature caveman fur vest with matching fur boots, and sported a walrus mustache and a Prince Valiant haircut. First Cher's voice threw you, then quickly nailed your attention: far lower than Sonny's, its rich contralto was startling in depth, especially when compared to the sound of the silky girl

groups from Motown or the perky chirps of London "birds" like Petula Clark. But Cher's voice was also the bait that drew you in to marvel at her willowy, boyish body, clad in frilly middy blouses and wide-tiered bell-bottoms, her cascade of glistening raven hair that, by the time Sonny and Cher had their own television show, fell down to the small of her back and was used with the flip of a nonchalant hand to toss back over her shoulder to punctuate a joke. You couldn't quite place her heritage, but she was exotic. None of her individual facial features was classically beautiful—a prominent nose, cheekbones more defined than Sophia Loren's, large almond Cleopatra-inspired lined eyes, and full pillow lips shielding a slight overbite—yet the amalgamation was mysterious and undeniably alluring.

Arm in arm, Sonny and Cher looked like a happy hippy couple from Haight-Ashbury who decided they wanted to go home for the holidays and make a good impression on their respective families. They presented counterculture not only as unthreatening but sealed with a kiss. No one in rock and roll—make that no one in entertainment—had created an act like it. And mainstream America ate them up with a spoon.

Naturally, Hollywood came calling. But their debut film, *Good Times* (1967), was anything but that. Television proved a much better idea. CBS introduced *The Sonny & Cher Comedy Hour* in August 1971 on Sunday nights as summer replacement filler, but enough folks got home from weekends at the beach in time to watch them. The show was a hit, and CBS brought it back in December in the same time slot. CBS liked their weekend variety programming. Deservedly revered, *The Carol Burnett Show* owned Saturday night. But CBS had been aching to fill their Sunday slot with something similar since abruptly cancelling *The Smothers Brothers Show* two years earlier in a nasty censorship dispute.

Sonny and Cher were so much safer. Their comedy was all domestic, in the mode of the legendary team of George Burns and Gracie Allen, but laced with less absurdity and more innuendo-laden quips aimed at their unlikely matchup. If Sonny would rave about his reviews on tour— "Fantastic in Vegas. . . .dynamic in Los Angeles," Cher

would cut him off with "Boring at home." She made fun of his height and voice. He made fun of her nose and flat-chestedness. It was adorably harmless because you knew they went home together. As sketch comedians, they were no Burnett and her brilliant sidekick Harvey Korman, but they were self-effacing and game.

The bulk of the show, though, revolved around all things Cher: her voice, which had grown fuller; her notable confidence as a solo performer; and a penchant for outrageous, even risqué, costumes that had viewers all over the country fervently summoning family members to the den with, "Come in here and get a look at her—NOW!" As her career-long stalwart costumer and friend Bob Mackie proudly recalls, "She had everyone tuning in just to see what the hell she was wearing."

"It didn't take a lot to make Cher look amazing," says Mackie. "She was so multiethnic, so not of that era, her body perfect for fashion. You could try anything. . . .There was a section of the show called 'Vamp' where Cher would impersonate seductive women in history. She'd be Helen of Troy one minute, Blanche DuBois the next. She didn't even know who half these people were, and didn't care. She just loved dressing up and being outrageous. She made women love fashion." Not that Cher inspired imitation, mind you. Mackie even admits that "these were costumes, not clothes." But with Woodstock still fresh in everyone's memory, it was surprising to see a woman in a rock duo embracing what we would now call red-carpet glamour with such vivid panache. So perhaps what she inspired was more like variety, daring, the fun of putting together a wardrobe that resonated on more than one note. More than anything, she reminded women, for all their drive for liberation and equality, that sometimes it was really cool to be the center of attention simply because you looked smashing.

Cher went through as many as twenty changes per show, with her most photo-ready look used to complement her weekly high-drama solo ballad. "The problem was," according to Mackie, "I was also doing Carol's [Burnett] show, and sometimes Cher didn't decide until the last minute what she was singing. When we could plan, we could set her in an art gallery surrounded by and looking like a Modigliani, singing something like 'That Face.' But at other times, she'd be covered in diamonds doing a folk song, or worse, in a full Indian headdress doing 'He Ain't Heavy, He's My Brother,' the song she always fell back on when she could not decide on another number. Nobody cared. They loved her."

Unfortunately, Sonny and Cher fell out of love. The *Comedy Hour* ended 1974, the couple divorced in 1975, and they each returned to television with solo shows. Sonny's lasted three months; Cher's, a year. During that time, the couple didn't reconcile, but they did reach a rapprochement. A desperate CBS persuaded them to come home and in 1976, *The Sonny & Cher Show*, returned in the same time slot, with America's first ever, oh-so genial-if-not-that-gay divorcées as hosts. With divorce still somewhat taboo at the time, audiences at first found it tantalizing to see Cher pull a blonde hair off Sonny's jacket, have Sonny quickly claim it came from their daughter Chastity, and hear Cher snap, "The baby doesn't have black roots." Because both singers spent less time on set, there was less costuming. Mackie would simply "wrap three yards of jersey around her, put fresh orchids in her hair, and it still worked." But then Cher became pregnant with Gregg Allman's child. The larger she got, the more uneasy it became for Sonny and Cher to be onstage together. An uncomfortable audience felt the same way. The reunion show barely lasted two years.

Less than a week after their divorce became final, Cher wed Gregg Allman. She filed for divorce nine days later. But if her later life proved unlucky in love (David Geffen?), she achieved success on the screen, with Golden Globe Awards for *Silkwood* (1983) and *Moonstruck* (1987) as well as an Academy Award for the latter. On the concert stage, Cher began her first incredibly lucrative "Cher Farewell Tour" in 2002. It lasted for three years. Then she performed to sell-out crowds in Las Vegas for another three. She has been "farewell touring" ever since. Of course, what Cher became most celebrated for was her spectacular red-carpet collaborations with Mackie, the most famous of which, The Black Beaded Mohawk, was prompted by her being snubbed for a nomination for *Mask* (1986). Red-carpet

coverage still mourns her absence. Sonny remarried, was elected mayor of Palm Springs in 1988, and in 1994 was elected to Congress as a representative from California's 44th Congressional District.

On November 13, 1997, less than two months before his death in a skiing accident, Sonny and Cher appeared together on *Late Night with David Letterman*. Letterman asked them to sing. Cher claimed her throat hurt, but Letterman wasn't having it. He directed the two over to Paul Schaffer's band. They began to play. Sonny and Cher followed along, late and tentatively at first. But as "I Got You, Babe" progressed, their voices grew bolder and their manner loosened. They finished the song the way they always had, with Cher's arm round Sonny's shoulder. It wasn't a storybook ending. But even Dave was smiling.

LOVE IS COLOR-BLIND

The Idolatry of James Dean, 1955

"Hello, pretty boy!"—these are the first words said to James Dean in his debut film, *East of Eden* (1953). And boy, was he pretty, forever searching for answers with those lagoon-blue eyes. His honey-blond hair rushed forward on his right side and swept back so dramatically high on his left that had it been water, surfers would have called it the perfect wave. He had an adorable right dimple that almost reached his cheekbone. His lips were so full and beckoning millions of young women lipstick-smudged the pages of *Photoplay* wherever his face appeared. And if his profile had been on a coin, they would have never spent it.

But the frenzy Dean's film debut generated was due to more than looks. In the film, an almost equally handsome actor named Richard Davalos plays his brother. He barely registers. On celluloid, James Dean is one of those blessed—like Paul Newman, Clark Gable, and Sean Connery—with the indefinable power to command the audience's full attention, no matter who else is in the frame.

Dean would have been a star in any era, but he was certainly the first teen screen idol. True, Mickey Rooney was a top Hollywood box-office attraction during the 1930s, but cute as he was, he was a teenage anomaly, and certainly not as handsome as Dean. No one identified with, or wanted to be him. But from the moment Dean made his screen debut as Cal Trask in *Eden,* it seemed the not-so-secret wish of every girl turning sweet sixteen to date him, and the objective of all of her suitors to be just like him.

In 1955, Nicholas Ray's *Rebel Without a Cause* was the first Hollywood feature ever to focus on teen life from their

point of view, revealing there was more in adolescents' minds and hearts than who would make varsity or get asked to the prom, and declaring that whether or not adults were willing to take them seriously, teenage problems were real to them. Though the film hasn't aged well, *Rebel* connected with 1950s youth with Taylor Swiftian speed because it cleared the smokescreen of postwar familial harmony that was being pumped through American television via regular doses of the placidly blissful *Father Knows Best, The Donna Reed Show, Leave It to Beaver,* and *The Adventures of Ozzie and Harriet.*

Kids related to James Dean's Jim Stark, Natalie Wood's Judy, and Sal Mineo's Plato because they are confused, and eager to be understood and to belong. Most important, all suffer from the desperate, sometimes feverish desire that drives and torments each of James Dean's three roles during his brief career. For Dean's Trask, Stark, and Jett Rink (*Giant,* 1956), nothing they do in life means anything if they aren't accepted and, above all, loved.

Dean introduced a new kind of male sex symbol. Vulnerable, unsure, and manifesting a hunger to be embraced that practically vibrated, he was not only younger than but bore little resemblance to the brawnier, more macho male stars of the generation before him, like Humphrey Bogart, Gary Cooper, and Gregory Peck. Even Marlon Brando, only seven years Dean's senior, appears more mature and more prone to internalize his sensitivity. But from the moment we first see Dean in *Rebel,* it's evident that his character wears his heart on the sleeve of his red nylon jacket.

Ray used the red Windbreaker to point to Dean's Jim as the expression of all that was out of balance in our society. Not that we needed a marker. There are no sex scenes in *Rebel.* Jim doesn't even kiss Judy until near the film's end, but Dean's emotions are so raw, and his gestures so tensely exotic that when he and Wood finally reach out to touch each other's hands after the film's fatal game of

"chicken," their final connection generates a heaving sigh of relief from pain for them. Compared to Judy's stoic, withholding father and overcompensating boyfriend who died while playing the game, Jim is the man she always hoped she'd find, "someone who can be gentle and sweet."

Teenage boys had already heard the message, for high schools were populated with countless James Dean look-alikes. Dean's death by head-on collision in his Porsche Spyder one month before the release of *Rebel Without a Cause* only compounded the power of his image. Young men adopted Jim's work boots, his deep indigo washed Lee Rider 101 jeans (though Dean wore Levi's more often in real life), and the snug white T-shirt with the sleeves partially rolled up. Jim smoked, so they smoked too.

But despite there being numerous versions of a "James Dean leather jacket" available online today, the actor never wears the clothing he is often most associated with in any of his three movies. Corey Allen, who plays Jim's adversary Buzz, wears one in *Rebel,* but Dean stays zipped up in his red Windbreaker, not an easy color for any guy who isn't sure about how cool he really is to adopt. Offscreen, however, Dean was photographed so often wearing his black Schott Perfecto leather jacket—the same style Marlon Brando wore on his motorcycle in *The Wild One*—it seemed like second skin. With both actors having chosen the garment, the Schott Perfecto became so popular that, according to the manufacturer, "the jackets were banned by school systems around the country because they symbolized a burgeoning teen demographic, the hoodlum." The jacket, like Dean's T-shirt, jeans, pompadour, and work boots, is timeless, has been worn by all those inarguably judged as cool, like the Ramones, Johnny Depp, Patti Smith, and Jared Leto, and remains one of Schott's bestsellers today. With male objectification now a covetable norm, being called "pretty boy" is no longer the taunt that stings. Now it's a compliment.

LONG AFTER THE CAMELLIAS HAVE FADED

Chanel Nº5: The Film, 2004

Because Coco Chanel espoused such an emphatic, uncompromising, and consistent aesthetic, it's funny that of the eighty ingredients formulated in Chanel Nº5, the scent of camellias, the designer's signature flower, is not one of them. And though other flowers are incorporated into the perfume—may roses, jasmine, lilies—as well as oils such as bergamot, lemon, sandalwood, and neroli, Chanel Nº5 isn't dominated by any of their aromas either.

The fact is, Chanel wasn't fond of perfume. She dismissed most of them as blatantly girly, a trait she loathed equally in dressing and behavior. She found perfume oppressive, the smell triggering memories of her early employment as a seam-stress doing fittings on well-to-do women reeking of musk and lavender to cover body odors. One of her fondest recollections of her teenage years spent at Aubazine Abbey's convent—whose stained-glass windows just happen to resemble a series of interlocking Cs—where she was sent, and learned to sew, following the death of her unmarried mother, was how every-one at the abbey always smelled clean, not a widespread trait in the early half of the twentieth century. Chanel found the scent of soap and freshly washed skin invigorating.

So, in 1921, after successfully opening dress shops funded by paramours in Paris, Deauville, and Biarritz, Chanel commissioned perfumer Ernest Beaux to formulate a fragrance "like nothing else. A woman's perfume that reflected the scent of a woman." Beaux took the mission further, aiming for "the odor of clean linen after drying outside in cold air" or "the smell of water from the Arctic Circle at midnight." He presented Chanel with ten choices numbered 1 through 5 and 20 through 24. For choice Nº5,

Beaux had added an experimental chemical called aldehyde that extended the aroma of a perfume. On its own, aldehyde smells like soap. Chanel's choice? No contest.

Chanel rejected the fantasy that dousing one's body in florid essence from a Lalique atomizer ensured a woman a night of violins and flaming cherries jubilee, housing the scent in a straightforward bottle designed for "transparency" and stoic ivory and black-edged packaging. She believed that every woman alive who loved Chanel Nº5 would use its crisp freshness to herald the arrival of a complex being whose individuality, independence, and passions made her a tantalizing creature like no other.

Consequently, when Australian director Baz Luhrmann was hired to create a short film to reestablish Chanel Nº5 as first among equals in the increasingly crowded field of designer fragrances, he immediately envisioned a lavish tale of fame, desire, escape, and sacrifice centered on a woman of mystery. How handy that Luhrmann's recent film *Moulin Rouge* (2001) followed much the same plotline. Luckily, for him, Chanel designer Karl Lagerfeld adored both the movie and its star.

Not everybody agreed. At a time when this movie genre had been left for dead, *Moulin Rouge*, Luhrmann's doomed but exultant love affair between a celebrated music hall performer (Nicole Kidman) and penniless writer (Ewan McGregor) billed itself as a musical but had little in common with those starring Judy, Julie, Gene, or Fred. *Moulin Rouge*'s visuals are a gaudy mash-up of Toulouse-Lautrec's lush paintings of Parisian nightlife before the turn of the twentieth century, the decadence expressed in Aubrey Beardsley's black ink art nouveau drawings and over-the-top Ziegfeldian camp. The film's camera work is nonstop and ever-swirling, its musical numbers alternate between heart-stopping and head-scratching, and its emotions begin at fever pitch and then smash the mercury on its explosive way skyward. Even those who love the film admit that its first twenty minutes are such a deliberate, sensual assault that, at an advance screening for fashion press, an incensed Amy Spindler—the most erudite chief fashion critic the *New York Times* was lucky enough ever to have—aimed expletive-filled invective at anyone within earshot who had a kind word to say about the film.

Yes, those twenty minutes are a miscalculated aspirin-inducing chore. If Luhrmann ever created his own perfume, he should call it Excess. But after that, *Moulin Rouge* turns daring and intoxicating, like swigging a bottle of absinthe and vowing to fall in love with the next person you kiss. If every poor writer romanced like Ewan McGregor, no freelancer with a laptop would ever wake up alone. And no one could play Satine more ravishingly than Nicole Kidman. If Helen of Troy was this beautiful, then you can't blame Menelaus for starting a war.

For Chanel's film, Luhrmann recast Kidman not merely as a star, but as the most famous woman in the world, a cross between Marilyn Monroe (who once claimed all she wore to bed was "five drops of Chanel N°5") and Grace Kelly. As the Chanel film opens, a swarthy, handsome man (Brazilian actor Rodrigo Santoro) with perfectly strewn forelocks, sporting a white shirt, black jeans, and glasses is on his rooftop, poised against the back of a sign—its words are illegible to the viewer—regarding a city skyline awash with numerous klieg lights sweeping across the night sky like giant windshield wipers.

Then the film cuts to Times Square, which Luhrmann has shot in black-and-white like a 1950s newsreel. The scene is congested, and the crossroads are bumper-to-bumper with taxis, when suddenly a woman flees a limo into the traffic, the train of her voluminous gown trailing her by nearly half a block.

As we hear the male's raspy voice ask, "When did I wake into this dream? I must have been the only person in the world who didn't know who she was…" the film returns to color, revealing that the spectacular sweeping dress is tinted the color of pink freesias, crafted of 140 meters of silk tulle, 10 meters of silk organza, 250 ostrich feathers, and 2,000 silver crystals that took ten *petites mains* (couture seamstresses) seven hundred hours to create. Kidman opens the door of a taxi poised to escape the snarl and somehow manages to stuff in that entire silk yardage, except the cab is already occupied—by him, the swarthy, spectacled beauty with the fabulous forelocks. But from the moment Kidman whispers to the cabbie "Drive!" with one unhinged strand of her titian hair straying over her aquamarine eyes, you understand why the man claims "[his] life would never be the same again."

What follows in only thirty seconds is an abbreviated version of the ecstatic, false-hope-filled romance that occupies nearly half the running time of *Moulin Rouge.*

He takes her to the roof. She marvels at her freedom, trades her gown for his white shirt, while he, now clad in a white tank top, dips her into a kiss as the sky explodes in fireworks to the swelling strings of Claude Debussy's "Clair de Lune" ("Moonlight").

Then reality descends. She must return to her spotlit world. She resists. He insists. And she is gone. The sky is once again ablaze. We pan down from an Empire State Building–like skyscraper topped by interlocked Cs to an extremely wide red-carpeted staircase as the star, alone with her back toward us, ascends toward a grand golden hall (the Metropolitan Opera House at Lincoln Center). No longer dressed in her cotton-candy fantasy, she is attired in a more modern, knowing, and brand-conscious, sleek, backless cascade of black velvet. The camera cuts to a shot of the man once again, sitting on the rooftop sign. As he asks, "Has she forgotten? I know I will not," he is sitting on his rooftop's sign that turns out to read: CHANEL. As the camera returns to Kidman, she finally turns so we can see her face; she looks off in the distance, and though the man is miles away, her eyes and a smile that beats Mona Lisa at her own game tells us whom she sees. As his voice whispers, "Our kiss . . . her smile . . ." the camera comes in closer toward the 26.5-karat lariat of diamonds cascading down Kidman's back. Then he says, "Her perfume," and a starry close-up reveals that the pendant at the end of the necklace spells out Nº5 inside a circle of diamonds.

We never learn the man's name, or the woman's. You never see her applying perfume. Nor is the iconic bottle visible in any shot. The commercial, which cost more than $30 million, is listed as running three minutes, (it was short-ened for television) but it only contains two minutes of film. The rest is credits. However, in those 120 seconds, Luhrmann created a film that is tighter, sharper, more trans-porting and thoroughly rapturous than the feature he was riffing on. More important, he depicted the ultimate goal of Coco Chanel's quest for a fragrance—that it envelops only those women who believe themselves unforgettable.

Because Chanel is a privately held company, its owners, the Wertheimer family, do not release sales figures for individual products, although estimated annual sales top $7 billion. But at $98 for 1.7 ounces, a bottle of Chanel Nº5 is sold somewhere in the world every thirty seconds. Who knows what they could charge if it came with a kiss from Rodrigo Santoro.

GOING MY WAY

Annie Hall Gives
Alvy Singer a Ride,
Annie Hall, 1977

She's dressed in pieces she could have stolen from Willy Loman's closet. He is the grown-up version of the kid in class you'd cheat off of but wouldn't talk to. They've just come off the tennis court, where, through the introduction of mutual friends, they played doubles opposite each other. It's virtually impossible to describe their first encounter, because their conversation is nearly incoherent, barely qualifying as English:

> Annie: *Hi. Hi, hi.*
> Alvy: *Oh, hi. Hi.*
> Annie: (After hesitation) *Well, 'bye.*
> Alvy: *You-you play very well.*
> Annie: *Oh, yeah? So do you. Oh, God, whatta, er, whatta dumb thing to say, right? I mean, you say it,* (laugh/snort) *"You play well," and right away . . . I have to say, "You play well." Oh, oh, God, Annie. Well . . . oh well, la-de-da, la-de-da, la-la . . . yeah . . .*
> Alvy: *Uh, you-you want a lift?*
> Annie: *Oh, why-uh, y-y-you gotta car?*
> Alvy: *No, um . . . I was gonna take a cab.*
> Annie: *Oh, no, I have a car* (laugh).
> Alvy: *You have a car? So . . . um, I don't understand wh-why . . . if you have a car, so then-then wh-why did you say, "Do you have a car?" like you wanted a lift?* (laugh)
> Annie: *I don't . . . ah . . . I don't . . . Ah, jeez I don't know. I wasn't* (sticks out her tongue and makes a big noisy raspberry). *It's . . . I got this VW out there . . .* (snort/laugh) *. . . What a jerk, yeah. Would you like a lift?* (Snort/laugh)

On the printed page, as a "meet cute," it's a neck-and-neck race to Losertown. Yet, this film is all it took for Woody Allen and everyone else in the world to fall head over heels for Diane Keaton as Annie Hall and for the public to fuse the couple's factual and fictional personas forever.

Keaton's film career has been astonishingly varied; her notable range displayed in *The Godfather*, *Looking for Mr. Goodbar*, *Shoot the Moon*, *Reds,* and *Something's Got to Give* goes way beyond Annie's quirky charm. She insists, "I never said *la-di-dah* in my real life, until he [Woody] wrote it." However, she also admits, "I was a person who couldn't complete a sentence, so he did get that right." On talk and award shows over the decades, her radiant but scattershot speech pattern has proven consistent.

But her lifelong tether to her Academy Award–winning role for best actress in Allen's Academy Award–winning Best Picture goes deeper, and not just because Keaton's real last name is Hall. Allen nailed her wardrobe, which was curated by costume designer Ruth Morley, who combined vintage pieces with items from Ralph Lauren, and a lot from Keaton's own closet. The result was an assemblage devoid of any affectation of femininity, and yet Keaton is absolutely captivating. When delivering the dialogue reprinted here, she is wearing a man's white oxford cloth shirt; an oversize black vest; full-legged high-waisted khakis; a wide, diamond-patterned man's tie that is too long in the front; and a fedora with the brim turned down. Later on she dons a pair of green khakis with a dark plaid shirt buttoned up to the neck and a black blazer. Even in Keaton's most bewitching scene—seated on a stool in a club singing a wistful version of "Seems Like Old Times," she is in a tuxedo with satin lapels and a white carnation. Girlish affectation has no place in Annie's world, but with each scene Keaton's "irresistible" quotient just grows. It's no surprise then that the Annie Hall look was soon copied the world over.

Even today, Keaton consistently opts for hats, big ties, wide pants, and being as covered up as possible. She showed up for an interview with me at the Beverly Hills Hotel wearing a long-sleeved bottle-green wool Dries Van Noten coat, black turtleneck, long leather gloves, and a hat.

It was ninety-four degrees that day in Los Angeles. "I don't like showing skin," she said. "It's not an age thing. I'm just always cold, and I like feeling safe." I have to admit, I didn't really hear the quote clearly until I played back the tape because I couldn't take my eyes off her. Keaton is a case-closed argument that they don't sell sex appeal at Nordstrom, and it isn't guaranteed if you wear spaghetti straps either.

Like Annie, over the years Keaton has toyed with the idea of singing in jazz clubs or making albums, but has never committed. And like Annie, she has never married. Each of her major relationships—Allen, Warren Beatty, and Al Pacino—has lasted roughly the same length of time: five years. Her daughter, Dexter, and son, Duke, are her lengthiest love affairs since leaving behind Grammy Hall.

Allen and Keaton made eight films together, including several after their offscreen relationship ended. Given our knowledge now of Allen's life and loves, it's hard for some to view his early work, career, and stature without a tainted eye, yet the director's first film not played for flat-out comedy is infused with uncynical, yearning innocence. His passion for New York and for finding and sustaining true love in his hometown at this stage of his life is pure and forthright. Coming attractions for the film labeled *Annie Hall* "a nervous romance," but what made it memorable was its buoyancy and its ability to rise above and avoid—if only for a while— all of Allen's thorny layers of urban sophistication and to revel in two people, unexpectedly meant for each other.

It's funny how even the people most eager to talk about their favorite scenes in the film (the lobster-boiling scene is Marx Brothers–worthy slapstick) rarely note that Alvy and Annie don't end up together. But they don't quite end up apart either. In fact, after she leaves him, Alvy goes to his dreaded California, where Annie has moved, to show her the play that he's written about them. In the play, the two of them live happily ever after. Unfortunately, for them, and us, the reel-life conclusion is more bittersweet. Annie prefers to stay in Los Angeles. Alvy can't breathe outside New York. But there's a hint that they will see each other again. And when they do, we hope it will seem like old times.

FIGHTS
IN BRIGHT
SATIN

Krystle and Alexis's Catfights
on *Dynasty*, 1983

For all its embrace of new technologies, fashion repeatedly recycles its past. How can a designer focus on sophistication without a nod to the 1930s? The 1950s beckon anyone who admires classic reserve. No generation has ever been as funky as youth in the 1970s. And in the mid-1990s, the Italians brought back the notion that there is only one way to dress, and that's for sex, to an AIDS-scarred industry.

Yet no one yearns to revive the 1980s. Ever. Need a reason? Not if you were old enough to dress yourself back then and have a photo album handy. For those too young to remember the era, this is what's captured on Kodachrome: relentlessly shiny fabrics in colors to shame a rainbow draped by the yard, often beaded as if burlesque had never died; plunging necklines that ended just shy of the navel; and slit skirts rising to new highs. Towering above all is the hallmark of the decade: shoulder pads big enough to rival any starting lineup in the NFL.

What the hell were we thinking?

I'll tell you exactly: we wanted to imitate life as depicted on *Dynasty*.

Few now admit without apology that they never missed an episode of the series, but at the height of its popularity, *Dynasty* had a global viewership of more than one hundred million. Part comedy, part melodrama, and thoroughly ridiculous, this defining series of the yuppie's reign of conspicuous consumption was very much like the overpopulated, endlessly wealthy Carrington family it chronicled—it possessed too much of everything. Each week lust, treachery, adultery, betrayal, and false alliances were carried out in penthouses, villas, and mansions that seemingly devoted 40 percent of their square footage to walk-in closets.

With a weekly costume budget of $35,000, clothing designer Nolan Miller proved that nothing succeeds like excess: he fielded more than five thousand requests a month for sketches of his ruched and ratcheted-up confections.

But despite overwrought taste and plotlines, at the core of *Dynasty* was a love story: tycoon Blake Carrington's (John Forsythe) unbridled adoration of his good-as-gold-laméed second wife, Krystle (Linda Evans). Unfortunately for them, but happily for fans, an omnipresent serpent was ever ready to search and destroy their Denver-based Eden—Blake's envious and overdressed first wife, Alexis Carrington Colby (Joan Collins).

It didn't take long for producer Aaron Spelling to realize that though love is lovelier the second time around, jealousy is much more fun to watch. While aspirational fantasy did much to drive the show into the Nielsen rating's top twenty, *Dynasty*'s big boost was due to two deliciously sloppy cat-fights. In the season two episode entitled "The Baby," Krystle is tipped off by Alexis's stableman that a gun fired by her nemesis is what caused her horse to throw her, bringing on her miscarriage. So good pays an unexpected visit to evil at Alexis's illogical and oddly tacky white-brick-clad artist's garret (in Denver?), where she is sketching in a periwinkle-blue, accordion-ruched silk shirtwaist featuring jaunty pleated culottes and sporting major curled bangs. Clad in a silk jabot blouse sporting a gift-box-sized bow and shoulders almost as wide as her palazzo pants, all in phosphorescent burgundy, Krystle pitches her accusation. Alexis pitches a lame right hook, and off they go, tussling over the bed, floor, sofa, and stairs. Vases are shattered (no cuts visible), feather pillows erupt, lamps tumble, until the apartment looks far more beaten to a pulp than they do, though Alexis does wind up slumped in a corner with her culottes in thigh-high disarray and her portrait of Blake smashed by her side.

Round two, however, which occurs in episode twenty-three of season three may be *Dynasty*'s paramount moment of green-eyed foolishness. A pensive Krystle sits by a lily pad–strewn reflecting pool, incongruously garbed in a voluminous sapphire silk dressing gown with draped mutton sleeves and a full gam-baring slit that would suit a Vegas chorine. Swiftly striding to the water's edge,

Alexis, in a black-and-white coatdress with a matching wide-brimmed hat that could fit right into *My Fair Lady*'s "Ascot Gavotte," not only accuses Krystle of having an unlawful marriage but throws in one more jab at her bar-renness. However, calling her an "empty-armed Madonna" is a low blow, even for Alexis. With her normally placid demeanor instantly at full boil, Krystle hurls both a "You miserable bitch!" and Alexis into the deeper-than-expected pool, where they claw and punch but somehow only get wet. Blake, fortuitously passing by in a limo, halts the brawl, demanding that his present and former loves never feud over him again.

But why mess up a good thing? The overt love-hate dynamic of *Dynasty* had driven it to number one in the ratings. And for one brief shining moment, Denver became an international fashion capital. After the 1970s, when fashion reveled in an overwhelming clash of styles such as minis versus maxis, and Halston's cashmere minimalism versus disco-ready polyester kick pleats and gold chains, *Dynasty*'s strict dress code coerced fashion to return to one dominant mood. No matter how wince-worthy it appears in retrospect, glamour kicked casual to every curb in the neighborhood during the 1980s. Marshall Field featured a Carrington Christmas clothing line. Due to the prevalence of oversize headgear, both in and out of pools, Neiman Marcus and Saks Fifth Avenue took the cue and expanded their hat departments, Bloomingdale's launched an exclusive *Dynasty* collection, and at one point during its nine-year run, Nolan Miller had his name attached to eight retail lines simultaneously. Rarely mentioned but impossible to ignore, is that Linda Evans, in her forties during the show's nine-year run, and Joan Collins, in her fifties, became TV's most influential clotheshorses. Not only did the women on other serial dramas like *Falcon Crest* and *Knots Landing* seem to be raiding Krystle's and Alexis's closets, but the two became role models, sartorially if not morally, by presenting a style tutorial for baby boomer fans who were also approaching middle age. And not only could you look great, you could smell great too. *Dynasty* even had its own fragrance. It was one of the few products to bear the label that came without shoulder pads.

I LOVE
THE WAY
YOU LIE

The Kiss in
The Thomas Crown Affair,
1968

The Thomas Crown Affair is classified as a caper film, but the complexities of its central heist are more confusing than compelling. If its good guys and bad guys looked the way they usually do and were dressed the way they usually are in movies like this, you wouldn't even remember it, if you saw it at all. Its story offers no moral or insight about the human condition. Even its director, Norman Jewison, flippantly described the film as "a love affair between two shits."

Then what is it about the film that has kept designers like Tom Ford, Ralph Lauren, Michael Kors, and millions of ardent fans raving, rewatching, and riffing on it for more than forty years? Well, you could start with that first close-up of a carved solid gold Patek Philippe pocket watch with the Phi Beta Kappa key as it slides into the vest pocket of Crown's custom-made Prince of Wales plaid Douglas Hayward suit. Then there's the throwaway shot of the insurance investigator's atypical mode of transport: a 1967 ruby red Ferrari 275/GTB convertible—one of only ten ever made—a roadster that makes all of James Bond's Aston Martins look like bumper cars.

Of course, there's the delicious shock when we discover the identity of the dogged investigator. As Michael Kors recalls, "The moment Faye Dunaway stalked onto the screen in a pink-and-white suit with that big brimmed hat, you knew the dolly girls and hippie chicks of the 1960s were over. Here was the new ultimate power bitch. She blew me out of my seat." And finally, there's the unexpected casting of the master thief himself. After seventeen films as the willing heir to Humphrey Bogart's and Robert Mitchum's laconic tough guy, here was Steve McQueen, his locks dyed the same golden blond as Dunaway's, abandoning his trademark leather jacket, jeans, and motorcycle for nip-waisted, two-button, three-piece suits by Ralph Lauren's Savile Row tailor; a gotta-have-'em pair of blue-mirror-tinted Persol 714 foldable sunglasses (still available), driving a Rolls-Royce Silver Shadow with personalized license plates that read TC100, as he picks up his out-for-blood adversary, Dunaway, for a date to play chess, without ever wiping the canary-eating grin off his face.

If there was ever a movie where style was the substance, it's *The Thomas Crown Affair*. The movie serves as the source book for everything glamorous and enviable about the jet-setting 1960s. Directed, photographed, and edited by three Oscar winners— Jewison, Haskell Wexler, and Hal Ashby—who became key architects of Hollywood's dynamic filmmaking renaissance of the 1970s, the film is a mesmerizing catalog of distracting radiance. From the blinding yellow of Crown's glider to Dunaway's oversize gold-ball earrings and McQueen's bright blue suit linings, the film dive-bombs your concentration with glittering diversions. Its dialogue is clipped and staccato, at odds with the lazy laid-back lingo of the era, so you can't listen casually. Its deliberate, hyperkinetic pace is driven both by the anxious tempo of its oft-repeated Oscar-winning theme song, "The Windmills of Your Mind," and the cinematography's extensive reliance on the then revolutionary, now dated-looking use of split-screen technique—at one point the action subdivides into a grid featuring fifty-four separate frames.

Thomas Crown is no antihero and miles beyond cool. He is devilishly bad; a millionaire who steals $26 million for the thrill of it and embarks on this cat-and-mouse chase with the same gusto he brings to playing polo and hang gliding (McQueen learned to do both for the film). He is both poster child of the establishment and its definitive thumb noser.

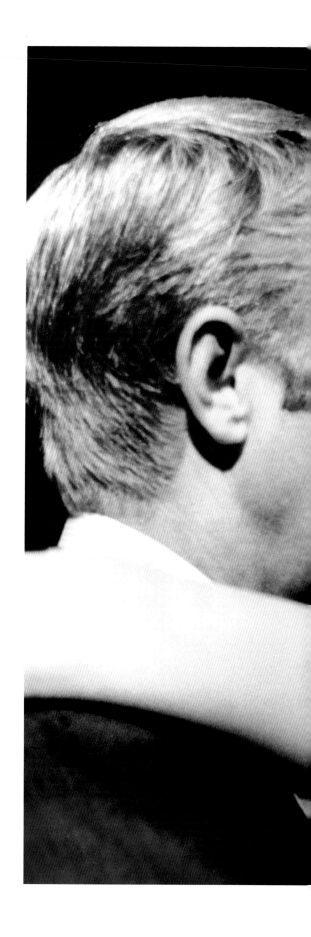

No wonder Dunaway's mercenary investigator, Vicki Anderson, is torn between destroying him and surrendering completely. Either way, Crown is the ultimate get. What heightens the intrigue is that she has made herself into the ultimate foil. She eschews the strong-arm techniques of her trade like isolated interrogations and force. Her weapon of choice is sex, which is why she is always dressed to kill. After initially accusing costume designer Theodora Van Runkle of "making her look like a boy" in *Bonnie and Clyde,* Dunaway recanted after the film's commercial and sartorial success, not only having Van Runkle dress her for the 1968 Oscars, but demanding her for *Crown.* Each of her twenty-nine outfits aims to outdo model Jean Shrimpton on her best day. Her angular suits reminiscent of Courrèges's stark silhouettes in lavender, moss green, and black trimmed in icy white are the attention-getting antithesis of Saint Laurent's subdued, prim clothes for Catherine Deneuve in *Belle de Jour,* released in the United States the same year. Vicki accessorizes with intimidating hats and unusually small nonutilitarian bags. She wears her hair pulled sleek until it explodes into a thickly braided, heavily lacquered, looped-under ponytail; her nails and lips glazed to Ming-porcelain finish; and false-lashed eyes kohled like the kids in a Margaret Keane painting. A lover of fashion might be tempted to look for Diana Vreeland's name among the credits because there is no difference between twenty-six-year-old Dunaway's imperious beauty in *Crown* and her *Vogue* cover shoot with fashion photographer Jerry Schatzberg (and later, her lover) that coincided with the film's release.

What makes Crown and Anderson's calculated stances more enticing than exhausting, however, is that Dunaway and McQueen don't simply turn each other on. They drive each other insane with consuming lust, so we have the fun of watching two people who know full well they are asking for trouble go "what the hell?"

The most celebrated scene in *Thomas Crown* is the fabled chess match, where the two sit fully clothed, reenacting a grandmaster game played in Vienna in 1899. Instead of dialogue, the camera comes in tighter with each move

as an act of foreplay. In 1968, Dunaway's slow stroking of the bishop, McQueen's brush of her hand and leg, and both sucking on forefingers in deep thought seemed risqué innuendo, similar to the once ribald but now coy eating scene in *Tom Jones* (1963) where Albert Finney and Joyce Redman notoriously tear into chicken bones and succulent pears. Unfortunately, today we see the same enticements in commercials for Greek yogurt.

But it's the kissing scene that follows the game that still causes palpitations. Vicki gets Crown's queen in the chess game, or Crown lets her. He then rises, says nothing for what seems an eternity, and then offers her his hand, saying, "Let's play something else." Starting with a darkened close-up where all one can discern are lips locking, the camera starts to circle the hungrily enmeshed pair. Though now a technique so common it was repeated on *Glee* once a week, Wexler's triple 360 rotation around the couple was the first time this was ever done on film. The shot took three days to get. Former president Jimmy Carter, not the first name that comes to mind when you contemplate steamy sex, admits to having watched the scene sixteen times.

The Thomas Crown Affair is not about finding love; the immoral lovers aren't destined for an ever after. But the movie did happily reunite sensuality and high style after years of fashion's flirtation with mod androgyny. Looking at McQueen, men saw a successful businessman's stature increase when he added panache to his wardrobe instead of sobriety. Dunaway made it obvious that brandishing one's femininity in public was as persuasive as using it in the bedroom.

At one point, Dunaway's investigator offers a gift to the police detective she is working with, played by Paul Burke, who doesn't approve of her methods but can't help but be impressed by her results. First he refuses to take it, citing company policy. Naturally, she thrusts it back at him. He opens it and cracks up at the placard she has had made for his desk, which reads, THINK DIRTY. She tells him it works every time, just as long as you are dressed in style. And that's why we keep watching this movie.

AIN'T LIFE SWELL?

Ralph Lauren's First
Advertorial Campaign,
1981

Face it. Your world will never be as ravishing as the one realized in a Ralph Lauren ad. How could it? Is your flaxen, sun-streaked hair forever in place? Does an amber light hit you directly above the cheekbone every time your picture is taken—always on your good side? Do your sweaters never pill and your jeans never fade? Is your children's skin of alabaster translucence and are their hand-knit Fair Isle sweaters unstained by peanut butter and jelly? Is your polo pony groomed and saddled, your sailboat ready to leave the marina the moment you can catch the wind, your Bugatti polished to perfection and waiting just outside your door?

One might think defining the good life within such unattainable parameters would turn off anyone who doesn't come home to an estate that boasts a roaring fireplace in every room. But who born between the Depression and the baby boom never imagined living in Laurenland? Like Ralph, most were the first-generation children of immigrants, with lineage less likely to stretch back to the Mayflower than it was to Ellis Island. Frankly, what the ambitious Jewish kid from the Bronx imagined was a heritage as foreign to him as it was desirable to everyone he knew in his old neighborhood. Except Ralph knew just what that world looked like.

By 1966, less than fifteen years after starting out with a suitcase filled with wide-knotted ties that got picked up by Neiman Marcus, Ralph Lauren's product lines had expanded so vastly that he decided to produce a marketing campaign that would bring together all of his label's merchandise—and *only* his merchandise—in a single editorial-driven context. At the time, the scope of the concept was unheard of. Neither designed as a separate insert, nor perforated to

be a pull out, Lauren's nearly two-dozen-page-long visual narrative of personal style curated solely by the designer (working with a photographer and crew of his choosing) was so fluidly incorporated into the publication's traditionally bound-in real estate, that his advertising became nearly indistinguishable from the magazine's produced pictorials. With the creation and placement of this "advertorial," Lauren, in essence, paid for the privilege of subverting the magazine's editorial point of view, ignoring both the arbiters on its mastheads as well as other retailers who might be selecting his products in their promotions, in order to present a singular vision: his. For Lauren, the "advertorial" was the optimal way to seduce the reader with the least amount of outside interference. "I was always inspired by the movies, so running multiple pages was a way of telling a story," says Lauren. "I wanted to convey the romance of living."

The male and female models photographer Bruce Weber chose for the initial campaign epitomized a scrubbed, unblemished, gently windswept, and sun-kissed aristocratic beauty. The cast of friends and families he created could have been the members of a venerable, old New England family possibly descended from Burke's Peerage. The photographs were free from tension, lust, yearning, or grand gestures, for what they communicated was that—in Ralph's world—dressing well was symbolic of a life going blissfully and beautifully according to plan. The images sought to evoke feelings of satisfaction, confidence, and grace, all of which could be had with polished sportswear that looked lived-in and in settings where wealth was apparent but never ostentatious. In other words, the china was perfect, but people were eating off it; the suit was impeccable, but the man was working; the dress conveyed easy glamour, but the woman wearing it wasn't posing— she was holding her child's hand.

There wasn't a sofa you didn't want to sit in. A car you didn't want to drive. "Sometimes the pictures weren't even about the clothes," Lauren says. "They were about a home, a car, or a table set under a tree—it was all about creating a spirit and the mood of a place. We'd find a manor house or a sailboat and prop it for weeks with the things that created our aesthetic: the right dogs, cars and pickups and people who weren't really models but surfers, and architects, painters, and musicians that Bruce [Weber] still never ceases looking for. We were photographing a real person in a real location doing something you could relate to or strive for. It wasn't simply about buying something."

The millions of consumers who have bought into Laurenland remain the envy of the industry. Over the decades, Lauren has proven the flexibility of his artistic vision by varying settings: the Hamptons, Martha's Vineyard, the English countryside, a Manhattan penthouse, a Hollywood movie set, Jamaica, Capri, Africa, Hawaii, and a good chunk of the southeast corner of Colorado, where Lauren has built the vast Double RL Ranch. The multibillion-dollar, multilabel Polo Ralph Lauren brand remains one of most vital fashion houses in history, and is actually in the midst of a major global expansion, because, Lauren says with the calm assurance of a man who holds all the keys to his kingdom, "people like to dream with us. They want to be part of our world."

HER VERY FIRST TIME

Madonna on the
MTV Music Awards, 1984

The opening lyrics of the Cole Porter song "Anything Goes" claim, "In olden days a glimpse of stocking was looked on as something shocking. Now, heaven knows, anything goes." As a tunesmith, no one was better. As a sociologist, Porter isn't so bad either, because, in retrospect, few celebrated cultural assaults retain their power to traumatize for long. After forty years, the rape scene in Stanley Kubrick's *A Clockwork Orange* (1971) will still leave you shaken. If you can track down a bootleg copy (there weren't a lot of music videos produced in 1972) of Alice Cooper hanging himself in a straitjacket and then coming "back from the dead" to sing "School's Out" you're guaranteed to shriek in horror before the first chorus. But Madonna in a wedding dress writhing on the stage floor and singing "Like a Virgin" at the first MTV Music Awards is hardly going to make you blush.

Watch the performance now on YouTube and your face can't help but scrunch upon hearing how pinched and reedy her voice sounds, how often she runs out of breath or her pitch wavers, how the stage is bare except for a community-theater-worthy seventeen-foot-tall wedding cake, and how her wedding dress and veil look chosen from whatever was left behind after a final clearance sale at David's Bridal. The number comes off more under-rehearsed than vulgar. These days, we are an easily offended but not very shockable public.

However, the day after the show, Madonna's unlike-a-virgin antics seemed to be all anyone was talking about. Whether viewers thought her performance hysterical or whether it upset them, its instantaneous notoriety becomes even more impressive when you realize there was nowhere to post or Vine in 1984. Unlike the hundred million views

Miley Cyrus, Beyoncé, or Taylor Swift can rack up after a few days on social media, MTV was not an instant hit when the music network premiered. Cable was a relatively new entertainment alternative, and record-label honchos remained too skeptical of video's effectiveness as a marketing tool to commit to producing them for every artist. Factor in the nascent network's limited budget, and it was hardly a revelation that music's top artists were less than eager to appear on MTV's award-show debut. The broadcast's hosts, Dan Aykroyd and Bette Midler, were not exactly youthful torchbearers for rock music's future either.

Madonna started her career in 1982, the same year as MTV's launch, and though she already had several hit records ("Holiday," "Lucky Star," "Borderline"), she had yet to tour, so she lacked a large fan base. Nevertheless, Mary Lambert's video for "Like a Virgin," which got played in heavy rotation on MTV, is polished, well produced, and, thanks to a series of quick cuts interweaving two narratives, exploits the untrained singer's raw bravado to her best advantage. Set in Venice, Madonna looks sensational in two guises. During one half of the film, she sings and slinks in a gondola, her hair bouncing in flattering, streaked, and curled disarray, her black midriff-baring dress bedecked in ropes of pearls, crosses, and chains, and worn over purple leggings. She wears a belt with a buckle that reads BOY TOY. During the other half, Madonna is at her soft-focus prettiest: smoky eyes searching, hair pinned in a perfect chignon, body swathed in an Elizabethan-style, floor-length wedding gown with a lace bodice and an elaborate pearl bib. She is being pursued through the city's narrow streets by a lion. At one point she does get on all fours in the wedding dress, but the shot is tight and her movement more provocative than overt. At the song's end, she is willingly carried away via gondola by a man wearing a black suit and a lion mask.

For her first live MTV appearance, Madonna requested her betrothed be a white Bengal tiger. When the producers refused, she chose to go solo and standing atop an oversize wedding cake alongside a mannequin groom. Instead of the gown she wore as pretty Madonna in the video, she chose a look the hipper Madonna would more likely have worn on her big day—a lace bustier top; a short, dotted, tulle skirt with a handkerchief hem; and the soon-to-be-ever-present

BOY TOY buckled belt. But while descending from atop the three-tiered cake, one of her shoes kept slipping off. Rather than attempt to secure it, the singer chose "to pretend [she] meant to do this and then [she] dove on the floor and rolled around." Somewhere in mid-roll, Madonna exposed her underwear. Then, after a few strokes of the veil between her legs, Madonna got up somewhat gracelessly, snatched her veil off the floor, and took a bow. The number was over in three and a half minutes.

Numerous industry executives in the audience believed the performance was career killing. But key people disagreed. "Was it perfect?" said Madonna's former manager Freddy DeMann. "No, but it worked. I think we all know she had

a few drinks, because she had the nerve to crawl around the way she did." MTV executives thought she stole the show. So did the public. "Like a Virgin" became Madonna's first number one hit, and the attention she generated did much to ensure that MTV Music Awards wouldn't be a one-hit wonder. The next year, the telecast attracted the much cooler and much younger Eddie Murphy as host.

But more important, in 1985, Madonna both costarred in the surprise hit film *Desperately Seeking Susan*, playing a character dressed and styled exactly the same way she was in the spunkier half of the "Like a Virgin" video but with the addition of fingerless gloves, and launched her maiden Virgin Tour. The combined force of that film and her better-rehearsed, enthusiastic live performances transformed tens of millions of preteen and teenage girls into a rabidly devoted global fashion cult of "Madonna wannabes," who continued to dress as streetwise urchins in leggings and tulle miniskirts, bows in ther hair and black-rubber bracelets bedecking their arms, long after the pop star had moved on to reimagine herself as the second coming of Marilyn Monroe for her Blond Ambition Tour.

During that tour, Madonna still sang "Like a Virgin," but not in a wedding gown. Instead, the Material Girl slithered on a red-velvet-covered bed wearing a new, higher-end outfit, one that incorporated the iconic cone bra designed for her by couturier Jean Paul Gaultier.

WHAT I DID FOR LOVE

The Marriage of the Duke and
Duchess of Windsor, 1937

"Since I can't be
pretty, I try to look
sophisticated."

–The Duchess of Windsor,
Vogue, 1943

The relationship of the Duke and Duchess of Windsor may be one the most chronicled and least envied of our times. King Edward VIII's empire-be-damned need to be with "the woman [he] love[d]" necessitated modern history's ultimate career sacrifice, one never betrayed with the slightest regret. And despite being labeled a "Yankee harlot" by the British press and enduring decades of her royal in-laws unrepentant disdain, Wallis Simpson crafted her own version of regal serenity. In virtually every photograph of them during their long, globe-trotting, aimless marriage, the couple looks simply sensational: softly tailored of-the-moment Parisian ensembles handsomely flatter her boyish body and frame her nearly crown-gems-worthy jewelry collection; his every outfit a reaffirmation of Diana Vreeland's edict that "He [was] the best-dressed man in all of history." Disney, Grimm, or Harlequin could not have packaged love more triumphantly.

Nonetheless, the marriage of the Duke and Duchess of Windsor gives one the creeps. From the beginning, their union was unseemly: Prince Edward first met his bride-to-be alongside her second husband, Baltimore businessman Ernest Simpson, at the home of Edward's lover, Thelma Furness (who was also married at the time to a member of Parliament). Further, the future king wielded the power of his station to cultivate a close friendship with Simpson in order to gain permission for weekly lunches à deux with his wife. Then there's the deliberately childlike language Edward consistently used in his furious flurry of mash notes and often thrice-daily phone calls to his intended. In the letters—which bear an unnerving resemblance to the published ones Prince Charles wrote to his future wife Camilla Parker Bowles, the Duchess of Cornwall—the prince calls his love "Mummie." In fact, the constant role-playing, coupled with his letters' increasingly obsessive tone—sometimes threatening suicide and starvation if she does not end up at his side forever—has generated speculation that the prince may have suffered from Asperger's syndrome, autism, manic depression, even anorexia, as he was more fixated on his weight than she was.

As for Mrs. Simpson, her predatory flirtatiousness—she called her paramour "Peter Pan"—was as unapologetic as her social ambitions were extraordinary. Though the general public knew nothing of their affair until Edward had made his desire to abdicate the throne known to his disapproving parents, she openly enjoyed her position as the future king's mistress in their circles. She even enlisted her best friend, Mary Kirk, to keep her husband company while she went off with the prince—and Kirk later married him. The illicit couple's passion, however, was less apparent. There were rumors of her special sexual talents. Others insisted their relationship wasn't physical. In public, Mrs. Simpson once declared, "No man is allowed to touch me below the Mason-Dixon Line." Also, in letters written after their betrothal, the duchess refers to her soon-to-be ex-husband as "the love of her life" and infers that if not for his escalating, all-consuming ardor, she would have been content to remain Edward's mistress.

But with Edward's abdication on December 6, 1936, his bride's revised mission became clear. When they married on June 3, 1937, the Duchess chose an atypically royal but oh-so-au-courant Mainbocher silk, high-collared, heart-shape-skirted dress in a soon-to-be-widely copied color called Wallis Blue (named by Mainbocher to match her eyes). Instead of a veil, she crowned her costume with a coq-feather-brimmed straw hat designed to look like a halo by Caroline Reboux. (Cecil Beaton, the chosen wedding photographer, loathed it.) A Cartier bracelet of nine ruby-, diamond-, emerald-, and sapphire-encrusted crosses dangled from her wrist. However, there was nothing trendsetting about the newlyweds' two trips to Nazi Germany later that year, including a jovial meeting with Adolf Hitler. To squelch the ex–future king's newfound friendship with the Nazis, the duke was eventually made the governor of the Bahamas, where the couple remained in sun-kissed exile for the duration of World War II.

The duke and duchess never returned home. They moved to Paris as a postwar base, then routinely jet-setted around the world, accompanied by their Dior-perfumed pugs, and were consistently feted by high society, simply because they were a lot more likely to accept a dinner invitation than Queen Elizabeth II. Unlike England's current royals, the couple never used their position or influence to generate any significant humanitarian or charitable effort. But they were ranked as Hall of Famers on the International Best-Dressed List. In fact, when the duke died in 1972, Givenchy's atelier stayed open all night to finish the simple black coat with a waist-length chiffon veil that the duchess wore to the funeral, where she maintained perfect composure. Millions of others around the world remained dry-eyed as well.

CLASS GONE IN A FLASH

Flashdance's Seduction by
Sweatshirt, 1983

When I was a kid, you got dressed up to go to the theater. You got dressed up to board an airplane. You got dressed up when going out to dinner. You got dressed up for a night of dancing. You wore ripped jeans to paint the deck furniture and work boots to plant and weed the garden. Sweatshirts looked best at a pep rally, and if you weren't a dancer, the only time you wore leggings was under your ski pants. Now people routinely wear all of the latter to do all of the former. And it's all Jennifer Beals's fault.

Okay, Adrian Lyne and Michael Kaplan should shoulder some of the blame, because while Beals was the star of *Flashdance*, the film's director and costume designer must also be held accountable for instigating the casualization of America's dress code. *Flashdance* was brusquely dismissed by film critics as a series of overproduced music videos strung together by a thin Cinderella story, but screening rooms full of middle-aged cineasts scrawling notes in the dark was never the film's intended audience.

Instead, the movie aimed true and shot a bull's-eye into the zeitgeist of 1983, becoming the third highest-grossing film of the year. Looking at it three decades later, the reason for the film's surprise success is obvious. *Flashdance* looks like high-gloss, paper-thin entertainment, but it is actually an invaluable time capsule, uncannily incorporating seismic changes in how almost every element of youth culture— from sex to style—was drastically shifting away from the mores and manners of the previous generation.

Though Tom Hedley's original screenplay is based on an eighteen-year-old girl who worked as a sandblaster at her boyfriend's construction company in Buffalo by day and danced at the local bar at night (under the name Gina-Gina, the Sex Machine), it's doubtful that the real-life couple resembled Jennifer Beals and Michael Nouri. Beals, as the dancing steelworker—when she's not hidden under a welder's mask with the ambiguous name ALEX stamped on its visor—and Nouri as her boss, Nick, don't exactly look like potential lovers. If it weren't for a notable age difference, their equally olive-toned skin, dark brooding eyes, slight but broad-shouldered frames, and full manes of semi-tamed curls, one could uneasily mistake them for fraternal twins. In fact, when they first meet on a lunch break in the steel yard, Alex and Nick are not only wearing interchangeable outfits but they are also wearing the exact same colors. The androgyny is no coincidence. By neutralizing clothing as a source of gender power, the courtship starts with neither having the upper hand.

Simultaneously, although on a higher economic plane, women entering the white-collar workplace quickly realized that donning frill-free suits with padded shoulders in colors that adhered near to the "greige" of Armani menswear might help get them taken more seriously. Raising the stakes even higher, the world of ready-to-wear was being hijacked by

Japanese designers, like Yohji Yamamoto, Junya Watanabe, and Rei Kawakubo, who hardly saw sex or urbanity as a driving force in their conceptual creations.

To make *Flashdance*'s dynamic even more confusing, at least as far as the Cinderella myth goes, Alex could intimidate most fairy godmothers. A little rough around the edges, with a fuse as ready to short-circuit as the wiring in her ungentrified loft, she is the aggressor in this steel-beamed fable. Always peddling on her bike, talking tough, owning a dog that could guard the River Styx, throwing a rock through Nick's window when she becomes jealous, leaving him in bed the morning after spending the night there, so she can get to work on time (he comes in late)—she is easily the more macho of the two.

It may seem cliché today, but thirty years ago, Alex's take-no-shit attitude struck a resounding chord with young women trying to find their own way. Six million copies of the sound track weren't sold just because people liked the music. No, women wanted to be a "Maniac" (one of the big dance hits on the record) just like Alex, dancing like they've never danced before. They were so taken with Alex's gutsy ways that her mode of dressing became an unofficial uniform for teenage girls and college women— and it still is. Consider her army-navy-store-inspired wardrobe of men's anoraks, work boots, green army jackets, multiple scarves wrapped round the neck, oversize cardigans, torn sweaters, ripped jeans, and military coats—there's nothing in her wardrobe any cool, self-respecting young woman couldn't or wouldn't wear now.

And then there is the sweatshirt that changed everything. Beals claims its design was an accident; that she had to cut the neck out of Alex's sweatshirt to pull it over her head after she had taken it home and shrunk it by mistake in the wash. But more likely, the sweatshirt's torn incarnation was due to costumer Kaplan's astute observation on how ballet dancers dress when in rehearsal. Because many dance studios used to be drafty and badly heated, and dancers need to keep their muscles warm, they often stretched and slashed sweats and sweaters to allow heat to be trapped between them and their leotards while still providing freedom of movement.

As for imitating Alex's unschooled but riveting dance moves, well, luckily there were plenty of places where you could don fleece and leggings and go "dancing for your life." Two years before *Flashdance*, a new form of exercise called aerobics swiftly gained widespread popularity and raised heartbeats nationwide. As for the sport's dancer-reflective garb, it received a jolt of recognition in 1981, when Olivia Newton-John released one of the biggest hits of her career, "Physical," with a video featuring her in turquoise shirt, white unitard and headband, and boysenberry leggings, set in possibly the nelliest gay gym ever put on tape. Then in 1982, Jane Fonda confirmed this getup right for women of all ages with the launch of the first of twenty *Jane Fonda Workout* tapes, *Workout: Starring Jane Fonda*, the bestselling exercise video of all time, in which she wears similar body-hugging gear.

But few remember the directorial stroke of genius director Lyne added to make the scene with Beals sitting spread-eagled in her sweatshirt (she actually has a leather skirt on but it's hidden) so indelible in our collective consciousness. On their first date, Alex comes home, slips into the off-the-shoulder sweat, and plops herself down across from Nick. As she begins talking about herself, she is also matter-of-factly and rather skillfully removing her lace bra, pulling it out from underneath and tossing it without saying a word about it. It's obvious, from the shot of Nick's eyes nearly rolling to the back of his head, that neither he, nor any man in the audience watching *Flashdance*, ever heard a word she said. All he and those of his sex were thinking about was how nice it would be to cry, "What a feeling!"

HOW TO MAKE A SHOULDER-BARING SWEATSHIRT IN SIX EASY STEPS

1. Measure from your left side of your neck to one inch below your right shoulder. Cut the number of inches (rounded off) in half.

2. Starting from a mark in the center of your chosen sweatshirt collar, use the halved number to measure on a diagonal to a point on the shoulder seam.

3. Now cut in an arc from one point to the other only on the front of the sweatshirt. Do not worry if the cut isn't perfect.

4. Peel back the cut piece and trim off the remaining collar around the neck.

5. Cut the border hem of the sweatshirt and cut the sleeves off at the inset seaming.

6. Throw the sweatshirt in the wash, so that the newly cut edges will curl. Throw over your head. Bra not required.

THE GREAT FAKE-OUT AT VERSAILLES

John Galliano's *Matrix*
Collection, 1999

"John Galliano at the home of Louis XIV!" gushed the effusive editor as she seated herself on haute couture's traditional gold chair next to me. "Can you imagine anything more perfect? It's going to be so over the top, just like the opera house, only more!"

Oh, it was over the top all right, but a night at the opera it wasn't.

In his first three years as creative director of Christian Dior, John Galliano had cast a spell over what had become a moribund atelier, turning it into an epicenter of lavish creativity for the haute couture, resulting in the fashion world scurrying around him like courtiers in a newly dubbed king's court.

Dutifully following Christian Dior's edict to "save the world from nature" and childishly enthralled by all the craft, freedom, and money Dior had placed at his disposal, the former punk designer kept turning up—and literally, out—the volume with each successive haute couture and ready-to-wear collection, generating reams of publicity and a steady increase in Dior's revenue. The powers of Dior's parent company, LVMH, therefore saw no reason to curb his free rein. Racing forward with a deeply researched yet intensely fantasized vision of beauty, clothing women in as much splendor as he could bead, brocade, and layer around them, Galliano held his presentations in equally elaborate settings, such as São Schlumberger's abandoned Parisian villa, the Palais Garnier, and the Gare d'Austerlitz train station.

So naturally, when the invitation for the Dior fall/winter 1999 haute couture show indicated it would be staged at the Palace of Versailles, potential guests swooned at the possibilities of grandeur beyond comprehension. But this time Galliano had other ideas. He recalls, "While I was very grateful for all the attention and accolades, I was starting to feel like a slave to the DNA of the house, a bit trapped by what we had created at Dior." The excesses had also sparked criticism from contemporaries—or rivals—such as Valentino, who mused that Galliano "has a wonderful imagination, but I am not sure if he knows everything about how to make a dress." Galliano was not unaffected. For all his flamboyance on the runway, he is not only quite shy in private but was also devoted to and humbled by the people who made up his design team at the time: designer Bill Gaytten, milliner Stephen Jones, and the late Steven Robinson, Galliano's right-hand man since his school days at Central Saint Martin's, as well as the veteran artisans at Dior's atelier whom Galliano considered his teachers. The designer decided that "[he] had to reach for something that showed that [he] had wrested [his] creative flow and sent it in a new direction." His inspiration: a little movie that had just opened called *The Matrix*.

For those who don't recall much about the film other than Keanu Reeves's long coat (which figures as a key element in Galliano's inspiration), *The Matrix* is the Wachowski brothers' simultaneously visionary and pretentious look into a potential future of doom for humankind if computer hacker Neo (Reeves) rejects his anointment as the potential messiah to save the world from becoming lost in a virtual reality of cyber-escapism. (Don't really follow? Neither did anybody else.) More important, however, was that this blockbuster, which the *New York Times* called "a special effects tornado," was a smashingly stylized film whose swaggering black-as-a death-star costuming blew motocross chic, Goth, and punk out of the water and into a discarded parallel universe.

Galliano was mad about the look of *The Matrix*. No doubt it brought back memories of his first well-attended Paris show (thanks to the support of *Vogue* editors Anna Wintour and André Leon Talley), where he made virtually every dress, jacket, and coat out of the same bolt of black satin crepe because it was all he could afford at the time. "I realized this haute couture collection could be my turning point to show that I was more than just a designer paying homage to another. Initially, Sidney [Toledano, president of Dior] was alarmed by my ideas. But then he remembered my controversial Paris Tramps collection

[spring/summer 2000 haute couture] that resulted in so many bestselling denim accessories. So, with his blessing I decided to indulge in my new mix of glamour and savagery."

And so, guests entering Versailles were immediately distracted from the parquet floors, gilded mirrors, and crystal chandeliers by a one-hundred-foot-long, undulating runway that was lit from underneath, which made it seem as if it were almost buoyant, not unlike a partially filled waterbed. Once seated, the audience was hit with sounds of static, like a computer board short-circuiting, followed by composer Don Davis's pumping, ominously driving theme for *The Matrix*. As soon as the first model stepped out onto the runway, it was apparent all references to past Galliano shows for Dior had been left behind.

The model, with raccoon eyes smudged black from the lower lid to way above the eyebrow and stopping just short of her only sole accessory of color, a blood red beret worn over her long flat-ironed hair, strode down the runway as if entrusted with a serious mission. She wore a version of Reeves's long black trench, reconceived by Galliano as a cropped leather jacket with an asymmetrical collar and beaded banding on its diagonal closure, which was open to expose her bare midriff. Below, she wore a matte-black leather ankle-length skirt slashed to the left hip and wrapped around the waist with a gun belt. She also wore knee-high, flat-heeled, black leather boots, garters, and one glove. Not a girl who would be quick to curtsy.

Next Galliano sent out a tall, wafer-thin, long-haired, and bare-chested male model, clad only in a similar slashed black skirt and knee boots. And so the show went. It was all black leather: vinylized, waxed, patented, and cut at every angle possible, worn as pants, bustiers, bandeaus, shorts, belted shifts, and gauntlets. Then the show switched to attire replete with a heady mix of black beading, black macramé, black tulle, and black lace, all with Galliano's signature stunning extravagance but with an impact as hard as a backhanded smack.

Just as the clothing started to get familiar, the same angular shapes were presented in acid yellow silk and patent leather worn under voluminous furs in the same shocking color. Then the designer's palette moved to fire-engine red in the form of long leather skirts lined with scarlet sequins and big knits trimmed in massive pelts of

vermillion-dyed fox. Next he presented stunning white variations on the *Matrix* coat accompanied by monumental hats crafted by Stephen Jones that featured stuffed pheasants surrounded by whole taxidermied foxes or forest foliage framing boar heads.

Then, as the music switched from techno to Madonna, shredded suede hunting gear followed, alternating with variations on British military redcoats. The makeup got softer, the hats got more aggressive. One model carried a rifle and cocked it. Then, in a discordant twist, Galliano sent out a few dozen of the ornate bias-cut, sequined, sheer, and diaphanous stunners that seemed as if they had wandered in from another season and at one time would've seemed pure Galliano. But those gowns had to have been there to lull the crowd as a setup for one final sartorial goose. Gisele Bündchen stepped out onto the runway— her face painted in warrior camouflage, her hair braided like a looped tomahawk—in a pop art version of Saint Laurent's signature Mondrian dress rendered in lavender and purple, followed by a series of similarly dressed Day-Glo Amazons, and closing with Carmen Kass walking down the runway, an enormous bright-red-and-pink silk parachute cape that she held above her head sailing behind her.

The next day, the headline for Suzy Menkes's column in the *International Herald Tribune* read, "Versailles Hosts Dior Delirium," and she described the show's "Gothic fright makeup, clothes apparently made over from discarded battle dress, and headgear composed of dead birds and animals" as "the most staggering example of self-indulgent luxury since Louis XIV held court at Versailles . . . a megalomaniac moment." That didn't matter though, because one animated couture client, who will remain anonymous, had a slightly different take on the presentation, saying to a reporter, "Monsieur Galliano has changed my eye." Strip away the blackened war paint, the bounty-hunter hats, and the deliberately obscuring layering, and what remained was a tough, sleek, incredibly modern "new" Dior image, less referential to the past, and more connected to the street energy that other brands had tapped into with great success (including Galliano when he began), but Dior had previously resisted. Within two years, retail sales had increased another 40 percent.

"I wanted to show the inner workings of haute couture," says Galliano, "not just surface finery. All that beading and workmanship was still done by Lesage [the world's finest embroidery house]. Cutting that fabric on the bias is like dealing with oily water running through your fingers. Taming that is what I dream of. Sometimes you have to destroy something so you can re-create it a new way. Haute couture is my laboratory, and this collection allowed me to go back to the ready-to-wear with new ideas I could adapt to make clothes that were not just ornate but modern. In some ways, it is the collection I am most proud of, because it showed that besides loving women, I love the limitlessness of design, the mysteries to unlock with each new fabric, and the chance to reimagine beauty for the future."

Diane von Furstenberg summed up Galliano's talent and vision succinctly in Michael Specter's 2003 profile of the designer in *The New Yorker*, when she said, "John is really the reference point for the rest of us. Because we are making clothes, and he is making magic."

DEATH BECOMES HER

Vertigo, 1958

If the foundation of true love is unconditional acceptance, what could be crueler than an obsession with transforming someone into the person you wish they were? And what could be more disheartening than watching someone agree to change the way they walk and dress, even how they wear their hair, in their desperate need to be loved? No one in Alfred Hitchcock's *Vertigo* wields a kitchen knife, a gun, or is chased by angry birds. In fact, there is no obvious evil, and yet it's the director's most chilling and emotionally demoralizing film, because it uses love as a murder weapon.

James Stewart as Scottie Ferguson, a retired detective whose undiagnosed agoraphobia sets off an attack of vertigo that unintentionally caused the death of a fellow cop, initially refuses an old college chum's request to trail his wife, Madeleine (Kim Novak), whose sanity is in question. But from the moment Scottie sees Madeleine in a restaurant, swathed in an emerald-green opera cape that sets off her carefully pinned platinum hair, Scottie is transfixed by her furtive sensuality. He follows her relentlessly, rescues her when her inner demons drive her to jump into San Francisco Bay, and is soon so blindly besotted that he believes if he can purge her ghosts they will be together forever. Madeleine returns his affections but can't escape her spectral tormentors, who send her running to the top of a Spanish mission bell tower she claims to have seen in her dreams. Scottie tries to stop her, but again his vertigo immobilizes him, condemning him to watch helplessly as his love leaps to her death.

A year passes. Having finally recovered from a nervous breakdown, a gaunt and haunted Scottie wanders

San Francisco "seeing" Madeleine everywhere. But suddenly one day, there she is, chatting with friends on the street. She looks different. Her hair is brown and worn in a flip instead of Madeleine's sculpted French twist. Her clothes and makeup are more provocative—suggesting the attire of a single woman—and her manner is more feral than ethereal, yet Scottie has no doubt that it is her. But when he shows up unannounced at her apartment, she states her name is Judy and angrily rebuffs his insistent questioning. Heartsick and in obvious pain, he refuses to leave. Finally, Judy takes pity on Scottie and agrees to see him for dinner.

If the reversal seems odd and sudden, that's because everything that's happened up to now in *Vertigo* has been a hoax. Judy *is* the woman he fell in love with. Scottie's college buddy hired her to impersonate his wife so he could stage her murder. He was already atop the bell tower with the body of the real Madeleine. When Judy reached the summit, he threw the body from the belfry window. Scottie's vertigo prevented his climb to witness the switch (his supposed old friend had learned of his condition, setting him up to fail). The hitch in this coldhearted plan is that Judy truly did fall in love with Scottie, so she fled, but now that he's found her again she realizes she doesn't want to lose him. Yet how can she tell him the truth?

Scottie's problem, however, goes deeper than merely being in the dark. He is in love with the dead. He becomes equally obsessed with Judy, in an unbecoming and disturbing way. When she warms to him, he recoils. "Couldn't you like me just the way I am?" she asks. But the only way back into his heart is for Judy to let him turn her back into the woman she wasn't. And so we witness a perverse Pygmalion set out to re-create his lost Galatea.

There is a scene early in the film that seems incongruous on first viewing (*Vertigo* is a film that becomes richer, more complex, and more twisted with each watching). Scottie takes Madeleine to Sequoia National Park and rhapsodizes about the trees' inherent majesty, their incredible longevity, and the fact that sequoias remain eternally green, deducing green to be the color of life.

When Scottie first sees Judy as Madeleine, she's wearing a green cloak. However, once their relationship starts, her wardrobe shifts solely to black, white, and gray—as if

her life force is being extinguished. She stands in front of green curtains in Scottie's apartment. She drives a green car. But she no longer wears it: Hitchcock transfers his use of the vital color to inanimate objects. The wardrobe Edith Head created for Novak often hides the actress's ample curves in folds. Her figure is only revealed via severe tailoring. For Madeleine's feigned demise, Novak wears a rigidly structured, limestone-gray skirt suit. In fact, Novak objected to it, rightly stating the shade was unflattering on blondes and the silhouette asexual. Hitchcock, however, fully aware of Novak's curvaceousness (he was delighted she refused to wear a bra), chose it for these very reasons in order to amplify the depths of her duped lover's infatuation.

When Scottie first spies Judy, she is notably buxom in a green sweater and matching skirt and appears in the color again several times. The neon hotel sign right outside her window burns bright green. Now Scottie is the one snuffing her life. He convinces Judy to go to a fancy dress shop ostensibly to buy her new clothes. But it's immediately apparent that he is looking for only one outfit, Madeleine's gray suit (the original is hidden in Judy's closet). He dismisses one variation after another with increasing frustration. When Judy professes liking one, his eyes narrow as he callously dismisses her opinion. The saleswoman, realizing that "the gentleman certainly knows what he wants," sends someone to the stockroom, where they locate the identical so-last-season suit. When he sees it, Stewart's gleeful expression terrifies Judy. His eyes flash as if he can already see Madeleine reborn.

But not yet. Judy's hair, makeup, shoes—they all must change. His humorless exactitude turns Stewart, an actor renowned for universal likability, into a real demon instead of an imagined one. It also turns him into an eerie alter ego for Hitchcock, whose unsettling enchantment for casting blondes was no secret: Vera Miles, Tippi Hedren, Janet Leigh, Eva Marie Saint, Doris Day, and Grace Kelly. He reveled in presenting them as patricians in public and temptresses in the bedroom. The majority of his American films revolve around placing them in peril so that their veneer of placidity escalates to unbridled emotion, like Day's classic scream at the climax of *The Man Who Knew Too Much*. In Hedren's case, he literally tortured her while

making *The Birds*, tying her live feathered attackers to her arms with elastic bands so that she couldn't escape them during filming.

This aberrant virgin-vixen duality, overseen by Hitchcock's chief designer, Edith Head, was achieved with wardrobes marked by nipped, structured day clothes, and Palm Beach country club–appropriate eveningwear—the one exception being Kelly's costumes for *To Catch a Thief*. Not only has Hitchcock's repeating motif of repressed sensuality inspired countless photo shoots in fashion magazines for years, but it has served as the spark for designers as diverse as Alexander McQueen, Miu Miu, Alice Temperley, Badgley Mischka, and Marc Jacobs.

But no Hitchcock scene featuring a blond actress is more nerve-racking than the moment Kim Novak's transformation is complete. When Judy returns as a blonde wearing the gray suit, her hair is down the way she wore it as a brunette. Judy claims she and the hairdresser didn't like it up. Scottie, beside himself for still landing short of his deviant dream date wails, "It can't matter to you!" Judy goes into the bathroom, slamming the door on her way in. But when she emerges, framed in the green light of the hotel sign coming through the window, she is Madeleine raised from the dead. As Hitchcock states in the book *Hitchcock* by François Truffaut, this moment is the height "of necrophilia."

Unfortunately, Scottie's rekindled ecstasy is short-lived, when Judy, dressing for their celebratory dinner, puts on a necklace that Madeleine once wore. "You shouldn't have been that sentimental," he whispers piecing the deception together a little too quickly. Judy confesses all but declares her love. A traumatized Scottie insists on returning to the mission to reenact the crime and "save" her, and to see if the shock of her betrayal has expunged his vertigo. The good news is that it did. The bad news is that though he stops her, Judy becomes frightened by a dark figure coming up the stairs (a nun), and slips, falling to a real death this time.

In the film's last scene, Hitchcock shows Scottie standing on the tower ledge in despair, lost in a world of gray. Alfred, Lord Tennyson once said, "'Tis better to have loved and lost than never to have loved at all." He obviously never saw *Vertigo*.

I'M SO INTO YOUR EARRINGS

The Legacy of
Will & Grace, 1998

I serve on the board of Live Out Loud, an organization devoted to generating and sustaining harmonious environments for lesbian, gay, bisexual, and transgender youth. Each year, we award college scholarships to LGBT students whose unstoppable optimism and unnerving organizational skills have built bridges of understanding in their high schools and communities. Ten years ago, honorees either came alone or with a scholastic adviser. In 2014, each winner was surrounded by family—mom, dad, siblings, grandparents—all beaming at their special kid.

Prior to the ceremony, I asked our recipients whom they believed most responsible for the seismic turnaround in the public's perception of gays and same-sex relationships. Names cited included Governor Andrew Cuomo, who spearheaded the passage of marriage-equality legislation in the key state of New York; Edie Windsor, whose domestic partnership case had forced the catalytic 2013 Supreme Court rulings; and the high-profile comings out of Ellen DeGeneres, Neil Patrick Harris, and Apple CEO Tim Cook. However, one silent student appeared bewildered and bemused by the choices of his fellow honorees. Noting his dissension, I asked his opinion, at which point he perked up with that knowing grin people flash when they're confident everyone else has missed the obvious. "*Will & Grace*," he said. "*Will & Grace* made *all* the difference. The two guys who thought up that show should get medals. Not just because they made me laugh, but because they saved lives." Then the other honorees smiled back because they knew he was right.

Will & Grace's heroes are the writing team of David Kohan and Max Mutchnick. Kohan is openly straight;

Mutchnick, openly gay. "The foremost goal of any sitcom is laughter," says Kohan. "But *Will & Grace* was also a romance, about two people who have an insurmountable object to their romantic love." Director Sydney Pollack (*Tootsie, The Way We Were, Out of Africa*) once told me that when telling a tale of boy meets girl, "the narrative is essentially over once the boy and the girl kiss. So the story is only as good as what keeps them from kissing." As obstacles go, not being physically turned on by the person you love most is hard to beat.

Will wasn't the first gay character on television. Billy Crystal played Jodie on *Soap* (1977–1981), a sitcom that parodied daytime television, but poor Jodie wanted a sex change, then fathered a child with a woman. Tony Randall was supposed to be gay on *Love, Sidney* (1981–1983), but NBC (the same network that later broadcast *Will & Grace*), became skittish about the character's sexuality, so for two years, we never saw Sidney love anyone. The reason constantly threaded through the story line was that he was "shy." DeGeneres's character on her hit show *Ellen* wasn't gay when she came out on the cover of *Time*, but the show then made the mistake of trying to ignore the fact, or at least not make her sexuality a big deal. But audiences knew the truth, and it *was* a big deal. The show deservedly died.

No wonder NBC was nervous that Eric McCormack's Will was the first gay man not hiding his sexuality or hurting

because of it. He was a successful lawyer. At work, where he was out, he wasn't dodging gay slurs. He was also handsome, smart, compassionate, and both sexes found him charming. Will looked like your friendly coworker in the next cubicle, or your helpful neighbor with two kids. Yet he flirted—with men. He had sex—with men. And he wanted to fall in love with one. But that didn't seem to be happening anytime soon, and until it did, the love of his life was Grace.

Grace was, according to Debra Messing, who played her, "a marvelous mess, like about every woman I know at one time in her life. She was talented and loyal. She was smart and really good at her job [interior designer]. And she knew her love life was stunted because she compared every man to Will."

Why did this anything-but-odd-looking odd couple create such an impact in our society? It's amazing how irresistible people become to each other—especially attractive, sexy ones—when they are so very funny. In twenty-two minutes, the quartet of Will, Grace, Will's stereotypically flamboyant but rapier-tongued best friend Jack, and the ridiculously self-possessed Karen ricocheted so many sharp, catty, risqué, culturally spot-on, rude, and vulgar jokes, who wouldn't want to hang out with these people? The beautiful part is how they thrived on and appreciated one another's wit. You can't help but root for people who can take a joke and then give as good as they get.

The humor was neither fueled by cruelty nor drenched in euphemisms solely about being gay. Thankfully, the script happily exploited the great bond between gay men and women: vanity. "Grace believed she had a flair for fashion," says Messing. "But she couldn't quite get it right, to her friends' delight. One day she walked into her office wearing a white pony-skin skirt covered in little black spots, and Karen looked up and asked, 'Got milk?' Another time she walked in wearing a Valentino burgundy body suit blouse slashed to the belly button. Jack wanted to know if Grace should be out so soon after open-heart surgery. But frankly, if Grace always had it right, I don't think we would have liked her. We did because, like all of us, she was trying."

Their humor made them enviable. Their flaws made them real. Will became jealous when Grace ignored him for a new boyfriend. She felt judged every time she brought a new beau home. Will's parents weren't ashamed, but why didn't they "get him?" Jack couldn't understand why no one saw his true talent, though he had none. Karen acted as impenetrable as her lacquered chignon because she was anything but. There was a foible for everyone to relate to. When times get the best of you, friends and lovers don't have to be perfect, or gay, or straight. What matters is that they show up.

Kohan and Mutchnick were smart and shrewd. They let the laughs turn *Will & Grace* into a success first. Then, in the third season we learned how Will and Grace's relationship began. Entitled "Lows in the Mid-Eighties," this key episode (Kohan's favorite) is set at a fraternity party at the time the two had started dating, and Will was in the closet. While other guys are whispering to their dates, "I'm so into you!" Will squeals to Grace, "I am so into your earrings!" They are perfectly dressed like extras in *Flashdance*. Will has a mullet and a fluorescent-blue Lacoste with the collar up. Grace has a red off-the-shoulder sweater, lips so lacquered you could see your own reflection, and a frizzy,

overtly intellectual asymmetrical haircut. Despite the fact that Will has taught her the secret to keeping a scrunchie in her hair, that she's observed that "he looks just like an old-time movie star like Rock Hudson or Montgomery Clift," and that he thinks they should wait before they "do it" because they are each other's destiny, she is clueless as to Will's sexuality.

But when the two go home to Grace's family for Thanksgiving, she comes on to him in her bedroom. As she desperately smothers him with kisses, Will can't stop staring at a poster of Kevin Bacon on her wall. In a last-ditch effort to avoid sex, he proposes marriage. She tells her family. They plan a spontaneous celebration. She asks if he's hungry. He answers that he is gay and that he realized it when he became fixated on "the guy toweling himself off in the Zest commercial." Grace throws him out. They don't talk for a year. Then she finds out he actually slept with a woman and painfully confronts him. Will admits he did, and it was awful. She replies, "Why couldn't you make it awful with me?" Will answers softly that he had to be sure, and that "[he] had to do it with someone [he] didn't love." You could snicker at the 1980s' getups and Grace's frizzy do, but you had to have tissues handy nonetheless.

My young honoree was right. Audiences learned about devotion and acceptance while chuckling at these funny people. They realized that gays aren't foreign, frightening, or predatory, at least, no more so than anyone else. For eight years, Will, Grace, Jack, and Karen convinced us you can get through anything as long as you have love, laughs, and hope. Well, almost anything. "She's wearing synthetic plaid," says Karen of an unwitting bystander. "That's a four-day drive *and* a boat trip to a place called hope." Okay, it wouldn't hurt to get yourself a good wardrobe.

DON'T QUIT YOUR DAY JOB

Belle de Jour, 1967

"It's more interesting
to discover the sex
in a woman than it is to
have it thrown at you."

—Alfred Hitchcock, *Alfred Hitchcock:
Interviews,* 1972

True to his word, the director's preference for reticence can be applied to nearly every "Hitchcock blonde," the classification even infrequent filmgoers know describes the master of suspense's procession of elegant, emotionally distant, flaxen-tressed heroines, whose sexual energy is stimulated only after being placed in grave danger. Hitchcock relished frontloading his thrillers with repressed sexual dynamics. But like the tease of an eternal virgin, he nearly always confined his lovers to foreplay with no follow-through. Visually, Hitchcock was a prude.

It took Luis Buñuel to kidnap and relocate the Hitchcock blonde somewhere she could realize her suppressed ambition—to be an eager slave to her fantasies. Hitchcock reveled in what you couldn't see. Buñuel seduced you into staring at what would shock. For the surrealist director, "watching a movie is a bit like being raped."

When we see her walking down the Rue Saint Honoré or dining at an après-ski chalet in *Belle de Jour,* Catherine Deneuve's chic and immaculate Séverine could pass for a separated-at-birth sister to Hitchcock's deified patrician muse Grace Kelly. Still radiating the expected glow of a newlywed, Séverine has been married for one year to Pierre, a gentle, adoring, classically handsome, and exceedingly patient doctor. He's quite the catch, but alas, Séverine is never in the mood to reel him in. Deflections, forehead pecks, and separate beds define their love. Séverine is as frigid as Hitchcock's Marnie.

But Marnie's brutal dreams scare her. Not so for Séverine. In her ever-increasingly brutal, vivid, and sexually humiliating visions, Séverine (whose name is a variation of Severin, the protagonist of the 1870 novel *Venus in Furs* by Leopold von Sacher-Masoch, from whose name we get the word *masochist*) finds such orgasmic fulfillment that she is both startled and saddened each time she awakens and finds herself back in her sumptuously placid reality.

Consequently, she is as transfixed as she is terrified upon realizing that by working afternoons in a brothel her two worlds can become one. Buñuel and his screenwriter Jean-Claude Carrière interviewed scores of women about their secret reveries in order to create Séverine's. The dreams are presented with the clarity of daylight and without judgment, which is what makes them so compelling. What made them shocking for a 1967 film audience is that when Séverine's shame-filled fantasies are actualized within the brothel, they generate only pleasure. We never see the intimacies of Séverine's first encounter there—with a rotund Asian man who carries a box containing something buzzing furiously—but Buñuel makes us very aware of two things when the man leaves: the stain of bright red blood on the white sheets and a facedown Séverine raising her head from the bed just enough for us to see that she is smiling for the first time in the film.

To create the quintessential French bourgeoisie/ Hitchcock blonde, Buñuel made two brilliant choices: to have Catherine Deneuve play Séverine and to have Yves Saint Laurent dress her. Whether you analyze Deneuve feature by feature or revel in their sum, her beauty defines perfection. Stare at her face too long and you're destined to lose your place in the drama. She has no flaws. No wonder France selected Deneuve as the symbolic representation of Marianne, a national symbol of the French republic.

Yves Saint Laurent is the most influential French couturier in history. Countless designers have been inspired by his limitless range, for he produced such iconic and signature work as the tuxedo, the Safari jacket, the peacoat, the jumpsuit, the chubby, the Mondrian-inspired dresses, and the legendary Russian Ballet and Opera Collection. Nonetheless, his clothes for *Belle de Jour* may be the most copied wardrobe he ever created.

Saint Laurent didn't do as he pleased when designing for the film, as Buñuel insisted that despite the current fashion on the streets of Paris, Séverine was not to wear minis, go-go boots, or any other item that would give away the period. The director believed that women of every era had experienced these urges; he didn't want Séverine's desires to be a sign of the times.

Before she begins to work at the brothel, Séverine is an elegant, modest minimalist: we see her in a fully buttoned, double-breasted, black military coat with black Roger Vivier pilgrim flats; a pale cable-knit sweater buttoned to the neck; pristine tennis whites with headband; and a chocolate-brown high-necked, unadorned A-line

shift that comes to the knee. In her dreams though, her double-breasted military coat is scarlet and worn open, her dress, a white, flowing, gossamer gown. But as her double life merges, the red coat turns up at a clandestine meeting with her gangster boyfriend; her brown leather and fur trench is replaced by one of black vinyl. But regardless of the context in which they appear, there is not a single item of clothing in *Belle de Jour* any fashionable woman wouldn't be happy to step into. What's more, each item is currently available at what is now called simply SAINT LAURENT, with a sometimes cocky but often respectful Hedi Slimane now at the label's helm.

Yves Saint Laurent's precisely tailored clothing for Séverine, used to mask her sexual desire that has repeatedly proved seductive to fashion houses as diverse as Burberry, Tom Ford, Calvin Klein, Akris, Lanvin, Giambattista Valli, Tommy Hilfiger, and Carven. Saint Laurent's most famous dress in the film, the instantly recognizable black "schoolgirl" dress with white cuffs and collars that Séverine dons after her worlds collide and tragedy strikes was reinterpreted as recently as fall 2013 in a homage-like collection to Saint Laurent by Maria Grazia Chiuri and Pierpaolo Piccioli for Valentino. Even Madewell has a version.

Though Deneuve had worn Saint Laurent's clothes before, the film marked the first time the designer had worked directly with her. Their ensuing friendship as well as her devotion and patronage lasted the rest of the designer's lifetime. At his funeral, Deneuve wore a double-breasted black satin trench, not unlike the vinyl one she wore in *Belle de Jour*, and black Roger Vivier flats.

WE ALL WANT TO BE SASHA FIERCE

Beyoncé's "Single Ladies"
Video, 2008

What do the following groups and people have in common: Matt DePauw, Mr. Hononegah High School of 2013; three Filipino drag queens; Rowan Atkinson; the BBC news team; Justin Timberlake; one hundred women in Piccadilly Circus; the McKinley High football team (on *Glee*); Alvin and the Chipmunks' girlfriends, the Chippettes; and three guys at a wedding named Clark, Dan, and Gus?

Here's a hint: "Wha-uh-oh-oh–oh-oh…"

Right. Each of the above made a video in which they dance to Beyoncé's "Single Ladies." Everyone at one time or another in 2008, yes, everyone, even Barack Obama, either donned a leotard, attempted the head-down, double-step-forward strut during the "oh-oh-oh" part, or, at the very least, mimicked the twisting jazz hands used during the chorus.

With more than 400,000,000 views (and counting) on Vevo, "Single Ladies (Put a Ring on It)," marked the first dance craze sparked via the Internet, with critics comparing the song to enduring anthems of female strength, like Aretha Franklin's "Respect" and Gloria Gaynor's "I Will Survive." The recording, which sold eight million copies worldwide, won three 2009 Grammys, including Song of the Year.

The recording was released simultaneously with another eventual hit, "If I Were a Boy," from Beyoncé's *I Am Sasha Fierce* dual-personality concept album, the conceit being that each single showed a different aspect of the singer's on- and offstage personalities. "Single Ladies" is clearly Beyoncé as Fierce: despite the incredibly catchy hook and

inescapably engaging, hip-popping rhythm, the tone of the woman singing is defiant. Fed up with being strung along by her man, with no proposal in sight, she breaks up with him, goes to a club, gets hit on, and likes it. Then her ex shows up and gets jealous. Really? Well, she isn't giving him any attention because if he liked it, he should have put a ring on it.

The mood is very much in the same vein as Beyoncé's previous "I've had enough of this shit" anthem, the 2006 song "Irreplaceable," which in concert, invariably incites every woman in the audience to jump to her feet and eagerly swing her hands "to the left, to the left" on the chorus when the loser boyfriend's things get thrown out of her house.

The difference is that "Single Ladies" is an all-dancing video. Starkly shot in black and white with very few cuts and against a white scrim, Beyoncé and her other two dancers, Ebony Williams and Ashley Everett, are dressed

nearly identically in black leotards (designed by Beyoncé's mother, Tina Knowles) and heels. Beyoncé stands out because her leotard is one-shouldered; her left arm is gloved in a cyborg-worthy prosthetic of gleaming, jointed titanium designed by jeweler and friend Lorraine Schwartz; and, well, because she is Beyoncé—ridiculously beautiful, full-bodied, blessed with still untapped talent, and as formidable as a new dictator.

The choreography by Frank Gatson and JaQuel Knight is deceptively simple. Snarky blogs accused Beyoncé of cribbing directly from a Bob Fosse number, "Mexican Breakfast," choreographed for a female trio led by Gwen Verdon that was performed on *The Ed Sullivan Show* in 1969. Beyoncé freely admitted to watching and admiring the dance, although the key difference is that Verdon and company are coyly and unsuggestively dancing frug-like moves to a bubbly tune in white blouses and Day-Glo separates as if they were secretaries

from the office-party scene in the musical *Promises, Promises*—also choreographed by Fosse and playing a few blocks away on Broadway at that time.

However, "Single Ladies" employs a repetitious-into-the-floor-style inspired by J-stepping, named after the women's step-dance troupe at Jackson State University, in Jackson, Mississippi (designer Rick Owens used step dancers to model his spring 2014 ready-to-wear collection to great acclaim). The idea was that the repetition would make it easy for fans to pick up and imitate the moves. And we all tried. But unless you have thighs of steel, gyroscopic hips, and raunchy self-assurance, well, good luck. In fact, only two people came close to matching Beyoncé's writhability. Dressed scantily, a New York dancer named Shane Mercado performed a YouTube rendition that became such a sensation he was invited to meet the singer, an event that caused another social media hit. But the most

impressive copycat was Justin Timberlake, who was so disturbingly limber and sultry—with sensational legs—in the now classic *Saturday Night Live* parody that starred Beyoncé and also featured (but who noticed?) Bobby Moynihan and Andy Samberg that the singer's management suggested she bail on the number.

Always a lady, however, she ends the video like no one else could. In 2008, whether sitting for an in-depth interview or riffing on a red carpet, she and her boyfriend, Jay Z, would shut down when asked about where their relationship was headed—a topic not open for discussion. However, after the final "uh-oh-ohs," the video cuts in for a close-up, revealing the slightly winded singer smiling and twisting her metal glove for one last time, revealing an eighteen-karat diamond solitaire. Evidently, Jay Z liked it—and put a helluva ring on it. And that's all Beyoncé had to say about it.

IN PRAISE OF OLDER WOMEN

The Dance in The Thomas Crown Affair, 1999

Technically, the movie is classified a remake, with the same title of the original made three decades earlier. Though fine art is now the prize instead of hard cash, the plot once again revolves around two meticulously planned heists. All the trappings of the lush life—the cars, the glider, the high-end accessories—are appropriately updated. And the intrigue that drives the film remains the romantic entanglement of very attractive adversaries. But beyond that, the two versions of *The Thomas Crown Affair* have little in common.

The original *Thomas Crown Affair* was designed to dazzle— a kaleidoscopic rush across lacquered surfaces and polished facets so eager to show off its pretty cast and their shiny possessions with splashy cinematic technique it often lost interest in simply telling the tale, jettisoning any reflection about life that didn't involve sparkle, or taking the audience anywhere, either emotionally or physically. Watching it was like being trapped in space defined by four curtain walls of Swarovski crystals. Even its compelling lovers end up displaced and alone. While it forever stands out as one of the most stylish scrapbooks of the late 1960s, it is one chilly film.

The remake of *The Thomas Crown Affair* is a more involving, even sexier take of the story; the dynamic between the characters is less cryptic. Pierce Brosnan's Crown and Rene Russo's Catherine Banning—the woman sent to entrap him this time—project a startlingly different, far more blood-pressure-rising magnetism than Dunaway and McQueen. Brosnan—a much subtler actor than his James Bond

credentials would indicate—plays a man delighted to find himself fascinated and feeling mischievous about his overly confident foe. As for Russo's Banning, she tells her associates she's simply setting up her prey, but she almost immediately gets her foot caught in the trap and hardly struggles to get out.

In this film, the romantic set piece happens on a dance floor, where Crown gets on Banning's good side during one rhythmically grinding and entwining, go-get-a-room seduction. Dirty dancing is hardly a new move on film, but what is refreshing here is the age of the dancers.

Faye Dunaway was twenty-six when the first *Crown* film was made; McQueen, thirty-seven. In the remake, Russo was forty-five; her partner, forty-six. Brosnan and Russo are grown-ups, meant to be playing grown-ups, unashamedly lustful, sweating, groping, and hungry for sex. What makes the scene as noteworthy as it is steamy is that they manage to get us rooting for them as a couple against all odds and despite our knowing how the original film ends.

Michael Kors, who dressed Russo for the film, was drawn to this sexually mature character. "I grew up obsessed with movies," recalls Kors. "In fact, I was mad for the first *Thomas Crown Affair*. But it's a perfect example of a movie in which a woman Rene's age would never be cast as the knockout. Instead, she would be the older, wiser friend, or the mom, though who knows how she had kids, because she obviously never had sex." Kors had dressed Russo, a former model who had graced many a magazine cover

offscreen ("my kind of girl"), so when the film's producers called upon her recommendation, he said, "I jumped at the opportunity knowing we couldn't go the same hard-edged, fashion-magazine route as Dunaway."

Kors, who had begun designing for Céline the year before, used his first fall/winter collection for the brand—praised at the time for understated affluence—as his template for Catherine Banning. "I find it very sexy when a woman knows and enjoys being in charge," says Kors. "Russo was playing a woman who calls her own shots, sets her price, lives big, but who also works with cops. So her glamour can't be garish or overt. She takes advantage of her sexuality, but in ways that should be imposing, maybe even a little intimidating." For Banning, Kors chose what have now become his signature looks: plush cashmere turtlenecks; leather pencil skirts; man-tailored, double-breasted wool coats thrown over the shoulders. "It looks familiar now, the essence of classic urban dressing in today's world," Kors says, "but imagine seeing a woman dressed this way after having gone through the overstated 1980s and the dressed-down look of the early 1990s. It gave Rene this tremendous swagger. Plus I love it when it looks like a woman has borrowed something from the boys."

Kors also takes credit for one more key stylistic stroke. "Rene's hair was crucial. Remember how Faye's hair was so perfect in the first film it was like sculpture? Instead, we dyed Rene's hair that deep red and then cut it so that it always looked a little mussed and wild. It's not a do you would normally expect on this kind of woman, but that constant bed head made everything Rene wore just a little more provocative."

Going beyond provocative, the beaded, sheer navy gown Russo wears during that tantalizing tango scene was not designed by Kors, who wasn't contacted until after this scene had been shot, but by Randolph Duke, and it seems a coarse, atypical choice for her character, especially when Russo is no less captivating in another scene wearing a black beaded sheath with a nearly clerical collar by Kors that shows off her incredible figure. Kors may be a bit optimistic when he claims, "Older women saw themselves on the screen," when they looked at Russo, but what they could readily acknowledge was that the woman starting the fire was not young enough to be their daughter.

Despite youth-obsessed social media, the public now routinely accepts beauty and fashion campaigns featuring women over forty, including Julia Roberts, Cate Blanchett, Julianna Margulies, and Tilda Swinton, and even over sixty, such as Jessica Lange, Diane Keaton, Charlotte Rampling, and Helen Mirren, as well as Jane Fonda, who's over seventy. "When I design clothes, now," says Kors, "I look to appeal to three generations of women. A woman of a certain age? What does that mean anymore? All she needs to be certain of is that she looks great. You've got to give Rene Russo a lot of credit for showing women how's it done."

And though male stars have always, if unfairly, managed to extend their sexual shelf life, the fact that Brosnan played Crown to Russo's Banning—chronologically, intellectually, physically, and emotionally—is why these two wily operators eventually steal your heart. And that brings up the final reason why the second *The Thomas Crown Affair* is a more satisfying film than the first. Just as we hoped, the lovers do end up together. After all, living happily ever after sure as hell beats—to paraphrase the original film's theme song—being stranded in the windmills of your mind anytime.

YOU DON'T REMEMBER THIS

The Finale of *Casablanca, 1942*

The film alternates between being labeled the most popular movie ever made and the golden age of Hollywood's greatest romance. It's a rare amalgam of exotic locale, the hovering threat of war, undercurrent of espionage, noble but illicit passion, unexpected heroism involving the ultimate sacrifice, two rising stars with smoldering chemistry, and a hell of a lot of fog that created a film whose fight for love and glory remains an irresistible story even more than seven decades after its release.

Casablanca was nominated for eight Academy Awards and won three, including Best Picture. Its Oscar-winning script is routinely quoted by both film buffs and those who don't even know where its immortal lines like "Here's looking at you, kid" come from. The film made a romantic lead out of Humphrey Bogart, who possessed a mug rather than a handsome countenance comprised of chiseled features, and it propelled Ingrid Bergman to international stardom to rival Marlene Dietrich and Greta Garbo. "As Time Goes By" will always be one of the great quarter-to-three piano bar tunes. And most stylishly,

the film magically transformed the trench coat—a garment first popularized when Aquascutum and Burberry turned out waterproof versions for British soldiers during World War I—into the universal, slightly androgynous, eternal cloak of love and intrigue, thanks to that memorable, misty, final double close-up of its two paramours.

Except, there's a problem. It's obvious Rick is wearing a trench when he flashes back to reading Ilsa's good-bye letter in a heavy rain at the Paris train station. And he is wearing that same trench at the airport when he selflessly sends her away to safety at the end of the film. But when Rick is surprised to discover her in Casablanca, prompting him to later say, "Of all the gin joints, in all the towns, in all the world, she walks into mine," Ilsa is wearing a pale suit. When she heaves, "Kiss me. Kiss me as if it were for the last time," Ilsa has on a silk dressing gown. Her wardrobe also includes a mutton-sleeved white coat, a man-tailored suit with wide lapels, a sleeveless white suit with a striped pull-over, and a dark paisley blouse worn over black pants.

As for the climactic heart-wrenching farewell when Rick admits, "It doesn't take much to see that the problems of three little people don't amount to a hill of beans in this crazy world," Ilsa is wearing a beige suit. Granted, thanks to the film's densely atmospheric black-and-white cinematography, her jacket appears to be the same shade of gray as Bogart's outerwear. In addition, both garments have wide, notched collars, and each is wearing a hat with the same pale wide brim.

But Ingrid Bergman *never* wears a trench coat in *Casablanca*. Oddly enough, her rivals Dietrich and Garbo wore trenches more often both on-screen and off. Garbo first wore one on-screen in *A Woman of Affairs* (1928);

Dietrich in *A Foreign Affair* (1948); offscreen, Garbo spent her final years walking around inconspicuously, always clad in a trench, on the streets of New York, while Dietrich wore one to entertain the troops during World War II. But the sustained popularity of the trench rekindled by the film proves that legend trumps truth. Prior to *Casablanca*'s release, the trench was seen merely as a utilitarian garment in its home country, because after World War I, the British military was left with such a surplus of them they gave them to the public for free. Hollywood used the trench as a trademark look for tough guys. But Bogart was a tough guy with a soft heart, and after *Casablanca*, sales of the trench spiked for both men and women. Its aura of seduction has been sustained by such screen idols as Audrey Hepburn (*Breakfast at Tiffany's*, 1961), Cary Grant (*Charade*, 1963), Sophia Loren (*The Key*, 1958), Steve McQueen (*Bullitt*, 1968), Catherine Deneuve (*The Umbrellas of Cherbourg*, 1964), and John Cusack during the classic boom-box-over-his-head climax of the most romantic first-love film ever made, *Say Anything* (1989).

As for the hallowed place the trench still holds at home base, Burberry introduced its first scent of designer Christopher Bailey's era, Body, by having Mario Testino photograph model Rosie Huntington-Whiteley wearing nothing but a trench coat. The company launched the Art of the Trench website in 2009, and had one million Facebook fans within a year. For Christmas 2014, it produced a lavish music video featuring handsome, young, starry-eyed Romeo Beckham (son of David and Victoria) and what appears to be all of England dancing in Burberry trench coats and scarves, confirming that fashion's fundamental things get reapplied as time goes by.

VEILED REFERENCES

Angelina Jolie's
Wedding Dress, 2014

From the moment the public first saw her, the general consensus has been that Angelina Jolie was and is the great beauty of our age. Yet, despite her genetic blessings, that's not the main reason we search for her on the red carpet, or anywhere else for that matter, with a curiosity unlike our collective interest in her begowned contemporaries. Granted, arriving with Brad Pitt on your arm does dim the luster of just about every else's "it bag" or borrowed chunks of jewelry.

But our never-flagging fascination is based on the fact that she is that rare actress with an aura of mystery. Cate Blanchett routinely glides through the preawards show clamor with a wry air of unflappable, knowing elegance; Emma Stone sports a slightly tomboyish, quick-witted, can't-wait-to-kick-off-my-shoes swagger; and Sarah Jessica Parker beams like someone who has obviously had more fun dressing up than anyone else, but Jolie is a much tougher read, due to inerasable memories of an offscreen persona that once fluctuated as widely as roles and lovers. On morning-after roundups, other stars earned shout-outs for the potential influence of their one-of-a-kind attire, but it was Jolie's idiosyncratic actions—none of which were likely to start a trend—that were cited more often than what she wore.

At a post-awards party after winning a Golden Globe for her leading role in *Gia* (1998), an HBO film about the lesbian model who died of AIDS, Jolie jumped in a swimming pool, destroying her beaded Randolph Duke gown. She then showed up to events with her then girlfriend, model Jenny Shimizu. One year later, she and her

husband, Billy Bob Thornton, whom she had recently wed, appeared on the red carpet, showing off necklaces containing vials of each other's blood. (Years later, Thornton revealed they were "merely lockets normally holding a child's hair," but instead held a drop of blood smeared between glass and "not quart jars of blood, like we were vampires living in the basement.") In 2000, Jolie won an Academy Award for Best Supporting Actress in *Girl, Interrupted*, but even her stark visage in a Gothic black Morticia Addams–like Versace gown was upstaged by the extended unsisterly lip-lock she planted on her brother, James Haven.

Jolie had no peer as Hollywood's most unapologetic and oblivious bad girl. Her subsequent temporary exile from public events coincided with tensions created by the collapse of Brad Pitt's marriage to everyone's favorite Friend Jennifer Aniston and his burgeoning relationship with Jolie as well as her growing involvement in humanitarian efforts as a special envoy for the United Nations. It was this latter role, however, that initiated the shift in the public perception of her from naughty to noble.

That shift has now gone into overdrive due to three subsequent events: after three adoptions (two done on her own) and three natural births (one set of twins), Jolie and Pitt now corral a family of six children. On May 14, 2013, Jolie published "My Medical Decision," a soul-bearing op-ed in the *New York Times* that detailed her double mastectomy and made a forceful and forthright plea for women who have a family history of breast and ovarian cancer to go through genetic testing. The information she provided and universal praise she earned dominated the media for several weeks. On October 10, 2014, Queen Elizabeth II declared Jolie Honorary Dame Grand Cross of the Most Distinguished Order of Saint Michael and Saint George for her efforts to stem violence against women, a rare honor for a non-British citizen.

Jolie's evolving style throughout her elevation to earth goddess has been subtle and yet singular. While she still looks the bombshell, her red-carpet choices are more patrician than provocative. And though she's chosen pieces from designers as diverse as Emanuel Ungaro and Erdem and occasionally as right-here-right-now as Hedi Slimane for Saint Laurent's cropped, deconstructed version of the Le Smoking, her current ladylike mood is frequently rendered by Ralph & Russo, the bespoke atelier that became the first British label to be accepted by the Chambre Syndicale de la Haute Couture to produce a show during Paris Haute Couture Week and who outfitted her to accept her award from Queen Elizabeth.

Jolie's longest sartorial relationship, however, is with Donatella Versace, who has dressed her for more than a decade. Versace's gowns for Jolie bear little resemblance either to her runway collection or dresses she's created for more flamboyant stars like Nicki Minaj or Jennifer Lopez. Rather, Versace's designs for Jolie recall the curvaceous and conspicuously refined gowns Edith Head would craft for Grace Kelly when the actress was Alfred Hitchcock's unofficial muse.

Jolie did get a leg up—literally—on her competition along the red carpet at the 2012 Academy Awards when she deliberately and repeatedly took advantage of the deep slit in her strapless black velvet Versace gown to expose a bare right gam that generated almost as much press coverage as it did imitators on the Internet. But certainly Jolie's most singular—and likely to stay that way—fashion statement has to be her wedding dress. As reported by *People,*

which paid Jolie and Pitt for the exclusive rights to cover their nuptials (the couple donated the earnings to charity), Jolie again turned to the House of Versace. She asked Versace's master tailor and personal longtime friend Luigi Massi to design a simple white silk gown with shirred fitted bodice and full skirt similar to the shape worn by Princess Fiona when she married *Shrek*, as per the request of Jolie's brood of six. But the kids didn't stop there. Besides orchestrating and participating in most of the day's events, including making the wedding cake, what made Jolie's wedding ensemble so extraordinary—and perhaps the most warm-and-fuzzy creation ever to come out of the house of Versace—was the bridal veil, covered crown to hem with multicolored, hand-embroidered horses, birds,

planes, motorbikes, aliens, and family members drawn by the Jolie-Pitt children and then crafted in detail by the atelier's artisans. *People* writers Michelle Tauber and Mary Green described it perfectly when they called it "quite possibly the first example of haute couture meets refrigerator art."

But once again, as singular a star as she may be, Jolie may never be a style leader. In the time since the Jolie-Pitt wedding, I have asked three major bridal designers if they have gotten calls for a dress like this. They all said no, and I was surprised. After all, who wouldn't want to be married enveloped in so much love? "Think about it," replied one designer. "How many brides do you know get married in white after having six kids?"

Oh.

THANK HEAVEN FOR LITTLE GIRLS

Selling Stanley Kubrick's
Lolita, 1962

Whether she knows who he is or not, Britney Spears and her endless scout troop of successors and imitators owe their pubescent stardom to Vladimir Nabokov. With acutely seductive prose, the great Russian novelist hopelessly bewitched his protagonist, the middle-aged literature professor Humbert Humbert and, in turn, millions of readers with his creation of the intellectually bland, yet irresistibly dimpled, "apple sweet," twelve-year-old "nymphet" Dolores Haze. In case you haven't read the novel either, you might know her by her nickname—Lolita.

Today, it seems more scandalous that Nabokov was never awarded the Nobel Prize for Literature, but when it was published in 1955, *Lolita*'s wry domestication of pedophilia caused such an uproar that the novel—branded "repulsive" and "disgusting" in a hysterical rant by Orville Prescott in the *New York Times*—was even banned temporarily in more sexually liberal France. True, judged on plotline alone, the tale is repugnant. But the combined effect of the author's caustic vivisection of the American middle class's cultural totems as well as his revelatory insight into the psyche of the sexually frustrated middle-aged male coerces the reader into empathizing with and being wryly amused by Humbert's bid for happiness with his underage object of affection.

When seduction is by words alone, one can lay partial blame for suggestive images on a dirty mind. Realizing *Lolita* for the screen, however, created formidable challenges for the less than liberated morality of the early 1960s. Hollywood studios turned the story down left and right. Prominent stars like Laurence Olivier, Cary Grant, Rex Harrison, and David Niven refused to take on the role

How did they ever make a movie of LOLITA ?

LOLITA

METRO-GOLDWYN-MAYER presents in association with SEVEN ARTS PRODUCTIONS JAMES B. HARRIS and STANLEY KUBRICK'S

Starring JAMES MASON · SHELLEY WINTERS · PETER SELLERS as "Quilty" and Introducing SUE LYON as "Lolita"

Directed by STANLEY KUBRICK · Screenplay by VLADIMIR NABOKOV based on his novel "Lolita" Produced by JAMES B. HARRIS

Music composed and conducted by Nelson Riddle
Lolita Theme by Bob Harris

APPROVED BY THE PRODUCTION CODE ADMINISTRATION

62/262

of Humbert because they feared for their personal reputations. James Mason, who had been Kubrick's first choice because his screen persona readily projected both a wry intelligence and unforced vulnerability, initially passed on the role, choosing to perform in a stage play instead. Luckily for Kubrick, by the time he circled back to Mason one last time after the other rejections, the play had been postponed. No wonder, when finally released in 1962, Stanley Kubrick's film adaption of the infamous novel was promoted with the brilliantly provocative tagline: "How did they ever make a movie of *Lolita*?"

Gingerly, is the answer.

Kubrick doggedly pursued cinema-hating Nabokov to collaborate on the adaptation, relieving the author's revulsion with a check for $150,000. Despite its American setting, the director shot the entire film in London where, in this predownload era, it was impossible for Metro-Goldwyn-Mayer to demand scrutiny of the "dailies." Kubrick also altered three key elements of the novel to make the tale more palatable. First, Humbert's murder of his nemesis and rival, Clare Quilty, the even more callous seducer of Lolita, occurs at the opening rather than the end of the story, adding a layer of murder mystery as well as a dash of sympathy for the hopelessly smitten Humbert. Second, Humbert doesn't admit his ardor for Lolita until the novel's end, making his lust as repellant as it is compelling; in the film, his infatuation turns quickly into something more desperate and sincere. So in its own odd way, it is a love story. Finally, Dolores is only twelve in the novel, and her behavior is appropriately disconnected and childlike. Because the reader is nowhere nearly as captivated by her, Humbert's incessant musings of his nymphet goddess have to be judged as half-illusory. But without a nubile Lolita on-screen, the movie would have been unwatchable, so Kubrick aged the tween two years and cast fourteen-year-old Sue Lyon, a knockout who could easily pass for senior prom queen with the kind of natural pout *Playboy* magazine used to build an empire.

Yet the most seductive tease surrounding *Lolita* was its ad campaign. Bravo to the ad man who was savvy enough to create the "How did they . . ." tagline that was immediately engaging because it addressed the obvious question on the public's mind. The movie poster featured a close-up of its nubile star, with bright red glossy lips and matching heart-shaped sunglasses, sucking on a cherry lollipop. It was an obvious but attention-getting image, with Lyon's right eye looking just over the glasses directly at the viewer. Only the most stoic could resist blushing and curiosity.

The film was released with a "For Adults Only" rating (Sue Lyons was not allowed into the theater at its premiere), but there were enough fade-to-black sex scenes to escape a "Condemned" rating from the Catholic Legion of Decency, which in 1962 could still damage a film's distribution. Due to his crucial plot shifts, script changes, and brilliant casting (Mason, Lyon, Shelley Winters as Dolores's shrill mother, and a predatory Peter Sellers as Quilty), Kubrick refocused *Lolita* into a black comedy lampooning just about anything considered "normal" in America, so Humbert's twisted love just became one more off-kilter quirk in a story where all reasonable behavior became suspect.

The movie's controversial success resulted in the introduction of the noun *Lolita* into the dictionary, where it is defined as a "precociously seductive girl." These days, a tween or teen whose ability to ignite lascivious thoughts in the minds of others is widely accepted by the public as standard operating procedure.

Despite the youthquake of the 1960s, Lolita's successors weren't immediate. True, by the time she turned age sixteen, Twiggy's blond sprite-meets-schoolboy haircut and wide, thickly lashed eyes had become the face of Swinging London, while her brunette counterpart, Penelope Tree—she of the even wider, even more heavily lashed, woeful eyes—had been photographed by Richard Avedon and Cecil Beaton. However, neither had much in common with Humbert's muse besides youth.

But in 1980, a fourteen-year-old Brooke Shields, who possessed the same kind of early onset beauty as Elizabeth Taylor, came on television and asked, "You want to

know what comes between me and my Calvins?" Her answer, "Nothing," scandalized conservative groups, PTA committees, and religious leaders, while Calvin Klein sold millions of jeans. Shields was hardly fazed. Two years before, she had played a child prostitute in Louis Malle's film *Pretty Baby*.

Though the Lolita flame went dim again for a while, except in fashion, where designers remained fixated on the idea of sending teens down the runway in the guise of grown-ups, the true torch bearers came from the music world, beginning in 1998 with an eighteen-year-old Britney Spears, dressed in a schoolgirl uniform, standing with her legs apart, daring us to "Hit Me Baby, One More Time," and then asking for more because "Oops, I Did It Again." Today, though Spears is over thirty and firmly ensconced in Las Vegas, where she and her audience jointly relive their adolescence, we are now deep into the second decade of the golden age of Lolitas, with no end of singing nymphets in sight, thanks to Miley Cyrus, Taylor Swift, Demi Lovato, Selena Gomez, and Ariana Grande. At least there are signs that some singers are grateful to the

trailblazer before them. Both Taylor Swift and Katy Perry have been photographed wearing sweetheart-lensed red rimmed sunglasses.

In 1997, director Adrian Lyne made a remake of *Lolita* with Jeremy Irons and Dominique Swain. But despite less restrictions on language and more nudity, the movie generated more avoidance than curiosity. While many critics claimed the film was inferior and more crass than Kubrick's version, director Lyne had a more damning take, insisting that thanks to our ever-encroaching politically correct parameters, America has grown even more prudish than liberal, or as he put it, "It is a country where six-year-olds are sent home from school for kissing their classmates." But perhaps it's not fair to target conflicting attitudes concerning erotic boundaries solely in the United States. In 2012, Great Britain banned Marc Jacobs's ad for his new fragrance. The ruling criticized the photograph for "sexualizing" a seventeen-year-old Dakota Fanning by photographing her with an oversize flower-topped perfume bottle resting between her thighs. Jacobs had named the scent Lola.

GET ME
TO THE
CHURCH
SOMEHOW

Mick and Bianca Jagger's
Saint-Tropez Wedding, 1971

Brad Pitt and Angelina Jolie's August 2014 nuptials at their estate in France demonstrated that the famous can keep wedding plans a secret if they choose to. Just a few weeks later, George Clooney proved you can even let everyone know the details of your impending nuptials but still keep the uninvited at bay if you plan meticulously and spend big—a reported $13 million. So, there is something laughably disingenuous about rock 'n' roll's most idolized bad boy deciding to get married in the small but hardly hidden summer playground of Saint-Tropez, tipping off the press about it a few days in advance, and then throwing a series of hissy fits when hundreds of photographers and reporters plus a stadium's worth of vacationing fans show up to throw rice.

Good luck finding a close-up of either Mick Jagger or his bride Bianca Pérez-Mora Macias beaming, let alone one of them looking happy together, on their special day. At 3:00 P.M. on Wednesday, May 12, 1971, Saint-Tropez's mayor was stationed at the town hall waiting to marry the hardly happy couple. But at the appointed hour, the couple stayed put inside the four-year-old, celebrity-ridden Hôtel Byblos, while Jagger sent word that he wanted the streets and hall cleared prior to their arrival, claiming he wasn't going to get married "in a fish bowl." To his surprise, the mayor refused Jagger's demand, citing both locations as public places and, therefore, the people had every right to be there. An hour later, guided by a phalanx of bodyguards, Mick and his bride-to-be made their way through narrow streets that were so dense with crowds it was as if they had gathered to witness a road tour production of Pamplona's Running of the Bulls.

From looking at most of the black-and-white photographs of the day, the couple, whose obvious resemblance to each other was eerily incestuous, are often described as having dressed identically in white Tommy Nutter pantsuits, as Jagger was often outfitted by the Savile Row bespoke tailor. Two other factors fuel this assumption: it's very hard to see either of them from the waist down, and after their divorce, Bianca chose white pantsuits as her unofficial uniform when attending fashion shows, gallery openings, and charity events.

But color footage of the day reveals Mick to be in a tailored three-piece beige linen suit. Bianca actually is in all snow-white, complete with an oversize version of a beekeeper's hat with veiled brim, but she's not wearing pants. The longer-than-currently fashionable jacket covers a slightly flared maxi skirt. Both outfits were designed by Bianca's friend Yves Saint Laurent, who did his very best to hide the couple's secret: Bianca was four months pregnant with the Jagger's sole child, Jade, at the time.

After the brief civil ceremony, vows were repeated at a Roman Catholic service at the chapel of St. Anne's. The man who could arouse sympathy for the devil had been taking catechism lessons to please his bride-to-be and was granted a special dispensation by a bishop of the Church of England. Bianca walked down the aisle to selections she chose from Francis Lai's score for the year's smash romantic movie *Love Story.* Honest.

That night, at his wedding reception, Jagger blew off the strain of the day by jumping onstage to perform in an impromptu jam session with a group of musicians that included Stevie Nicks, Stephen Stills, and his favorite reggae band, the Rudies. Not everyone was as relieved. "My marriage ended on my wedding day," recalls Bianca Jagger. The couple divorced in 1976.

I dreamed
I barged down the Nile in my *maidenform* bra

Sweet Music*... Maidenform dream bra... features spoke-stitched cups for Cleopatra curves! All-elastic band for freedom of fit; reinforced undercups for everlasting uplift. White in A, B, C cups. This and seven other enchanting Sweet Music styles, from 2.50.

*REG. U. S. PAT. OFF. ©1962 BY MAIDENFORM, INC., MAKERS OF BRAS, GIRDLES AND SWIMSUITS

WHEN YOU WISH UPON A BRA

Maidenform's "I Dreamed . . ."
Campaign, 1949

Life got you down? Feeling unattractive and ignored? Wish you were anywhere but here? Who knew all it took to harness the passion and adventure to live out your dreams was strapping on the right brassiere?

According to one of longest-running ad campaigns in history, once you were hooked into your Maidenform bra, you could go on safari, escape to Paris, score a TKO, win an election, open the World Series, stop the show, sway a jury, hop on a fire truck, ride a roller coaster, drive a chariot, hail a streetcar, become a doctor or even a matador. And that was just for starters.

The people responsible for literally unbuttoning the advertising of intimates did not start out in the brassiere business. In the 1920s, the flapper look was all the rage, as the saying goes, and bras were appropriately crafted more like slips with interior bandaging that flattened the bust, perfect for wearing a chemise. But when Ida Rosenberg and Enid Bissett created Enid Frocks in 1922, they chose to make dresses for women who weren't dancing the night away or eager to hide their shape. Since these women needed some support, they built a little bra "like two pockets" inside each Enid Frock for an "uplift." But soon their customers, mainly curvy women uncomfortable with boyish-oriented lingerie, started asking if they could purchase the "uplifts" separately.

By 1928, the uplift business was so successful that the company stopped making dresses. Ida's husband, William, who was a sculptor, improved upon his wife's idea, using a fabric called swami (like nylon tricot) to construct a more structured bra, adding an elastic center, which helped raise and contour, emphasizing what Rosenthal believed was a woman's "maiden form."

I dreamed I was a knockout
in my *maidenform* bra

Arabesque*... *new Maidenform bra*... has bias-cut center-of-attraction for *superb*

separation... insert of elastic for *comfort*... floral circular stitching for the most *beautiful* contours!

White in A, B, C cups, just 2.50. Also pre-shaped (light foam lining) 3.50.

The Rosenthals renamed their company the Maidenform Brassiere Company in 1930. They also invented an on-assembly line, the first in the industry, to produce both long-line and fitted bras.

During World War II, Maidenform ceased bra production to help meet wartime demands for mattress covers, mosquito netting, and parachutes. Once the war was over, the company returned to making its products, but their customers were now changed women who had not only taken charge at home while their men were serving their country abroad but also liked it. The idea of an existence outside homemaking began to feel like a real possibility.

At the same time, enlisted men's attitudes toward sexuality had evolved as well. Exposed to foreign cultures that regarded sex more openly and attached less shame to the naked body, soldiers began covering their walls and lockers with provocative pinups of Hollywood beauties like Betty Grable, Veronica Lake, and Jane Russell. Add to this mix one more game-changing element: in 1947, Christian Dior upended the fashion world with the debut of his New Look, ignoring the previous need for fabric rationing in design or for utilitarian clothes, returning to fashion an overtly feminine silhouette that featured a highly cinched waist, emphasizing the hips and the bust in a way that demanded a structured bra.

The Rosenthals added up these factors and approached the advertising firm of Norman, Craig & Kummel to come up with a campaign that combined the post-war woman's dream of striking out on her own, the post-war male's more unbridled appreciation of his potential dream date, and Dior's dreamy new silhouette. The agency found the perfect inspiration—a complementary trend that had become popular in groundbreaking Broadway musicals such as *Oklahoma!*, *On the Town*, and *Carousel*. Each show underscored their restrained central love story with a "dream ballet" that invariably presented its central characters in a fantasy that drew a more sensual parallel on their current reality.

Maidenform's first "I dreamed . . ." ad in 1949 actually had the model doing something commonplace; that is, "I was going shopping," It wasn't the first time an ad had featured a woman in a bra. But it was the first time an ad featured that woman out in public. There she was in the supermarket, floating blissfully in midair surrounded by suspended fruits and veggies, clad in a becoming gossamer full skirt billowing below her waist. And above her waist, she wore a bra—and only a bra—usually the Chansonette, Maidenform's circular-stitched, pointy-cupped bestseller that was inspired by the outlines of the popular 1940s Hollywood pinups known as Sweater Girls. Kitty D'Alessio, a designer who worked on the initial ads and would later become president of Chanel, Inc. said, "The ads were created in a year when life was more intimate and simple. We tried to inject fashion as well as some humor, so the ads would be fun. People looked for them because they were campy. They certainly stopped traffic."

Church groups were horrified, the competition balked. But women went shopping. In the twenty years that the ads ran, Maidenform sales increased threefold, because despite the fantasy of the ads, there was a succinct, realistic strategy behind the campaign. The models, all of whom were required to be single and without children (to avoid the public scandal of photographing a mother in her undergarments) were in their mid to late twenties, older than traditional runway models, and had to fill a 34B cup at the very least to be in accordance with both the age and cup size of the target Maidenform customer. The "dream" woman was also almost exclusively Caucasian and looked middle-class because Maidenform considered itself an aspirational lingerie company.

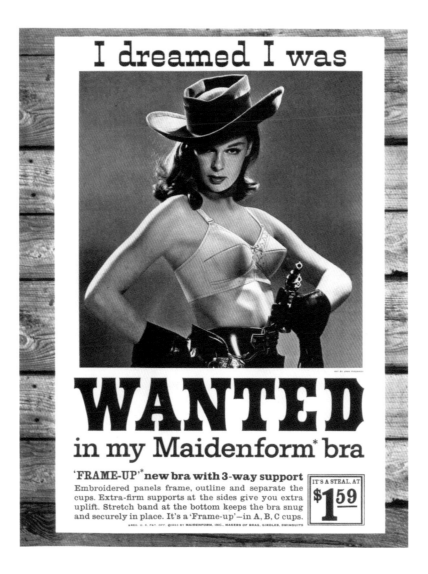

As the ads' popularity quickly morphed into pop-culture iconography, their production grew more lavish and the situations outrageous, discarding reality altogether as the woman barged down the Nile as Cleopatra (in several guises), posed à la Annie Oakley as "Queen of the West," or turned into "an outlaw" in the famous ad shot by Richard Avedon. By 1960, 30 percent of American women were wearing a Maidenform bra.

During the mid-1960s, both in conjunction with the introduction of the Dreamliner, a softer, less sexually aggressive-looking bra (there were even maternity and nursing versions), and to reduce criticism from a few progressive women's groups who took offense at the ads (or perhaps of wearing a bra in general), the campaign became less fantastical and more directed toward a woman's intangible emotions, such as the dream of "stealing the show," "being a classic beauty," or "turn[ing] on the magic of Venice." Maidenform devised contests like "Do You Dream of a College Scholarship?" offering multiple $10,000 cash prizes.

But no ad campaign, no matter how groundbreaking, runs forever. Maidenform ceased the "I Dreamed" campaign in 1969. In twenty years, Maidenform created 210 themed opportunities, all driven by a single philosophy: when a woman was proud of herself and respected her body, she could do anything a man could do—and be a lot sexier doing it. Since then, women have been tempted to cross their hearts, lift and separate, even don angel wings, all in the hopes of making their upper torso more shapely and appealing. But if any manufacturer thinks for one minute their campaign will ever eclipse what Maidenform did, they're just dreaming.

BATTING
.000

Playing by the numbers
in *10*, 1979

We will keep this short and sweet, because this film goes so sour so fast. But for one brief shining moment, there is a vision with the utmost glory.

Bo Derek's career didn't last much longer than a beach run and a Tarzan flick, but mention this film's title, and automatically her image appears on the Panavision screen inside your head, jauntily jogging along the shore across your cerebrum in soft-focus, slow-motion, Henry Mancini–scored bliss. Regardless of what follows, the image of her prancing in the Malibu surf may be the purest, least prurient image of sun-kissed head-to-toe healthy female beauty ever immortalized on film.

As long as she never says a word—and her silence thankfully lasts for the first two-thirds of the film—Bo Derek remains an idolizable golden goddess, the perfect avatar for the burgeoning resurgence of 1980s California beach culture. The first wave of 1960s California girls was defined by the Beach Boys' imaginary landscape of an entire state getting up at dawn to go surfing (the Pacific Ocean, by the way, is freezing most of the year), cruising away the afternoon in little deuce coupes, followed by a night of fun, fun, fun till their daddies took their T-birds away. The fact that most of what the Beach Boys sang about was mythical to as many Los Angelinos as it was to Clevelanders did nothing to stem its potent illusion of the Golden State as one big beach party.

Bo Derek, as dream girl Jenny Hanley, however, beamed the onset of a new image of California's good life, exhaustively chronicled for contrast in *The Soho Weekly News* and *Details* magazine when both publications were regarded as Manhattan's arbiters of downtown style. In 1979, New York was the international party mecca, disco Valhalla. Life began

sometime after sundown. Studio 54 was the holy of holies, where the dress code demanded outrageousness, last call was merely a suggestion, and after-hours clubs were not the last stop in the evening, unless, of course, you were stuck having to work for a living. Pass the Visine.

But the Los Angeles sprinting behind Derek was caught up in the rapidly escalating craze for aerobics, sunrise power walks in Runyon Canyon, sweating through Bikram yoga, chanting and celebrating your body as your own personal temple that ran on bean sprouts, mung beans, and the new age philosophy of the week, which you practiced while wearing loose cotton muslin or raw linen tunics. Compared to the vampirish hours of New Yorkers, or in *10*'s case, Dudley Moore's George Webber in midlife crisis, Jenny's regimen offered the promise of eternal youth in mind, spirit, and most of all, body.

I mean, look at her. Bathing suit manufacturers have Derek to thank (with a tip of the hat to big-haired Farrah Fawcett's famous red bathing suit poster) for skyrocketing maillot sales once women caught sight of Derek's flesh-colored one piece. Then in opposition to Farrah's über-ready disco flip was Bo's unexpected, race-shifting hairstyle, which was unfortunately copied by women on vacation the world over. To this day, you can barely hit a stretch of sand along the shores of the Caribbean, Hawaii, Tahiti, or Mexico that doesn't feature stalls doing a brisk business in cornrowing and beading tourists' hair, a do no white girl ever wore until Derek appeared looking so surprisingly adorable with streams of clicking blond braids.

Why stay so fixated on just this one scene in a hit film? Because it is the source of the movie's greatest influence. Once Derek's jogging Madonna opens her mouth to speak after learning of successful, happily married, universally adored, thoroughly selfish, and self-serving George's uncontrollable obsession with her, *10* sinks into a smutty, repellent, chauvinistic mess.

So, in the spirit of this movie, I suppose we should rate Bo Derek and her maillot a 10. Her hair ornamentation earns a 6, because cornrows really do look so bad on most non-island-native women, and the sensibility of *10* the movie, gets a 0, because you can't always get what you want, especially when you don't deserve it, and even if you could in this case, wouldn't the racket from the clicking of all those beads every time you had sex drive you nuts?

WE LOVED YOU, YEAH, YEAH, YEAH

The Beatles Make
Over the World, 1965

Ed Sullivan, the television host who had introduced the Fab Four to America on his Sunday night variety show to a record viewing audience of seventy-three million people, stood alone at a microphone on the flat, rectangular stage erected in Shea Stadium's center field.

"Now, ladies and gentlemen, honored by their country, decorated by their Queen, and loved here in America, here are the Beatles!"

And those were just about the last words anyone was able to clearly distinguish emanating from that platform. Once the Beatles bounded out of the Mets dugout and onto the stage, immediately launching into their version of the R & B classic "Twist and Shout," you couldn't hear much besides screaming, screeching, and wailing interrupted by hysterical sobbing, gasping for breath, and beseeching cries directed at one or all of the quartet, and the occasional thud as one more overcome and overheated teenage girl hit the ground in a faint.

A sports stadium is a commonplace venue now, but until the night of August 15, 1965, no entertainer had ever performed in one anywhere in the world. The Beatles, however, had no trouble amassing more than fifty-five thousand fans—at the time the largest concert audience in history.

Despite the impression given by published pictures that recall the event, the Beatles' audience was not a precursor to the Bieber/One Direction congress of females. There were plenty of male fans and families. The girls, however, were crazed. And though John Lennon compared the experience to seeing "the top of the mountain," the Beatles were equally stunned. Beatlemania had been the norm for several years in Great Britain, but this night at Shea was on a scale no one, not even Elvis, had ever experienced. "We were so far away from the audience," recalls Ringo Starr. "It was very big and very strange." And also very short. The Beatles' twelve-song encoreless set lasted barely more than thirty minutes. But their influence in songwriting, album production, world music, brand marketing, dress, and our perceptions of masculinity, however, have lasted a lifetime.

After their first appearance on *The Ed Sullivan Show*, *Newsweek* wrote, "Visually, they are a nightmare: tight, dandified, Edwardian/Beatnik suits and great pudding bowls of hair. Musically, they are a near-disaster . . . a merciless beat that does away with secondary rhythms, harmony, and melody. . . . The odds are they will fade away, as most adults confidently predict." Ludicrous as it reads now, the magazine wasn't alone in its smug disapproval. Granted, the Beatles' sound was fresh and raw, but it was hardly jarring if you knew the music of Chuck Berry, the Isley Brothers, the Miracles, or other R & B artists the Beatles admired. What was truly threatening though, was their look. It wasn't an image they originated either, but it was one they honed and modified with calculated precision.

When John formed his first band, the Quarrymen, he decided to dissent from the British tradition of ultimately dressing like one's father by taking on the look of a Teddy Boy. The Teddy-Boy style—bold-hued Edwardian jackets with velvet lapels, skinny drainpipe trousers (nicknamed "drainies"), hair slicked back with a DA (duck's ass) in the back and a quiff (a rolled pompadour with a dip) in the front—was revolutionary because it came from a rebelliousness born in the street. But its striking silhouette belied the fact that real Teddy Boys also carried knives and bike chains. They were angry punks. In fact, before joining the band, Ringo had also adopted Teddy-Boy gear, but less as a fashion statement and more as defensive garb because of the rough neighborhood he grew up in where Teddy-Boy gangs were all too common.

When Paul McCartney joined John's band, he vetoed dressing like "a weekend Ted," but was in complete agreement with John about the attention-getting power in a band having a unified look, having witnessed its power firsthand at a country-club swimming pool. "Out came five guys from Gateshead," said McCartney. "And they all looked alike. They each had on a tartan flat cap with a gray crewneck sweater, tartan shorts, [and] pumps, and they carried white towels under their arms. They walked in a line across the pool . . . and I noticed everyone's heads turn and go, 'Who's that?' In that second, a penny dropped." After several aborted attempts (including a beatnik guise that Lennon had lifted from his art-school classmates), the band found a uniform they all agreed upon while playing in Hamburg, Germany: black leather jackets, black turtlenecks, and either drainpipe or leather pants. There were more than four hundred bands in Liverpool's vibrant music scene in 1960. Not one of them was wearing leather onstage. Now the Beatles stood out. More important, their music not only gained a following, but so did their new mode of dress. Black leather jackets became a familiar sight in their audiences.

In November 1961, Brian Epstein, whose family owned the highly influential NEMS record chain, decided it was time he checked out the band. Known as Liverpool's best-dressed bachelor (his homosexuality wasn't made public until decades after his death in 1967), Epstein instantly had a clear vision of what they could become and offered to manage them, which they accepted.

Epstein also had a clear vision of how they should dress, and it didn't include anything they were currently wearing. The scruffy leather was immediately banished. First, Epstein had suits made for the boys by his tailor, but to mollify Lennon's cries that they were selling out, he compromised on forcing them to imitate his classic bespoke look. Instead, the jacket was tailored shorter and boxier to amplify the contrast of the drainpipe pants the quartet loved and insisted on keeping. The only other two elements Epstein kept of the previous wardrobe were the turtlenecks, which he thought would look good in photographs (hence the cover

of *Meet the Beatles*, the debut album in the United States), and the mop-top haircuts, which they had also picked up from their stint in Germany, because the floppy locks were intriguingly at odds with their new formal suiting. Once again, the Beatles stood out. But in Epstein's opinion this time it was a far more relatable way to theater managers and concert promoters. "He literally fucking cleaned us up," Lennon carped.

But even the band's unofficial leader had to admit the plan worked. With their gigs and income rapidly improving, more English "birds" swooning, and sales of turtlenecks skyrocketing, Epstein brought in celebrity tailor Dougie Millings, who designed the plaid jackets that identified Bill Haley and the Comets as well as Roy Orbison's trademark black suits, to modify and elevate the Beatles' current

silhouette into a more theatrical and photogenic variant. Millings designed four-button jackets that closed high with black velvet collars (like that of Teddy Boys), very narrow shoulders, and pants so tight they couldn't really sit down. Reproduced identically in five colors, the silhouette was slick, stark, unmistakable. Mick Jagger dubbed the band "the four-headed monster" and deliberately directed the Rolling Stones wardrobe toward Carnaby Street, the more extravagantly androgynous Beau Brummel–style started by John Stephen's groundbreaking London store, His Clothes, that was beginning to influence fashion on both sides of the Atlantic.

To keep the Beatles from appearing too staid, Millings whipped up a second set of suits for the band that became their calling card, the famous collarless round-necked jackets

with contrasting piping. Designer Pierre Cardin accused Millings of stealing this design from his 1960 "cylinder" menswear, and Lennon admits to having bought a similar jacket in Paris in 1961 but couldn't recall from where. Beatles historian Paolo Hewitt, however, claims the jacket has an earlier inspiration; a jacket made by Astrid Sutcliffe, a Hamburg designer and friend of the band, who made the jacket for Stuart Sutcliffe, an early band member later replaced by George Harrison. At the time, the band first opted for the leather jackets but had kept the collarless one because Astrid had made it. When they showed the jacket to Epstein, Epstein took a fancy to it and brought it to Millings. But Epstein began to fear that the combination of mop-top haircuts, collarless jackets, and Chelsea boots he discovered at the London cobbler Anello & Davide to which he added a high Cuban heel (they eventually became known as "Beatle boots") might come off as way too feminine-looking in a more-conservative America. Consequently, for their debut on *The Ed Sullivan Show*, the Beatles wore the less forward four-button suits with white shirts and black ties. For their performance at Shea the following year, they modified the collarless suit to one with a Nehru-like closure but kept the rest of the silhouette the same.

Their sound was different, their clothes were different, their hair was different, but the Beatles' almost immediate impact on our music, dress, and even our speech (the sudden ubiquity of the word *luv*, for example) was greatly aided by the fact that the Fab Four's rapturously anticipated arrival was the first uplifting event to occur in the United States since the devastating assassination of President John F. Kennedy barely two months before. A nation shaken to its core found it easier to look outside our country for joy. Consequently, more revelers from across the pond—the British Invasion—followed the Beatles to America and were heartily welcomed. Bands like the Dave Clark Five, the Animals, Gerry and the Pacemakers, and, of course, the Rolling Stones, were not only varied in song but provided more sartorial inspiration, as they wore both more preening and uninhibited versions of what British men were buying on Carnaby Street and Chelsea's Kings Road. Soon Cuban heels,

velvet, lace, Edwardian collars, mohair suits, Nehru collars, foulards, and stovepipe pants found their way into American menswear. Singers like Lulu, Petula Clark, and Marianne Faithfull, dressed in A-line minis by Mary Quant and pre–flower child Bohemian prints by Ossie Clark, influenced American style, as did his angel dresses (minis with trumpet sleeves). Models Jean Shrimpton and Twiggy were the arbiters of beauty. And retailers like Biba, Take Six, Kleptomania, and Habitat turned shopping into entertainment.

Premier Leonid Brezhnev tried to ban the Beatles haircut in the Soviet Union, deeming it a symbol of rebellion. But it was no use. The Beatles and Swinging London were a worldwide phenomenon. It was the Fab Four themselves who actually brought their style to an end. One could immediately tell from the cover of their music-industry-changing concept masterpiece *Sgt. Pepper's Lonely Hearts Club Band* (1967), the band's appearance had radically altered. *Pepper's* world was way more colorful, as if viewed through Lennon's new tinted wireframe "tea-shade" glasses.

But, however drastic it was for the Beatles, the military coats, edged shearling, paisley-print shirts, and flared bell-bottoms were not new; in fact, they were similar to what was already being worn in America from Haight-Ashbury to New York City's East Village. Their style no longer belonged only to them, though you can't discount how the universal popularity of *Sgt. Pepper* increased the mass appeal of such male flamboyance. John, Paul, George, and Ringo really did look incredible in their vintage band uniforms.

The Beatles disbanded in 1970. Thirty years after their split, on November 13, 2000, *1*, an album of all their number one hits was released and sold thirteen million copies in one month—more than any other album has sold in that period of time. For the millions of original Beatlemaniacs still alive, as well as the generations that have been introduced to the band by parents who either were at Shea Stadium that night or wished they were, at one time grew their hair long, and have am embroidered shearling hidden somewhere in the attic, the Beatles will always be here, there, and everywhere.

LEAPS
OF
FAITH

Tom Cruise Jumps
on Oprah's Couch, 2005

He had us way before a crinkly-eyed Renée Zellweger admitted she was a goner at "Hello." As Joel Goodsen, a teenager left home alone in *Risky Business* (1983), a baby-faced twenty-one-year-old Tom Cruise slid across the floor and into our daydreams as he lip-synched Bob Seger's "Old Time Rock and Roll" into a candlestick, played air guitar on an andiron, and shook his tush on Mom's sofa wearing only crew socks, a pink pinstripe shirt, and not too tighty-whities. After this bona fide star-making turn, his character slips a pair of Ray-Ban Wayfarers atop that smile that can be seen from space when he borrows his dad's Porsche. Within weeks of the film's release, sales of the sunglasses skyrocketed.

Not only did he reboot the same frenzy for aviator frames in *Top Gun* (1986) as Pete "Maverick" Mitchell, when Cruise decided it was an essential part of his "need for speed" wardrobe, but Avirex couldn't keep up with the demand for their copy of the navy G-1 flight jacket that Cruise and costar Val Kilmer wear throughout the film, perhaps the screen's highest-grossing testosterone-driven and inescapably homoerotic "bromance"—though it predates the word's origin by nearly two decades. With three Academy Award nominations and three Golden Globe wins to prove his range, and movies like *Jerry Maguire* to verify his sincerity, Cruise became a global dreamboat, with his films generating more than three billion dollars at the box office.

So the estrogen-spiking insanity that greeted Oprah Winfrey on May 23, 2005, when she brayed "He's in the building!" was no surprise. Cruise's long strides onto the *Oprah* set generated more than one minute of uncontrollable screeching, chest clutching, furious hand-fanning, and BFF hugging.

Cruise was overwhelmed and grinning nonstop, but it didn't appear as if the two feelings were connected. In fact, it was as if the audience's idolatry was distracting him from his already achieved ecstasy. Nevertheless, he was his usual gracious self, acknowledging the audience's emotional rush, thanking Oprah for inviting him to a charity event the night before, and blushing as he recounted getting a rose from Tina Turner, who wanted to meet him.

But the incessant grinning never dimmed. Naturally, Oprah asked him why she had never seen him like this before. And then he took off. But unlike what you've heard if you've never watched the segment, Tom Cruise *does not*

jump up and down on Oprah's couch. In sequence, it's far more complicated, riveting, and bizarre. First he stands and raises his hands in victory as if he'd won the Boston Marathon. Then he kneels like Tim Tebow after a touchdown, and clenches his fist and pulls back as if he'd scored with a seventy-five-yard run. Then he confesses he is "in love." Twice. And mutters that he is "not cool." Despite Oprah's constant questioning, he hardly speaks, and when he does he is incoherent.

Ten minutes into the interview, the love-drunk Cruise jumps onto Oprah's startlingly ugly mustard leather sectional, and then he jumps right off without saying a word, as if

the cushions were heated stones and he'd been barefoot. Oprah, a little ill at ease, declares, "He is gone!" Replying he doesn't care, Cruise quickly jumps on and off the couch again. What's disturbing is neither the leaps nor his declarations of happiness, which seem quite sincere, but his near mauling of Winfrey—furiously high-fiving her, hugging her, then literally grasping her hands and shaking her down until she is helplessly wedged into the corner of the horrid sofa.

But he is not done. Cruise insists on running backstage to find and fetch his soon-to-be fiancée and bring her out to show off. Though she eventually gets led on, it's obvious Katie Holmes has as much desire to be on set as she does to play three-handed bridge with Mimi Rogers and Nicole Kidman, Cruise's previous wives. But Cruise, feverish with bliss, can't be stopped.

Take away knowledge of Cruise's religious affiliation with Scientology and one might chalk his behavior up to Thackeray's quote that "love makes fools of us all." But that's like someone with a nut allergy trying to ignore there being any in the pecan brownies. How it looks is not how it was spun.

Within days, Cruise's overly elated antics were judged by blogs, syndicated celebrity-driven news, and virtually every venue of female-oriented daytime programming as creepy—so creepy, in fact, that while he is still instantly recognized globally, he is a megastar with a dimmed persona. Since his marriage to and subsequent divorce from Holmes in 2012, Cruise has made seven films. Except for *Rock of Ages,* where he plays a broad caricature of a rock star, all of them have been either high-tech thrillers or action films set in the future, where he is more likely to be running than kissing. None of them features the international star with a love interest. And box-office returns are trending downward.

To quote the last line of Philip Roth's sex-obsessed *Portnoy's Complaint*: "So [said the doctor]. Now vee may perhaps to begin. Yes?"

Ray-Ban Wayfarers are still way cool nonetheless.

LUCY IS ENCEINTE

*Lucille Ball Has a Baby
on I Love Lucy, 1952*

Lucy is *what*? Why would the title of one of the most celebrated *I Love Lucy* teleplays include an archaic French term for an impregnated woman? Was the hit show's beloved star, the Jamestown, New York–born Lucille Ball, a closet Francophile? Did Desi Arnaz, her Cuban-born husband, have obscure Gallic roots? Was being multilingual all the rage in Hollywood in the early 1950s?

None of the above. It may seem strange today, when the world has now devoured two heaping portions of the Duchess of Cambridge's trimester trivia, but in 1952, both the Columbia Broadcasting System (CBS), which aired America's favorite sitcom, and the show's principal sponsor were terrified of using the incendiary word *pregnant* on television. In fact, to ease jitters, a priest, a minister, and a rabbi vetted each of the series' seven "having a baby" scripts. Ironically, the clergymen unanimously recommended the network use the word *pregnant*. CBS refused.

Consequently, when Lucy Ricardo started feeling "dauncey" (a word Ball made up), she went to the doctor and discovered she was having a "blessed event" due to the "bun in her oven." The euphemisms flew. Ball was actually five months along when the second season of *I Love Lucy* began filming, so, unlike the first season, when she also was pregnant, only to suffer an early miscarriage, the decision was made not to try to camouflage her now obvious condition behind couches, laundry baskets, and groceries again.

Ball's wasn't television's first pregnancy. A lesser, unsuccessful show *Mary Kay and Johnny* staked that claim. But she was the medium's first major female star, and Lucy and Desi's decision to celebrate the art-imitating-life birth

of their second child after eleven years of off-camera marriage became a cultural benchmark. Though childbearing in the twentieth century had long since discarded torturous Victorian maternity corsets, billowy full-body aprons, and strict adherence to Empire-waist gowns, post–World War II moms-to-be were never described in the "glowing" terms chroniclers now routinely use to hail a Cate Blanchett or Angelina Jolie when they appear on red carpets in custom maternity gowns by Dries Van Noten and Max Mara respectively. In fact, Hermès's classic Kelly bag took on the last name of Grace, Princess of Monaco, because she ubiquitously used the purse to obscure her royal belly while carrying Prince Albert to term.

Lucy's maternity smocks, however, were flowing, voluminous, and colorful (though the show was shot in black and white), rendered in bold prints, plaids, and checks. With her scarlet-glossed lips, flame-red hair, and trademark zaniness unchecked by her condition, Ball sent out a message that having a baby need not mandate housebound exile and recession from public life.

More important, on-air Lucy and Ricky Ricardo emerged as an even more romantic couple. Despite their bizarre on-set sleeping arrangement (twin beds pushed together but separately made), Arnaz's passion for his real-life wife is obvious. "Lucy Is Enceinte" climaxes with Lucy, frustrated that Ricky is too preoccupied with work for her to tell him their wonderful news, goes to the Tropicana nightclub where he performs. She persuades the maître d' to hand the crooner a note stating that a woman in the audience wants him to break the news to her husband of their "blessed event" by singing "We're Having a Baby, My Baby and Me." Ricky, at first unaware of Lucy sitting solo at a table, asks four ringside couples if they're the lucky ones as he sings "Rock-a-Bye Baby." Then he notices a beaming Lucy, who blissfully nods. Ricky smiles and walks past, not connecting the dots. Then he does. The script called for Ricky to faint, but Arnaz was so in

the moment he continued to sing to his wife, his voice quivering with happiness.

On January 19, 1953, Lucy gave birth "on air" to Little Ricky. The episode was watched by 44 million people, a staggering number considering that the majority of Americans did not yet own a TV set. Ball scheduled a Caesarian on the same day so that the birth of Desiderios Alberto Arnaz y de Acha IV—Desi Jr.—would seemingly coincide with the broadcast, which was actually filmed in November of the previous year. But the millions of women who watched that night as well as the whole season of I Love Lucy got more than a lot of good laughs and a memorable milestone-in-television moment. The ease with which the show integrated Lucy's pregnancy with her schemes and antics was an affirmation that being with child was more than a fact of life to be dealt with but something to be proud of, and that it enhanced one's existence rather than impeded it. Ricky's unwavering affection gave evidence that a woman remained desirable, sometimes even adorable, when pregnant. The show suggested that rather than lay low in whatever they could find that covered their growing bellies, pregnant women should wear clothes that matched that glow that they are supposed to own.

That was a great idea, except where were those clothes? The answer came quickly. Lucy's on-air and offscreen wardrobes, which were constantly featured in the fan magazines of the day, kick-started the now nearly $5 billion maternity-wear industry. Lucy even helped out the still fledgling television industry, introducing a surefire way for any show to jolt their ratings—have someone get pregnant—and its effectiveness still holds true today.

One sardonic note: the show's sponsor who found the word *pregnant* so distasteful was the Philip Morris Tobacco Company, whose commercial tagline for their King Size smoke was "the most wonderful cigarette made in America today . . . your throat can tell." The mind reels.

DANCING WITH MOMMY

President and
Mrs. Ronald Reagan
at the Inaugural Ball, 1981

Thanks to headstrong women like Michelle Obama and Hillary Clinton, very few people expect the first lady of the United States to fill her day with ribbon cuttings and photo ops in the Rose Garden. But thirty years ago, the role was more rigidly defined. It was almost a mandate that the mistress of the White House would be a model of reserve. She would speak softly and carry a small purse.

Bess Truman, Mamie Eisenhower, and Pat Nixon (who once said that "[she] just want[ed] to go down in history as the wife of the president") had no problem filling the bill: they infrequently spoke in public, were devoid of personal initiatives, and were rarely photographed with their husbands outside of official events. Of course, a game-changing Jackie Kennedy incorporated memorable stylistic initiatives while using her position to incite global cultural exchanges, but she exuded flawless elegance rather than sensuality. And though she and Jack radiated the glow of an idyllic, pre–Ralph Laurenian couple, their partnership appeared more patrician than passionate (an observation not made in hindsight of later knowledge of the president's sexual escapades). Lady Bird Johnson was passionate—about highway beautification and not much else. In 1977, First Lady Rosalynn Carter interpreted Washington's new penchant for austerity perhaps a bit too literally by dragging out the same blue chiffon gown she had worn to her husband Jimmy's prior inauguration as governor of Georgia.

However, Nancy Reagan wasn't just any former governor's wife. Her résumé also included minor film actress, wife of a Hollywood movie star, and paragon Bel Air hostess. Here was a woman who knew what to do when she found herself center stage. Taking the approach that it was much more fun to move the accent off the word *inaugural* and onto the word *ball*, Reagan headed to her "local dressmaker," designer James Galanos, famous for his imperiously raised eyebrow and beak-nosed hauteur, as well as for the fact that he crafted impeccable gowns of haute couture quality without ever leaving Los Angeles. The collaboration resulted in a defiantly glamorous gown for the first lady of a country in the midst of a recession. As lavish as it was ill timed, the creation met with criticism. Many voiced outrage at its price tag (an estimated ten thousand dollars), at the cost of the rest of Mrs. Reagan's equally high-end inaugural trousseau, and at the insensitivity of raising the sartorial bar for first lady style sky-high at the same time the presidential administration was formulating the concept of trickle-down economics.

If Nancy Reagan was fazed by any of this, or her subsequent White House redecorating, then perhaps Hollywood should have invested more heavily in her. Because all that seemed to matter was that her number-one fan was delirious with schoolboy delight about her. The new president and his wife reveled in an unabashedly affectionate relationship. He never hid his enchantment with "Mommy" as he called her, or her powers of influence. She, in turn, was fiercely protective, engineered the dismissal of those disloyal to him, and, depending on the veracity of several accounts regarding the onset of his Alzheimer's disease, may have played a significant hand in the making of presidential policy during his second term.

It takes a heaping portion of bravado for a sixty-year-old mother to don a slim-fitting, sleeveless, one-shoulder-baring gown. But at the inaugural ball in January 1981, on a night with the world watching, Nancy Reagan chose to dress to please the man she still loved fox-trotting with rather than succumb to the unwritten restrictions of her new political position. And it was plain for all to see that as far as he was concerned, he was taking the prettiest girl in the world to his prom.

Four years later, at President Reagan's second inaugural ball, Nancy again wore a white Galanos gown, even more bedazzled and almost twice as costly as the first, but to far less controversy, probably because the jeweled jacket-like bodice covered her arms and shoulders, which at her age was probably wise. Plus, by the second presidential term, the first lady's extravagance was no longer a surprise. The public knew that she, like many celebrated hostesses, had never met an etched-gold china pattern she didn't like.

CLOSE YOUR EYES AND THINK OF ME

The Spector of Androgyny
in *Ghost*, 1990

The scene is barely more than three minutes long and less than two minutes at the location we remember best. A young woman with a wispy version of a boy's bowl-headed haircut and wearing only a man-tailored white shirt with the sleeves cut off is sitting at a potter's wheel, caressing the taupe clay into a long cylinder as it spins. Behind her comes a bare-chested young man with a head full of thick swooping curls clad only in a pair of jeans. He slides in behind her. He asks if he can help, but when he tries, he immediately messes up the clay's symmetry. She doesn't mind. With his arms wrapped round her, all four limbs take to the clay, touching it, molding it, its grayish gloss transferring to their arms until you can't figure out whose limbs are whose. Then, in shadow, he picks her up and carries her off. He kisses her in close up, but the darkness plays tricks on us. They both have such large, yearning eyes and such full lips—and they're backlit so it's hard to distinguish one sex from the other. The camera swirls and you're kind of lost in determining identity but somehow you don't care. All you hear is the Righteous Brothers making us wish we could release all our inhibitions to passion in their escalating version of "Unchained Melody." By the time the song ends we are in love with the lovers we are watching in *Ghost*.

One of the most beloved tearjerkers of all time, *Ghost* was a fairly low-budget production, released with little fanfare and expectation, yet the film resonated so viscerally with audiences worldwide that it not only reaped a blockbuster box office of more than a half billion dollars, making it the highest-grossing film of the year, but it enabled the

producers to cash in again a decade later with a special tenth-anniversary edition. And yet, despite all the tissue boxes it's helped empty, *Ghost* has escaped being filed under the dismissive category of "chick flick," unlike two other notable female-centric melodramas and one romantic comedy from the same period, *Steel Magnolias, Beaches,* and *Pretty Woman.*

True, *Ghost* is scarier than those three, and there's a prevailing sense of loss throughout its 129-minute run. The film begins with that young man's murder. Its story line is driven by betrayal. It features sleazy thieves and shrouded spirits from the dark side presented without irony, and its characters see dead people. Yet we feel soothed and satisfied when *Ghost* ends, because the movie is so successful in getting us to agree to the directive written across the top of its original promotional poster: BELIEVE.

Of course, it's a lot easier to put your faith in apparitions when the spirit of that young man resembles Patrick Swayze. Freshly installed as filmdom's newest deep crush

thanks to his role as Johnny, Baby's (Jennifer Grey) dreamy summer love in *Dirty Dancing* (1987), Swayze didn't resemble any of his fellow 1990 male box-office stars: Richard Gere, Arnold Schwarzenegger, Bruce Willis, Harrison Ford, and Michael J. Fox. Only Swayze looked like he'd fallen off a Harlequin Romance book jacket.

Certainly trusting in ghosts and mediums is standard procedure when watching films dealing with the supernatural, but that's not at the crux of the commitment *Ghost* is asking from you. What the movie demands is that you believe in the power of love beyond mere physical contact with your beloved to sustain personal happiness; it then gives you ample evidence of this life-affirming power via a subtly subversive and androgynous approach to sexuality and male-female role-playing.

As Sam, Swayze is a handsome hunk, with a deep buckwheat honey-laced Texas drawl that could slide you out of cowboy boots as easily as if they were ballet flats, but his features—full lips; crab-apple-shaped cheekbones;

limpid, always moist eyes; and tousled locks with a permanently curled forelock—and the grace with which he moves his lithe dancer's body, are distinctly feminine. It's no surprise that Swayze made for quite an attractive drag queen five years later in *To Wong Foo, Thanks for Everything! Julie Newmar*.

But Swayze is only half the attraction. Is that really Demi Moore playing Molly? She was the teen babe we first noticed in 1984's *Blame It on Rio* thanks to her hot bikini body and long raven hair. Then she frustrated us as Jules, the out-of-control young beauty who just couldn't get her life together in *St. Elmo's Fire*. Moore exudes a thoroughly different persona in *Ghost*: she's vulnerable, gentle, and achingly adorable in what has become her defining screen role. As Molly, she speaks with the similar raspy timbre to Swayze's but moves much more tomboyishly than he does. Adding to this gender-bending is the way Molly dresses. Her wardrobe consists solely of

overalls, button-down shirts, stretched out tees, and suspendered sweats. Molly never wears anything girlish. She doesn't wear makeup. And literally to top it off, Moore's thick, black locks have been drastically shorn into a dense pixie cut, even shorter than Swayze's, whose flowing gabardine shirts rustle in harmony with his flowing hair. The delicate drop earrings Molly always wears—a gift from Sam—are probably the only feminine things she owns. That's why it's difficult to distinguish one from another in the pottery scene.

Blurring or removing the obvious cultural signposts of male-female attraction is what imparts *Ghost*'s critical encounter with its enduring hold over us. Moore's pixie cut sparked the biggest hair-cropping craze among women since ice skater Dorothy Hamill's wedge cut a decade earlier. But her manner also reflects a faction of the fashion world that had begun exploring the appeal of androgyny. In opposition to the hypersexuality being expressed at the time by designers like Gianni Versace, Jean Paul Gaultier, and Dolce & Gabbana, designers such as Marc Jacobs, Calvin Klein, Ann Demeulemeester, Jil Sander, and even Giorgio Armani found that tamping down sexual dynamics was far more sensual and appealing to women, who had by this time grown tired of effusive color and exaggerated silhouettes. We don't see her that way now, but Kate Moss's extraordinarily lengthy modeling career was launched at the time too, and she was touted as the exemplar of a new androgyny. Her waiflike stance made her the anti-Naomi, the non-Cindy. And though Jacobs wouldn't put grunge on the runway for another two years, the movement was already spreading nationally in the music scene, its style very obviously characterized by the notion that a shirt is just a shirt. Is it for a man or a woman? Well, the answer depends on who wants to wear it.

As potent a romantic fantasy as the potter's wheel is, *Ghost*'s most moving scene, and the one that places it in

that rare subset of films we stop everything for and watch when we find it while channel surfing—no matter where in the story we've landed—is also where the drama takes an even bigger dramatic risk in subverting gender identity. It occurs near the end, when Sam takes over the clairvoyant Oda Mae's body (Whoopi Goldberg) to dance with Molly one last time before he goes heavenward.

This scene could have so easily been a cringe-worthy mess: a white man enters a black woman's physique so she can caress a white woman she's not attracted to in real life. But director Jerry Zucker and Academy Award–winning screenwriter Bruce Joel Rubin sensitively choreograph the encounter with a delicate balance of ambiguity and mystery. After Sam's spirit enters Oda Mae's body, we see a close-up of Oda's black hands touching Molly's white ones. But then she is gone and the film cuts to the approaching faces of Molly and Sam so closely you can

barely tell them apart. The camera keeps turning so that we view the sensations of only one face at a time. Never do either of their eyes open, so what each is feeling isn't compromised by reality. And because the couple we are watching seem such genderless mirror images of each other, the potential awkward carnality of the embrace vanishes and we begin to empathically sense what Molly is experiencing: it could be the memory of our father or mother, children or friends who are no longer with us but whose presence have helped us to feel safe. Or even more wondrous is the recollection of that one lost love who always cherished us and made us stronger and bolder and softer when we needed it most. Whether they were good kissers or had rocking bodies is now beside the point. We just want to believe they will never leave us even if they aren't beside us. Because time goes by so slowly without them.

HERE COMES THE BRIDE— AGAIN

Elizabeth Taylor's
Eight Marriages, 1950–1996

"I've only slept with men
I've been married to.
How many women
can make that claim?"

–Elizabeth Taylor, from *The Book of Lists*
by David Wallechinsky, 2009

What a sweet sentiment. That is, until you realize Elizabeth Taylor wasn't always married to these men when she first slept with them. Consequently, at various times she earned notoriety, as an ingenue, a goddess, harlot, home wrecker, opportunist, or recovering addict, but, regardless of the labeling, she didn't cower from the public or shun the media, neither defending nor apologizing for her choices. Taylor admittedly loved being in love, and to her, "love was synonymous with marriage." She said, "I couldn't just have a romance; it had to be a marriage."

To look at the list of men who lent her their last names, she certainly didn't have a type. Her consistency lay in a life spent doing what came naturally. Famous before she was a teen, she never whined about the downside of celebrity or paraded intimate details of her romantic and family life. Inevitably, that's what sustained the public's ceaseless fascination with her. She helped herself to the banquet of stardom with finger-licking relish: the constant attention, the privilege no matter where she traveled, the strategic benefits of role-playing, the platform to urge or shame others to doing good, plus a free pass to discovery, to fashion, and above all, to all things that sparkled. She said, "Who wouldn't love my life? Some people never find happiness. Look at all the opportunities I've been offered. They're been pretty spectacular."

So, for better or for worse, for richer or for poorer, let's take these alliances one by one.

MARRIAGE 1
Conrad "Nicky" Hilton

Elizabeth became engaged to hotel heir Nicky Hilton four months after meeting him in a Beverly Hills nightclub and then married him at the Bel Air Country Club on May 6, 1950. Her gown was designed by costume designer Helen Rose as a gift from MGM, who shrewdly held the release of Taylor's next film, *Father of the Bride*, until right after the wedding. Rose did not reproduce the gown she wore on film, though there are similarities with the one Taylor wore to marry Hilton. Taylor, as *Bride*'s Kay Banks, wore a more traditional gown with a deep, rounded, scoop neck and multiple folds down the front that border a lace center panel. Lace is also worked into the veil and illusion panel above the bust. It's a wedding dress any father (played by Spencer Tracy) could love.

For the real nuptials, Rose used twenty-five yards of shell white satin to create a gown with an extreme hourglass silhouette, which, though it sparked a major trend, was not that easily suitable for most women, as a built-in corset cinched in Taylor's already impressive twenty-two-inch waist by another two inches. The border of the shoulder-bearing, sweetheart neckline and the top of the clear illusion panel on the neck were embroidered with seed pearls and sequins, while draped garlands of the same encircled the full skirt. The silk veil train extended fifteen feet. The entire ensemble took fifteen people three months to make and was valued at about $1,500 at the time, or about $15,000 today.

Seven hundred people, including most of Hollywood's A-list, attended the wedding. Nicky Hilton spent most of the wedding night at the bar getting soused and hitting on other women. (He had already slept with his father Conrad Hilton's second wife, Zsa Zsa Gabor). According to Taylor, "My marriage lasted two weeks, as long as the honeymoon." After returning home, she filed for divorce, though she never exploited the verbal and physical abuse she endured on their honeymoon. The split was finalized on January 29, 1951. Taylor requested no alimony.

Helen Rose created a similar version of Taylor's gown for Grace Kelly's marriage to Prince Rainier in 1955, a dress that was cited as inspiration for Sarah Burton, creative director for Alexander McQueen, when designing Kate Middleton's gown for her wedding to Prince William in 2011. Taylor's gown has changed hands several times; in 2013 it was sold at auction for $188,000.

MARRIAGE 2
Michael Wilding

Taylor married Wilding on February 21, 1952, whom she met while making *Ivanhoe*, with much less fanfare in a ten-minute ceremony at the Caxton Hall registry office in London. Considering the venue, that this was a second marriage for both, and that Wilding was twenty years

Taylor's senior, Helen Rose recommended a conservative gray suit, once again with a cinched waist to emphasize Taylor's figure. A double layer of sweeping, rounded, white lapels accented the jacket, which had three-quarter-length sleeves with wide white turned-up cuffs. Taylor wore a matching white headpiece instead of a veil. The ensemble looked like something former British prime minister Margaret Thatcher would have worn to launch a ship.

That said, the engagement ring was a big hit. The domed cabochon sapphire surrounded by diamonds sparked a trend for sapphire engagement rings in Britain. The style's popularity seems assured with boosts from Princess Diana and the Duchess of Cambridge, who now wears Diana's ring.

The union was a rebound marriage for both Taylor and Wilding, and though it produced her two sons, Michael and Edward, the alternative quiet countryside life that Wilding favored went from refreshing to repressive in a hurry. The couple divorced on January 26, 1957. Taylor did not request alimony.

MARRIAGE 3
Michael Todd

Taylor married producer, impresario, and film innovator Mike Todd (he invented the Todd-AO widescreen film process) on February 3, 1957, in Acapulco, Mexico, one week after Taylor's divorce from Wilding became final. Singer Eddie Fisher acted as best man; Fisher's wife, actress Debbie Reynolds, was matron of honor.

Todd met Taylor several times socially while he was engaged to actress Evelyn Keyes and Taylor's marriage to Michael Wilding was falling apart. Whenever he saw her she was unhappy, so he began surprising her with a series of cheer-up phone calls. She, of course, loved the attention. On July 19, 1956, the Wildings separated. The next day,

Todd phoned Taylor and said he needed to see her about something important. She met him at MGM studios, where Todd bluntly stated that he was in love with her and was going to marry her. For the next six weeks he courted her lavishly, nonstop. By early September, she had said yes to his proposal. Todd broke off his engagement to Keyes via telephone. "A lot of guys grow up and they want to become president of the United States," said Todd. "With me, I just wanted to grow up and marry Elizabeth Taylor. And I did."

Since Todd was born Avrom Goldbogen, the son of an Orthodox rabbi, Taylor wanted to converted to Judaism, but feeling she was doing it just to please him, Todd talked her out of renouncing her Christian Science faith. Nevertheless, Taylor wore a white draped organza dress with a cowl neck front that dropped to a hood in the back so that her head could be covered during the ceremony, as is customary in Jewish weddings. Taylor's movement, however, was restricted by a back brace (she had spinal troubles throughout her life, having been thrown from a

who enjoyed the spotlight as much as she did; yet Taylor seemed delighted by his refusal to take a backseat to her celebrity. "He could con the gold out of your teeth," Taylor once said. Their Acapulco wedding featured fireworks that spelled out "E loves T" and "T loves E" in the sky. The honeymoon was turned into a worldwide promotional tour for Todd's newest blockbuster, *Around the World in 80 Days,* which won the Academy Award for Best Picture that year. "The Oscar and Elizabeth Taylor in one year," said Todd. "Not bad for luck."

On March 22, 1958, Todd boarded his private plane, *The Lucky Liz,* for a press screening of *80 Days* in Albuquerque. Because Taylor felt overworked from filming *Cat on a Hot Tin Roof,* Todd insisted she forgo the journey. Todd never made it to the screening. The plane, flying too high in icy conditions, experienced engine failure and crashed near Grants, New Mexico. There were no survivors.

MARRIAGE 4
Eddie Fisher

As one of Mike Todd's best friends and at his wife Debbie Reynolds's urging, Eddie Fisher started visiting Elizabeth to console her. Evidently, he did more than that. Taylor, who this time insisted on converting to Judaism out of respect for her former and future husband, married Fisher at Temple Beth Sholom in Las Vegas, on May 12, 1959.

Taylor's belted short chiffon dress with sheer sleeves and a hood was pretty except for the fact that it was an oddly somber olive green and its unbridelike hue was further accentuated by Taylor's bouquet of deep green orchids and lilies of the valley. Since it wasn't easy one-upping Todd's twenty-nine-karat solitaire, Fisher cleverly opted for a forty-karat diamond bracelet.

horse while making *National Velvet* when she was twelve), which was also the excuse given for the loose fit of the wedding dress (daughter Liza Todd was born six months after the wedding, which means Taylor was still married to Wilding when Liza was conceived). The star attraction of Taylor's wedding ensemble, however, was the starter piece in what was to become her incomparable collection of jewelry: a twenty-nine-karat diamond engagement ring. In addition, the triple-tiered rhinestone chandelier earrings she wore that night and throughout her life were later reset with diamonds by Todd as a surprise anniversary present.

Taylor always said that Todd was the first great love of her life. Ever the showman, he was also her first husband

Though Taylor was condemned in the press as a home wrecker, the Fisher-Reynolds marriage was already in trouble due to Fisher's constant infidelity. Fisher's eponymous NBC variety show was canceled not long after his marriage to Taylor, and though Taylor helped get Fisher cast in her Academy Award–winning film *Butterfield 8* (an award she often deemed a consolation prize for being overlooked for *Cat on a Hot Tin Roof* and coming back from the dead after a life-threatening tracheotomy), Fisher didn't have the acting chops for cinema idoldom. Taylor had a thing for machismo, and when you watch the film, both his character and screen presence come across as weak and diminished.

Fisher, of course, got the ultimate karmic kick in the nuts once Taylor left for Rome to shoot *Cleopatra* and embarked on a notorious romance with the Welshman playing Marc Antony. Taylor and Fisher divorced in 1964, although Fisher contested it. Debbie Reynolds and Taylor reconciled years later, and when Taylor died in 2011, she bequeathed her most famous suite of sapphire necklace, earrings, and bracelet to her former rival.

MARRIAGES 5&6
Richard Burton

The Taylor-Burton union began as the greatest celebrity scandal of them all, even topping Taylor's marriage to Fisher—and it's never been bested. The couple's illicit on-set coupling was chronicled daily around the world and overshadowed the release of *Cleopatra,* at the time the most expensive movie ever made. Taylor wed Burton on March 15, 1964, at the Ritz-Carlton Hotel in Montreal, as Burton was performing in *Hamlet* in Toronto, a little over an hour away by plane.

Taylor wore what may have been her trendiest and ungainliest wedding dress. Designed by *Cleopatra*'s Academy Award–winning costume designer Irene Sharaff in Taylor's favorite color, sunflower yellow, the modified mini chiffon dress had a scoop neck with too deep a fold that amplified Taylor's already ample bosom, while its bodice was one fitting shy of being flattering. The dress also had a draped panel in the back but that was mostly obscured by Taylor's Rapunzel-long braided hairpiece, which was woven through with yellow hyacinths and white lilies of the valley. The dress's only saving grace was the nineteen-karat Bulgari emerald brooch given to her by Burton, who once said, "The only Italian word Elizabeth knows is *Bulgari*." He later had the brooch configured to attach to an emerald necklace—which became one of Taylor's favorite adornments—as its matching centerpiece.

Although the Vatican declared their romance "erotic vagrancy," the Burtons became the most famous married couple in the world and were renowned for their overt approach to both the mundane and the sublime. She left no doubt that he was her second great and most enduring love. The couple made eleven films together, most notably *Who's Afraid of Virginia Woolf?*, in which Taylor's performance supported Burton's assertion that she was the most "underappreciated actress in film" and won her a second Academy Award for Best Actress.

Burton lavished Taylor with jewels throughout their marriage. To celebrate their fifth anniversary in 1969, Burton replaced her engagement ring with the more than thirty-three-karat Krupp diamond, which she wore every day.

Nonetheless, their life of excess took its toll. While Taylor often claimed her "wooden leg" allowed her to drink anyone under the table, Burton's alcoholism, fueled by insecurity over his falling status as a classical actor and discomfort with their rootless, jet-set ways that were second nature to Taylor, became too much for Burton. They divorced on June 26, 1974.

Absence and sobriety made their hearts grow fonder, for a while at least. Upon meeting in Switzerland to discuss arrangements for their divorce, the two reunited and later were married on October 10, 1975, in Botswana's Chobe National Park. Taylor loved caftans—there were more than forty at the 2011 Christie's auction of her estate, including the one she wore for the ceremony, a tie-dyed, bead-embroidered one by Italian designer Gina Fratini that went from green to turquoise and violet and was bordered in guinea feathers. She also wove indigenous flowers of Botswana into her hair.

The remarriage didn't last. While Taylor could still handle the occasional cocktail, Burton could not, and that put both his sobriety and the career he was trying to respectfully rebuild in jeopardy. Then he met Suzy Hunt, a popular and socially acute British model who kept him sober, and accompanied him to New York when he starred on Broadway in *Equus*.

Burton filed for divorce on November 29, 1976. The two remained close though, starring on Broadway together in *Private Lives* in 1983. As the 2012 book *The Richard Burton Diaries* reveals, the actor remained deeply in love with Taylor for the rest of his life. The feeling was mutual.

MARRIAGE 7
John Warner

Taylor met Republican senator John Warner when he was asked by the British ambassador to escort the star to a dinner Queen Elizabeth II was hosting at the British embassy in Washington, DC. Taylor was stunned that Warner drove to pick her up himself. She found his lack of airs, his love of horses, and his commitment to his constituency, both admirable and a satisfyingly complete break from her previous life with Burton. On December 4, 1976, they were married in a private family ceremony on a hilltop on his 160-year-old, 2,400-acre working Atoka farm in Virginia.

Perhaps because she was at her heaviest weight, Taylor shrouded herself in a smart violet cashmere dress under a red, violet, and gray tweed wrap coat with fur trim and a matching intricately wrapped tweed turban.

While she professed to love her quieter life as well as political wifery, she was bored. Warner's long hours at his congressional office, the uninspiring social life in the nation's capital, and her waning film career, left her alone too often with only food as her most accessible solace. Consequently, Taylor's weight fluctuated widely while she was with Warner, although she managed to pen a successful diet book entitled *Elizabeth Takes Off* during one of her rare lithe periods. But as she said, "Being a senator's wife is not easy. What I was really starving for was self-esteem." The couple divorced amicably on November 7, 1982.

MARRIAGE 8
Larry Fortensky

In 1988, without shame or secrecy, Taylor checked herself into the Betty Ford Clinic again to get sober and rid herself of a lifelong addiction to painkillers for her chronic back problems. Always prone to illness under stressful situations, she caught pneumonia during her stay. Larry Fortensky, a brawny construction worker and recovering addict who had befriended Taylor with a strong arm to lean on and a ready ear, stayed by her side to nurse her to health. She called him Larry the Lion and was impressed with his honesty and sincerity during the clinic's encounter sessions. She was also moved by the story of his unhappy childhood and the fact that his $4,000 stay at Betty Ford was paid for by the trucker's union so he could right his life again. Fortensky knew she was a star but was hardly a movie fan. They fell in love.

Taylor married Fortensky on October 6, 1991, at Michael Jackson's Neverland Ranch in Los Olivos, California. The wedding was a $2 million media spectacle. It's worth noting that in virtually every picture of the happy couple a paler-than-either-of-them Michael Jackson is standing to the bride's right.

For the ceremony, Taylor wore a $25,000 jonquil yellow off-the-shoulder Valentino ball gown with a scalloped Chantilly lace bodice, a cinched waist (Taylor was in another thin phase), and a double-tiered Chantilly lace skirt. Despite her huge black bouffant, she wove white flowers into her hair. Fortensky's blonde mane almost matched hers in volume, but he eschewed the foliage. The bride drank grape juice at the wedding. Eddie Fisher, husband number four, said at the time, "It's the first time Liz married a regular guy. This one should last." However, the Fortenskys had almost nothing in common. They managed to stay together for five years, and though Fortensky hired celebrity divorce lawyer Raoul Felder to try to overturn the prenup, Fortensky and Taylor remained friendly over the years. She left him a half million dollars in her will.

⋈

Taylor never married again. Instead, she put her energy into business and her great capacity for love into charitable works. She launched her first perfume, aptly named Passion, in 1987. Her next scent, White Diamonds, instantly became and remains one of the bestselling fragrances in the world, proving she was as savvy a businesswoman as she was an actress. In 1985, in response to her friend Rock Hudson's death from AIDS, she cofounded the American Foundation for AIDS Research (amfAR), and then in 1991, the Elizabeth Taylor AIDS Foundation, tirelessly crossing the globe to raise hundreds of millions of dollars for research and treatment for this still incurable disease, proving she was as great a humanitarian as she was an actress and celebrity. For two weeks in early December 2011, nine months after her death, Christie's held a massive auction of Taylor's clothes, artifacts, furniture, and jewelry. The sale generated $156,756,576.00, the highest ever for an auction of celebrity belongings, proving that she was the last great and most beloved star of them all.

BLOWN AWAY

Jordan Knight Sings
"Baby, I Believe in You," 1990

One Direction is currently the most popular singing group in the world. These constantly Tweeting, texting, and Instagramming former British *The X Factor* contestants are acknowledged social-media megastars. Already the subject of countless fashion shoots, they are recognized as international sex symbols. Having earned a half billion dollars and counting for themselves and their canny creator, impresario Simon Cowell, they are also certifiable money machines. But the one thing you will never hear One Direction called is "a boy band." Cowell probably has forbidden any verbal or written use of the innately derogatory term under penalty of news blackout, concert banishment, or selfie refusal. But "a boy band" is *exactly* what One Direction is. If you think boy bands can only be adorable and cuddly but never sexy, especially not in the way One Direction is sexy, then you obviously never caught New Kids on the Block when they were huge. One Direction huge.

Unlike the myth that all boy bands are manufactured with interchangeable parts run through Auto-Tune and propped up by better-than-they-are backup talent, the New Kids on the Block's start was quick, hard, and rough. The idea to assemble an all-white American soul group began with songwriter-producer Maurice Starr who had guided the all-black group New Edition, with lead singer Bobby Brown, to stardom only to be unceremoniously dumped by them. Rather than be a pop Pygmalion, Starr sought out kids who already could perform. He found

four of them in the Dorchester section of Boston, a low-income white community that bussed its kids to schools in the even poorer predominantly black inner-city of Roxbury due to zoning regulations. Not only did these four kids know how to sing and move, but thanks to their direct exposure to the growing urban contemporary sound, Donnie Wahlberg could instantly create a solid rap, Danny Wood excelled at break dancing, Jordan Knight led the school chorus with his fluid falsetto, and Jonathan Knight's voice blended naturally with his younger brother's. Short a crooner, Starr found Joey McIntyre crosstown. He was only twelve but could do a spot-on Frank Sinatra imitation.

Starr rehearsed them every day after school. He owned their weekends. He encouraged them to write music, to study the licks of groups like Parliament Funkadelic and to devise their own choreography. He booked his new

quintet, dubbed for a short time as NYNUK (a play on the faux 1922 documentary, *Nanook of the North)*, exclusively into venues with black audiences because he knew they would be tougher on cute, young white boys determined to get down. Accordingly, their music was only played on urban contemporary radio for two years, until a DJ in Florida picked up the first single off their second album, *Be My Girl*. The radio station was instantly flooded with requests.

Several months later, the rechristened New Kids on the Block starting touring, opening for teen sensation Tiffany. Halfway through this association, the order flipped, and Tiffany became the warm-up act. The New Kids on the Block now owned the streets.

I attended a concert on the 1989 "Hangin' Tough" tour, their first as headliners, as a columnist for *The New Yorker*, mainly to profile their frenzied female audience, referred to as "Blockheads" and "Kidiots." Having been part of 1960s Beatlemania, I doubted the furor could be as authentic and had only a cursory interest in its source. To my forehead-smacking astonishment, the trainer-bra-ripping passion all around me was not only feverishly real, it was also deserved. NKOTB were terrific performers. The most fervent gushing and bra tossing was reserved for Jordan, the handsomest, tallest, and most vocally soulful of the group. He sang his solo in a crisp, untucked white shirt that blew open with a wind machine to expose his T-shirt, further stimulating his adoring idolators with limber dance moves across a stage littered with A and a few random B cups. With the group always dressed in coordinated, rather than identical outfits like most of their contemporaries, Knight's billowing white shirt singled him out as both the most noticeable and the dreamiest member of NKOTB, who had now risen above their streetwise origins due to pure talent.

Just one year later, and the band's success had grown even greater: bigger venues and larger crowds. The Step by Step tour played to more than two million people in just sixty-three dates. There was an insatiable hunger for anything stamped NKOTB that was wearable, portable, sleep-on-able, or swoon-worthy. In 1990, New Kids on the Block merchandise, including shirts, hats, dresses, coats, scarves, lunch boxes, sheets, and sleeping bags grossed more than $400 million. This sum did take not into account concert ticket or album sales, making it one of retail's most successful mass-market clothing brands.

When I attended a Step by Step concert at Madison Square Garden, Knight was once again center stage to sing his new hit "Baby, I Believe in You." This time, he stood elevated on a black platform, the stage dark except for four spotlights trained on him from the sides and above. He looked a little taller, but that could have been the incredibly high hair. But he certainly looked a little bigger, despite wearing the same white button-down shirt and black pants. Once again he started with his now familiar pose—arched to the left torso, outstretched arms, with his back to the audience. But upon turning to face us, Knight was met by a blast of air that could have blown Dorothy right past Oz. And when his shirt blew open, the T-shirt he'd once worn underneath was no longer there. Jordan Knight, who had turned twenty years old earlier in the year, was now bare-chested and very buff.

The girl standing to my right hit me in frustrated ecstasy. As Knight sang, he caressed his six-pack and offered grinds that predated and bested some of the cast of *Magic Mike*. The white shirt, which used to frame such innocence was now wildly flowing perpendicular to his body in a gale force wind as if to announce a newfound sexuality. You couldn't really call NKOTB a boy band anymore, because that was undeniably a man up there. My former attacker now joined her other neighbor and thousands of other not-yet-women in heaving very grown-up breaths. It was obvious. Knight was no longer cute. He was hot. But feeling, as Mike Nichols once called critics, like a "eunuch at a gang bang," I took my leave.

Eighteen years later, in 2008, New Kids on the Block reunited on a surprisingly highly successful tour. I watched as, at age thirty-eight, a still handsome and muscular Knight let his white shirt fly back. And those slightly older Blockheads lost it yet again. But now it was been there, once wanted that. In 2010, after a winning one-off matchup at the American Music Awards, NKOTB joined forces with the Backstreet Boys for another tour that has now lasted four years. But the wind machine is gone. So I stopped going.

But I did just take my neighbor's kid to see One Direction.

HATS OFF TO BETTE

Now, Voyager, 1942

Touted in its time as a powerful chronicle of a woman who escapes the cruelty of a tyrannical parent to find emotional independence, by contemporary standards *Now, Voyager* is a tower of claptrap, underscored by amateur psychoanalysis, populated by characters mercurially reeling from one emotional extreme to another, and dominated by an absurd, indefensible romance that any rational woman would kick to the curb without breaking stride. *Now, Voyager* and another classic tale of self-loathing sacrifice, *Stella Dallas* (1937), are adapted from novels written by the same author, Olive Higgins Prouty, and rank as keystones of a genre of melodrama known in Hollywood's golden age as the "women's picture."

A women's picture is not to be confused with a "chick flick." What women's pictures (e.g., *Mildred Pierce, Old Acquaintance*, and *Humoresque*) and chick flicks (e.g., *Sleepless in Seattle, The Notebook*, and *Notting Hill*) have in common are plots that hinge on all-consuming affairs of the heart. Where they differ is that in the latter category, love always triumphs. By the time the final credits of a chick flick roll, your waterproof mascara may have betrayed you, but you will be smiling. But, oh my, the *geshreeying*—a great Yiddish word that means to repeatedly tear at one's heart with no relief—that goes on in a woman's picture! And it's all for naught, since, without fail, the heroine is destined to wind up unmarried, abandoned, or dead.

What made these women's pictures so successful, let alone bearable, were the strong actresses who took on these equally strong characters: Barbara Stanwyck played Stella

Dallas, and Joan Crawford, Mildred Pierce. The hallmark of the genre is that only those with deep resolve survive. The more indomitable the dame on-screen behaves against all odds, the more the female audience that endured the Great Depression and/or managed life at home during World War II identified with her. And when it came to seizing control in a woman's picture, no actress was more fearless, invincible, and relatable than Bette Davis.

Offscreen, Davis suffered no fools, stood her ground, and rarely gave in. She was even sued by her studio, Warner Brothers, for refusing to act in films she felt unworthy of her talent. On-screen, she was nominated for an Academy Award seven times in one decade (between 1935 and 1945), and ten times during her career. She stands alone among the great stars of her era in that she was neither intimidatingly beautiful like Myrna Loy or Rita Hayworth, nor provocatively sexy like Barbara Stanwyck or Vivien Leigh. Yet, whether the material matched her formidable skills or not, Bette Davis "taught Hollywood to follow the actress, instead of an actress following the camera," said Elaine Stritch, by commanding every scene with such piercing intelligence that even equally billed costars were reduced to supporting players.

What makes *Now, Voyager* compelling entertainment is the sight of Davis initially repressing this most powerful asset in order to surprise us with a bravura transformation from dowdy dejected duckling to glamorous steadfast swan. To play her character, Charlotte Vale, the unattractive and unloved spinster on the verge of a nervous breakdown, Davis originally planned to go to such physical extremes to make herself look so terrible that Hal Wallis, the film's producer, demanded Davis tone down her physical alteration for fear she'd frighten her core fans.

Nevertheless, after director Irving Rapper teases us with close-ups of a woman's hands nervously stubbing out cigarettes and then her halting descent down a staircase in black oxford shoes, we get our first full gander at Charlotte. Hunched and hidden in Davis's resident costume designer Orry-Kelly's overly padded, ill-fitting, grandmotherly dress with fussy lace trim, her sallow features dominated by centipede eyebrows nearly casting shade on her rimless eyeglasses, and framed by thick, unruly, graying tresses pulled into a low bun, Davis's guise is comic in its exaggeration.

What stifles any snickering at her physical characterization is the torrent of verbal abuse she immediately receives from her monstrous mother, played by Gladys Cooper, who delivers her verbal onslaught with Boston Brahmin imperiousness, and Davis's reaction: meek, downcast silence. This nearly catatonic creature is her mother's selfishly motivated handiwork, and when Mrs. Vale snaps at Dr. Jaquith's (Claude Rains) attempts to interfere, a psychiatrist brought in by Charlotte's concerned sister-in-law, Lisa (Ilka Chase), brusquely replies, "If you had deliberately and maliciously planned to destroy your daughter's life, you couldn't have done it more completely." Right on cue, the argument over her condition causes Charlotte to come unglued within minutes and to be taken straightaway to Cascade sanitarium.

After three months of counseling and support from the bromidic doctor, Charlotte is told she is well enough to leave. But since returning to such an unrepentant mother jeopardizes her fragile sanity, Charlotte's sister-in-law arranges for her to go on a cruise to South America to jump-start her new life—and she loans her a much spiffier wardrobe.

And this is where *Now, Voyager* becomes both delicious and memorable. It's one of the moments we recall when we cite Davis (along with Katharine Hepburn) as the screen's most potent female icon. And it's the scene that every plain

Charlotte Vale has been reborn triumphantly, and we're only a third of the way into the film.

But as we learn from the instructional note cards Lisa has pinned to each piece of Charlotte's attire that she reads with resentment but follows to the letter, clothes, for the moment are making the woman. Yet clearly they are doing their job, because she's already made quite an impression on fellow passenger Jerry Dorrance (Paul Henreid), a mature gentleman whose unforced charm and cashmere baritone both excites and unnerves her. Determined not to regress, Charlotte forges on and makes a bell-ringing entrance into the ship's dining room. With her hair dramatically swept off her neck into a high French twist, Davis reveals even more skin with a white, low-cut, cross-pleated, full-flowing gown that shows off Charlotte's significant weight loss and adds flourish to her look with a floor-sweeping cape embroidered with oversize sequined butterflies that are as dramatic as they are obviously symbolic. Despite her polish being all surface, never has Davis radiated such modernity as well as—especially for her core audience—such attainable sophistication.

It doesn't take long for Jerry to sense Charlotte's encroaching feelings of inferiority (then again, the note still pinned to the back of the cape is a pretty blatant tip-off). But his compassion not only initiates the first of the film's famous "double cigarette" moments, with Henreid igniting and inhaling two at once, then smoothly offering Davis one, but also stirs Charlotte's open confession about her tenuous mental state. How convenient that Jerry shows snapshots of his daughter, a budding version of the old Charlotte, due to the stress induced by his unseen, shrewish wife, a woman Jerry's friends are all too eager to imply has been swimming in the same gene pool as Charlotte's mother.

The insurmountable situation deems a shipboard romance both inevitable and finite, but thanks to her seemingly bottomless unofficial trousseau, our heroine literally blossoms: at the cruise's end, when the couple embraces passionately after agreeing to part forever, Davis has a crown of flowers in her hair.

Buoyed by newfound confidence and attired in an even bolder Orry-Kelly wardrobe, this time of her own choosing, the acknowledged belle of the boat returns home to the expected volley of vitriol, first directed at Charlotte's

Jane can look to and find hope and salvation. We are on the ship and its tony passengers are impatiently waiting to set sail, but they're missing one passenger. Where is Charlotte? Suddenly, the cruise director (the always fey Franklin Pangborn), spying her at the top of the gangplank, gushes, "Sssh, here she is." And once again, the camera comes in on a shoe, but this time it is a two-toned spectator pump with a distinctly low vamp. Then we see stockings instead of that heavy hose that once covered her legs, followed by a smart handbag, white elbow-length gloves, and a slimmer figure. So where is she already? But Rapper teases us even more as he moves to the top of a sleek, wide-trimmed chapeau. Oh, it's a fabulous hat. You would wear it today if you had the nerve. Finally, the camera pans down below the light veil to a face still in half shadow, but we can make out porcelain skin, those inimitable Bette Davis eyes made up in full force, and perfectly applied lipstick. The lady wears a crisply tailored, belted dark suit with wide stand-up white lapels; a sharp, cutaway peplum; and a pencil skirt. Best of all, those bushy eyebrows are now perfectly arched and plucked. This is a woman obviously worth waiting for.

slim black skirt suit set off by an exuberant placquette of white ruffles, and then activated by her mother's demand to reestablish their old way of life. Davis responds by showing up for dinner and startling her pinched and haughty relatives in an urbane, figure-hugging black velvet gown, with a spray of gardenias (courtesy of Jerry) pinned to her deep décolletage, and a forthright can't-scare-me attitude to match. So desperate is her mother to stunt Charlotte's liberation and return her to a state of ready manipulation, that she throws herself down a grand staircase. Not the smartest move, considering that the stunt doesn't work, and that after delivering one final insult to her daughter, the detestable oppressor dies, leaving Charlotte strong, assured, and rich.

But married? Not in a women's picture. Charlotte does attract another suitor but turns down his proposal once Jerry unexpectedly appears again and rekindles her love. However, Jerry's wife soon pulls a severe but undisclosed stunt that leaves him still mired in emotional quicksand and somehow sends his woebegone daughter to Cascade. Clad in a soigné broad-shouldered black coat and a beret, Charlotte visits and befriends the girl. She then convinces Dr. Jaquith that after all

she's been through she's as qualified as he is to get the girl well, and she does. Charlotte even takes her home to live with her.

At the end of the film, poor, eternally anchored Jerry visits Charlotte at home. Standing before a large window revealing a clear night sky, he says how glad he is to see his daughter so happy and agrees to let her stay with Charlotte. "Shall we just have a cigarette on it?" Jerry asks. Charlotte strides forward in a simple flowing high-necked blouse and long skirt and offers him the cigarette box as composer Max Steiner's theme swells one more time. Jerry asks if he can visit. "There are people here who love you," she replies, and then asks if he will help her "protect that little strip of territory that's ours," offering a way to avoid becoming too emotional when talking about his child. Jerry insists the girl is now "our child," and Charlotte thanks him. Then he asks if Charlotte will be happy. And in the softest, most feminine voice Davis has ever been able to muster, she replies, "Oh, Jerry, don't ask for the moon. We have the stars." And she has his daughter. In some states, this is called kidnapping. In a woman's picture, this is as happily ever after as it gets.

THE LAST DANCE

Alexander McQueen's
Spring/Summer 2004
"Deliverance" Collection

There's no debating that *Wuthering Heights* is one of literature's great sagas of love. However, it's surprising how many overlook the fact that it is also an equally powerful epic about the dark side of passion. Thanks to William Wyler's 1939 classic screen adaptation, for many the tale is captured in the glorious shot of the spirits of Cathy (Merle Oberon) and Heathcliff (Laurence Olivier) standing together, facing the heavens on a windblown heath. But Wyler's adaptation only covered seventeen of the novel's thirty-four chapters, and that indelible screen image is of a love imagined but never realized. In fact, much of the novel, especially the second half, is driven almost solely by jealousy and revenge. The novel is a more shadowy and richer tale because of author Emily Brontë's belief that pain and love are inextricably intertwined. Maybe that's why it's a shame that Alexander McQueen, a designer so vocal about how film inspired and ignited his imagination, never got to do costumes for a production of *Wuthering Heights*. It could have been a match made in purgatory.

McQueen admitted that he found "beauty in the grotesque, like most artists." It drove him to bind models in leather harnesses, trap them in wind tunnels, cover their faces in leather masks, or make them walk on heels nearly a foot high. But if his designs were meant solely as elegantly crafted torture, the world would not have been so bewitched and bothered by his unsettling creativity. Equipped with bespoke tailor training, blessed with a cinematic eye that rivaled the great surreal directors like Luis Buñuel and David Lynch, and addicted to a near maniacal fervor for craftsmanship, McQueen refused to celebrate the obvious signposts of beauty. Instead, he revealed it in the unlikeliest places: within the rigid

parameters of angularly exaggerated silhouettes he devised to match the rigors and set pieces of a chess game (spring 2005). He cloaked the woman he entrapped in the wind tunnel in gossamer fabrics that made her soar and triumph against the elements (fall 2003). He lifted sketches of insects and other creatures at the lower end of Darwin's *The Origin of the Species* and wove them into silk prints of wonder (spring 2010). Even with Edith Head's help, Hitchcock never dressed his blondes as chicly as McQueen did when he took up temporary residence within the director's kingdom of *The Birds* (spring 2005). And there may be no more hypnotic moment in any fashion show than that of Kate Moss as a holographic apparition floating mysteriously in cascades of organza while trapped inside a glass pyramid (fall 2006). For McQueen, romance was defined by tension not bliss. "People find my things sometimes aggressive," he said. "But I don't see it as aggressive. I see it as romantic, dealing with the dark side of personality."

For his spring/summer 2004 collection, McQueen stepped inside yet another film that sought love among the ruins. His inspiration for the evening was director Sydney Pollack's 1969 cinematic adaptation of Horace McCoy's nihilistic 1935 novel *They Shoot Horses, Don't They?*, which depicted Jane Fonda and Michael Sarrazin in one of the brutal, punishing dance marathons that were staged during the Great Depression as a microcosm for the era's inescapable desperation. Marathons were a perverse spectacle, more survival derby than flight of fancy (the one in the novel goes on for 879 hours), for the last couple left standing and still moving—forget about dancing—limped away with what most people during the Depression had too little of—cash.

To re-create the setting, the designer seated attendees around the perimeter of the main floor at the Salle Wagram, an ornate late-nineteenth-century venue in Paris that was once the site of aristocratic gatherings and numerous balls. As the room faded to black, a soft spotlight revealed the wide-eyed, Titian-tressed, spectral beauty of model Karen Elson, clad in sinuous silver lamé. But as she began to move, it wasn't to affect a model's customary lockstep. Elson started dancing—ballroom dancing. As her equally ravishing male partner swept her across the floor, she was joined there by a nonstop procession of light-footed women in godetted denim skirts, georgette florals, blue satin trenches, and diaphanous charmeuse gowns dancing with muscled sailors,

from black tank-topped lotharios with brilliantined hair to he-men in sequined T-shirts, each couple urgently caught up in executing precise choreography as if it were their only way of inhaling oxygen. Hypnotically lyrical as each outfit was, it was a challenge to focus on the gifted designer's consummate attention to detail and innovative tailoring because spectators were too busy swooning at this collectively whirling, rhythmic parade.

As a designer equally transfixed by a rose's thorns as its blossom, it's eerily logical that McQueen would set a collection of captivating allure against such an ominous backdrop, but what made the performance so memorable was McQueen's unexpected, wickedly infectious, almost gleeful take on the frenzy. To achieve authenticity, models and their partners rehearsed for two weeks under the tutelage of Scottish dancer and choreographer Michael Clark. But unlike the ever-diminishing pace of the luckless participants in the movie, this barely fifteen-minute "marathon" was marked by rapidly accelerating strides where dancers exhausted themselves by eagerly vying for our attention. The competition was fierce. Lace and tulle skirts accentuating each move of the tango gave way to a cha-cha done in intricately pieced denim over jeweled stockings. Both were then overrun by jitterbugging sprinters in pastel athletic wear, leaving in the dust spent beauties who seemed to crumble and fold into their tiers of handkerchief chiffon atop pearl encrusted boots. The marathon ended with Elson, dizzy and done in a shredded variation of her original silver gown, being carried aloft out of the hall to a standing ovation of blissful hysteria, while an uncharacteristically healthy, trim, and beaming McQueen appeared, well aware that he had created, as one critic wrote, "a show to die for."

A year after his death in 2010, the Metropolitan Museum of Art mounted an extensive exhibition of the designer's work called *Alexander McQueen: Savage Beauty*. The show was a blockbuster: the Met had to open earlier, stay open later, alter traffic patterns within the museum, and extend the exhibition's stay to accommodate visitor demand, which rivaled record attendances for previous exhibitions such as *The Treasures of King Tutankhamun* and Leonardo da Vinci's *Mona Lisa*. By the end of the four-month show, which included turn-away crowds on its last day, 661,509 visitors had come to the museum solely to witness McQueen's visions of beauty, a sure sign he was never alone in finding a romantic spirit in the dark.

LIKE THE BAHAMIAN SUN

Michelle Williams and
Heath Ledger at
the Academy Awards, 2006

With her gamine features, platinum pixie haircut, and ever-present wee-bit-reticent smile, she seems both unthreatening and instantly appealing. Plus anyone who grew up watching her as the mercurial Jen on *Dawson's Creek* can't help but feel like it would be no big deal to wave and say hello if you crossed shopping carts with Michelle Williams at Whole Foods. Even on a red carpet, which she should be used to traversing by now, since she has already been nominated for a trio of Golden Globes, BAFTAs, and Academy Awards, she poses graciously and can sustain about three questions worth of frothiness for each requisite stand-up interview, yet she certainly doesn't possess the commanding presence that seems to be second nature to Charlize Theron. But her self-effacement is precisely what made her 2011 performance as the greatest blond bombshell of them all in *My Week with Marilyn* so shockingly swell. Who knew she could be such a scene-stealer?

Well, if you were caught totally unawares, then your red-carpet memory is way too short, because in 2006, Williams blushed at the attention but literally outshone every actress on the ruby runner at the Academy Awards. Despite the CIA-like secrecy that surrounds Hollywood's ultimate peacock strut, to look around that night, it was as if everyone else knew she was coming and what she was wearing and decided not to get in her way. Sandra Bullock wore navy. Jennifer Lopez chose an atypical olive green. Amy Adams had on mocha brown. Meryl Streep was in taupe. Uma Thurman wore nude. Reese Witherspoon was in antique ivory vintage, and the majestic Theron wore

a Dior that could only be termed charcoal green. Color was virtually nowhere. And then, like the sun breaking through a sky of low clouds, there was Michelle Williams standing next to Heath Ledger in a gown of graceful folds that fanned sensually with her every footstep. But it was the color that killed. The press called the dress "saffron" and "marigold," but its designer, Vera Wang, insists it is "Bahamian yellow." Whatever name you choose, it marked a one-and-only red-carpet moment, the dress a beacon, directing the world's attention on a deserving star—and the couple of the hour.

"The color had me so worried," says Wang. "Kate Young, Michelle's stylist, asked me to do something for Michelle and had seen a dress similar to this one that we did in pale lavender. She loved the pleated collar and the ruched gathering under the stomach because it was young and fresh and the exact opposite of the endless procession of strapless bustier gowns that had become the Hollywood formula. I mean, I loved it, too—it is my dress—but it's not what people expect to see at awards shows, and you know how cruel they can be when you step away from the norm."

Everything changed, however, when the young couple, who had fallen in love in 2004 while shooting *Brokeback Mountain*, the film for which they were both nominated for awards, visited Wang at her design studio. "They were both dressed very casually, the way every other young couple living in Brooklyn before it got too chic for young couples to live there would dress to hang out. Heath was holding their baby, Matilda, in a car seat. Michelle kept beaming at Matilda. She just radiated light. And he was so warm and gracious and, well, he looked like Heath Ledger, which is a hell of an accessory; she could have worn jeans and been declared Best Dressed. Of course, I'm joking, sort of."

Consequently, Wang knew the soft, deconstructed flow and drape of the dress Williams favored would be perfect for her. The color, though, "was Heath's and Kate's idea. He liked the way it awakened her skin color because she is so pale. Michelle liked it because it made Matilda widen her eyes. Kate liked it because she knew no one else would have the guts to wear it and she figured they were this year's golden duo. And I finally came around because I thought it was a fascinating juxtaposition against a dress that had such an early 1930s feel to it."

Wang believes there are two factors that ensured the gown's current placement on virtually every all-time best-dressed Oscar list. "When you are working with silk tulle or chiffon you can never do a dress in just one color. Like the tangerine gown we did for Charlize [Theron] in 2000, there are layers and layers of different tonalities, like lemon, green, rose, and others lining this dress underneath to absorb the intense lights so that the surface color stays true." The other factor? "The bright red lip," insists Wang. "I wasn't in the room for the decision, but whoever thought that one up was a genius."

Neither Michelle nor Heath won Oscars that night, but they were the brightest stars on the red carpet and in the media. The couple separated in late 2007, and in January 2008, Ledger died of an accidental drug overdose in a rented loft in New York City. He won a posthumous Oscar the following year for his portrayal of the Joker in *The Dark Knight*. Williams has been nominated two more times for Academy Awards for her work in *Blue Valentine* and the aforementioned *Marilyn*. In 2014, she made three bold moves: she took on the role of Sally Bowles in the Broadway revival of *Cabaret*, she lent her tender beauty to Louis Vuitton's fall accessory campaign, and she sold the Brooklyn home that she had bought with Ledger, moving to Los Angeles. "I wish we all lived in the movies, the happily-ever-after ones anyway," says Wang. "But that night at the Oscars they were a love story."

FAMILY TIES

Maria's Handiwork in
The Sound of Music, 1965

The opening is simply get-ready-for-it thrilling, every single time, with that incredible tracking shot that first glides over the apexes of the Alps, then rises up the treacherous crags and down into the verdant valleys, until the camera discovers a lone woman on a sloping hillside delighted in her solitude, surrounded by all that she loves for now. The closer we come, the more the orchestra swells, the more she moves, the faster we breathe, the more eager we are to have her burst into song and then, by God, she does, and we swear the hills really are alive!

But lustrous as Julie Andrews and that clarion voice of hers are, that is not why the movie has a permanent hold on so many of our hearts. The answer is obvious, however, if you've ever been lucky enough to attend the best of all the sing-along *Sound of Music* events held around the world each year. On a night in late June, one of Los Angeles's most appealing landmarks, the deco-arched Hollywood Bowl, becomes the largest open-air theater in the world, its massive screen and near-perfect sound system attracts more than seventeen thousand hardly pitch-perfect fans, mainly moms, dads, their kids, grandparents, cousins, and friends, who come with picnic baskets and blankets to celebrate why this movie has had them singing, shouting, clapping, and hissing for fifty years. *The Sound of Music* swells chests and strains vocal cords because it is the medium's most extravagant valentine to the love of family. It's about the strength one acquires when you're reminded you don't have to face a challenge alone. It's about the happiness we derive from putting others first. And sweetest of all, it's about the fact that love may come when and from where you least expect it.

Captain von Trapp certainly didn't expect to fall for any-one who behaved or dressed like Maria. Granted, some artistic license has to be granted in the costuming for the film, because it must have been tough for Christopher Plummer as Captain von Trapp not to be immediately entranced by Julie Andrews, since the rest of the world was instantly smitten from the first time they saw her, whether it was her debut as Eliza Doolittle on Broadway in *My Fair Lady* (1956), playing Cinderella on television (1957), or making her Academy Award–winning screen debut as *Mary Poppins* (1964).

Nevertheless, the outfit the willful postulant turns up in at the von Trapp villa to begin her work as governess to the captain's brood of seven must have made things a little easier for Plummer. Though it is a pretty close approximation of what the real Maria Augusta Kutschera wore when she first met Georg von Trapp in 1926, it's a doozy. The shapeless, cropped, boxy taupe jacket with its high neck and oddly

overscaled buttons worn over a long slate-gray textured dirndl skirt look as if they could have been stitched up from hair shirts. To say the wide-brimmed straw hat completes the look is not a compliment. What's worse, when the cap-tain suggests Maria change clothes to meet the children, she states she hasn't anything else to wear, since potential nuns give all their worldly possessions to the poor. When the cap-tain then questions how this ensemble managed to remain behind, Maria flatly replies, "I guess nobody wanted it."

Photographs of the real Maria von Trapp leave no doubt that she was no beauty, and in her memoir *The Story of the Trapp Family Singers,* she frankly admits that it was the children she first fell in love with, not the captain. Her affection for him developed only after marriage. In the film, however, no matter how intensely costume designer Dorothy Jeakins tries to bury Andrews under sartorial injustices, there is no tamping down the incandescence of one of the

her ingenious, rebellious decision, so we don't witness her cutting, pinning, and sewing. Rather suddenly, the kids' colorless and restrictive sailor suits vanish and are replaced by complementary play clothes made from the curtains' damask-like brocade featuring an olive baroque pattern against a field of cream. Frankly, while the clothes fit very well and are certainly lively, they aren't really all that attractive. But what's noteworthy is that the kids are infused with the energy that comes with wearing a garment that offers them freedom and appreciation for the fact that Maria is dressed exactly the same way. Though the captain is furious when he spies his kids sporting repurposed window treatments, Maria is unrepentant. The new clothes certify Maria and the children as a unified front.

It only takes the sight of Maria in a short robin's-egg-blue chiffon dress almost the same color as Andrews's eyes to finally win the captain's heart. Well, that and a folk dance. At the ball the captain hosts at the insistence of his fiancée, the baroness, the children watch in awe as elegantly attired guests engage in an Austrian waltz-like folkdance called the ländler. As Maria begins teaching it to the children, the captain steps in to lend a hand by taking hers. The unlikely pair instantly move like competition ballroom dancers. And just as Maria's rising emotions cause her to hesitate, the captain firmly grasps her hand and, as the camera comes in close, they spin in a tight circle. Though the shot is taken from Maria's perspective, there is only one place the captain is gazing, and her eyes tell us the look they exchange is unambiguous. Maria blushes and pulls away, aghast and helpless upon realizing that her calling is not with god. The captain senses her confusion and doesn't say a word. Love may be wonderful the second time around, but the first time can be terrifying, especially when you had your mind set on celibacy. A panicked Maria retreats to the abbey.

Redirected by the Reverend Mother to climb every mountain but not until after she returns to the captain's villa, Maria goes back. Maria is embraced by the children, the captain kisses her in the gazebo, and cued by the brood's unequivocal blessing, the massive orchestra that serenaded her on the hillside now swells into a triumphal wedding march interpretation of "How Do You Solve a Problem like Maria?" as the camera cuts to the captain and his former governess exchanging vows in the abbey's cathedral.

After two hours of watching poor Julie outshine a prosaically unflattering wardrobe, Maria's wedding gown is

screen's most lovable stars, so it was wise of director Robert Wise to immediately induce and exploit a percolating sexual dynamic between her and Plummer. However, despite the liberties the musical takes with the actual family von Trapp timeline (Maria arrived years before Hitler's rise and the Germany-Austrian Anschluss. The three children she bore with the captain are edited out of the story), the film does faithfully begin with the new governess's courtship of the kids.

Maria wastes no time in ending the period of house arrest imposed on the children by their still-grieving widowed father. With her, they savor Salzburg, shopping in the al fresco markets, going on bike rides and boating trips, creating puppet shows and singing incessantly all the way. But what unites them most strongly for us are the new "uniforms" Maria makes for them. Though the captain has bolts of fabric delivered to the self-proclaimed seamstress's room almost before Maria can unpack her luggage, she appears uninterested in the selection. Instead, she is immediately fixated on her soon-to-be-discarded bedroom drapes. The movie is canny in not belaboring

Andrews's only overtly stylish moment. It is also a masterful example of a costumer's skill, for without betraying the sensibility of a woman who had initially chosen to be a nun, Dorothy Jeakins designed an extremely modest dress with undeniable sensuality. The long-sleeved, full-skirted, ivory silk gown frames Andrews's face with a regally high stand-up collar that rises from overlapping curved panels that cover its Empire bodice, but instead of a skirt that falls loosely from the bust as it does in a classic Empire silhouette, the gown is highly form-fitted at the waist. Due to her choice of film roles, Andrews's highly curvaceous figure was too often obscured or overlooked. Oddly enough, it's her wedding gown in *The Sound of Music* that most handsomely shows her off. The skirt falls full without pleats from the corseted waist and forms a short train in the back. After the film's release, the gown was stored for years at Western Costume Supply in Los Angeles, where it was constantly borrowed.

The long dress didn't necessarily start a trend though, since its silhouette and volume were in opposition to the most popular wedding dresses of the period, that is,

trapeze and A-line white minis, like the structured suit-dress Mia Farrow wore to wed Frank Sinatra in 1965, or the lacy shift Raquel Welch chose to wed her publicist Patrick Curtis one year later. Nevertheless, Andrews said, "I've never felt as beautiful as when I wore that wedding gown . . . before or since." The dress's only extravagantly cinematic feature is its long tulle veil that forms a train that goes way beyond the gown, seeming to span half the length of the cathedral when captured in the famous over-head shot during the processional.

At the Hollywood Bowl's *Sound of Music* sing-along, many come in costume. There aren't many wedding dresses because they take up too much room, but there are plenty of girls in white dresses with blue satin sashes and kids dressed as brown paper packages tied up with string. But my favorite costume may be the one worn by the evening's host, television actress Melissa Peterman. Almost every year, she opts for an evening gown, featuring a print nearly identical to the one that decorated the old drapes Maria made into play clothes. It doesn't look bad at all.

HER
ONE AND
ONLY

Carrie's Great Love on
Sex and the City, 2002

Sarah Jessica Parker may be the only New York City resident in the last two decades universally adored by a populace that takes undue pride in not agreeing on anything except for their love of Central Park and the Coney Island Cyclone. First of all, we owe her big-time. Rudy Giuliani cut down on crime, and Michael Bloomberg attracted big business and built those useless bike lanes, but it was Sarah's portrayal of Carrie Bradshaw and her stiletto-heeled gang on HBO's *Sex and the City* who notified the rest of the world that a fiscally rejuvenated New York City was once again the most round-the-clock thrilling, forever challenging, wish-fulfilling, obsessively spontaneous, who-knows-what's-around-the-corner, sexy city on the planet. And what made Carrie's rhapsodic testimonial even more seductive was she wasn't directing it at wide-eyed innocents.

Sex and the City was designed for grown-ups, specifically single women in their thirties and forties—and its message was as tantalizing as it was full of hope: your ship hasn't sailed; you're just docked in the wrong port. It presented Manhattan as an enchanted island where the life you crave was all about you; where you could exercise your ambition; go shopping for what ails you; have lots of dates; lots of lovers; and lots of sex; and then share lots of juicy talk about all of the above with friends who had your back.

Entertainment had never seen a circle of women as boldly striving and committed to each other as Carrie, Miranda, Samantha, and Charlotte, laying claim to a territory show creator Darren Star saw as more accessible than, yet just as alien as, the worlds visited by the *Starship Enterprise*. The women on *Sex and the City* were urban astronauts wearing flight suits from Bergdorf Goodman.

By its third season on HBO, it seemed that anyone who craved style, hipness, fun, and sex were dutifully following and imitating the quartet as they guiltlessly surrendered to their indulgences. Thanks to our lust for *Sex*, we revived martinis, couldn't down cosmopolitans fast enough, justified our Starbucks and BlackBerry addictions, and made Botox part of our beauty regimen. We discovered—with the brilliant costumer designer Pat Field's help—that to live the good life required dutiful patronage of Jimmy Choo; Christian Louboutin; vintage clothing stores; Chanel; Bed, Bath & Beyond; Dior; Dolce & Gabbana; Prada; Oscar de la Renta; Banana Republic; and the New York Knicks. The following four brands, however, will forever be in the show's debt: *Vogue*, which Carrie ranked up there with the Gutenberg Bible; the Fendi Baguette, which seemed Krazy Glued to Carrie's arm for the first few seasons; "Manolos," her Cinderella slipper of choice; and last, but hardly least, Magnolia Bakery. In fact, the transformation of the West Village's Bleecker Street from a funky collection of thrift shops, bookstores, and antiques emporiums to an unbroken designer row including a Marc Jacobs or Ralph Lauren store every fifty feet is directly due to upscale retailers' desire to cash in on the hordes that lined up outside Magnolia seeking the same cupcakes Carrie and Stanford couldn't resist.

Carrie had twenty-five boyfriends during *SATC*'s six-season run, including Aidan and Mr. Big. But there was only one she never broke up with or cheated on, and she reminded us of her true-blue affection when it was needed most. At the start of season five, New Yorkers were still trying to absorb and recover from the horror of the terrorist attacks of 9/11. They felt beaten, insecure, and scared. If that's not enough to deal with, the season begins with romantic disaster: all four women have been dumped, divorced, or separated. Cheering up is in order.

Ever the optimist, Carrie begins the first episode by meeting her friends for dinner after indulging in one of her favorite pastimes—going to the movies alone. Charlotte can't believe anyone would do that, fearful as she is of being looked at as "that poor, pathetic girl." Carrie retaliates by insisting that "you are never alone in New York," and that it's the perfect place to be single. When Miranda teases Carrie about having a crush on her hometown, Carrie says, "[I've been] dating the city for eighteen years and I think it's getting kind of serious. I think I'm in love."

Charlotte counters with something she read—and took as fact—in a magazine that claims you can only have two great loves in your lifetime. Having loved and lost Aidan and Mr. Big, Carrie shuts down Charlotte by asking if she is therefore "done." Luckily, the mood is lifted as the four leave the restaurant and immediately spot three smiling, adorable servicemen, a sure sign that it is Fleet Week: "That one week a year," says Carrie, "when our fair city is made even fairer by cute, sweet American sailors looking for fun." As it happens, Carrie gets saved from a punishing rainstorm by a handsome seaman who hails her a cab and invites her to a Fleet Week party. Miranda is sidelined with her new baby, but Carrie, Samantha, and Charlotte decide it's their patriotic duty to attend. Soon surrounded by lust-happy sailors, Samantha and Charlotte dive right in. But Carrie's not in a frivolous mood and is just about to leave when she runs into Louis, her chivalrous sailor who, in a drawl laced with tupelo honey, tells her, "I came all the way from Louisiana to dance with a New York City girl." Carrie blushingly obliges.

Louis is smooth and appealing, so Carrie asks him, "How many great loves do you think you have in a lifetime?" He says, "Maybe one, if you are lucky," and offers a great dimpled smile. Carrie cozies up and tells him that she's glad she stayed after all, especially "after the way the city kicked [her] ass this week." Louis then admits that it's his first trip to New York and that it's "not for [him] . . . the garbage, the noise . . . [he doesn't] know how [she] put[s] up with it," as he comes in for a kiss. Instead, Carrie pulls away, says thanks, and reaches for her clutch to leave. The stunned sailor asks her how she could go home all alone, as "it's rough out there." Carrie replies, "It isn't so bad," and gives him a salute.

As she walks down the streets of her hometown, we hear Parker's voiceover: "If Louis was right and you only get one great love, then New York may just be mine. And I can't have nobody talking shit about my boyfriend." The night the episode first aired, I don't know one New Yorker who watched and didn't cry like a baby. Carrie would have made a great mayor.

DESTINATION: UNFORGETTABLE

Marc Jacobs for Louis Vuitton,
Fall/Winter Collection, 2012

Marc Jacobs has no interest in sending clothes out on a raised pathway covered in white fabric that cuts through the middle of a bare, well-lit tent. "It's called a fashion *show*," says the designer emphatically, as if he has no idea how anyone could think otherwise. "To me it's simple logic to produce a theatrical experience, so that you walk in off a city street and find yourself in another world, engulfed in the sounds and vision of what you aren't used to. If that space creates a context of its own, you are bound to see the fashion presented with a fresh eye."

After two decades devoted to finding new ways to go through the looking glass, Jacobs has confirmed that his imagination is limitless. Who else has challenged us with collections as wide-ranging, often diametrically opposed to the highly praised one that came prior to it, and always exhibiting a brazen indifference to the trends his contemporaries are mining? For each of these singular wardrobes, Jacobs has triumphed in setting them in such unpredictable worlds of wonder, that with the exception of Karl Lagerfeld for Chanel, no other designers' shows in any of the four fashion capitals are greeted with the crazed anticipation normally reserved for a major rock star—and that goes for presentations he does for his own label as well as the ones he produced in his fifteen years as creative director for Louis Vuitton.

For his Marc Jacobs line, the elaborate concepts he brings to fruition in one of two Manhattan armories are more stylistically cerebral, transporting the audience to a rock- candy apocalypse, a Dickensian main street, a ten-cents-a-dance hall, or to a plateau under five hundred dove-gray clouds with a serenely weary Jessica Lange narrating the lyrics of "Happy Days Are Here Again."

As hypnotic, sometimes odd, but always provocative as the armory shows have been, there was a reason why, no matter how exhausted journalists, retailers, and buyers may have been of the monthlong fashion week marathon, no one dared to take an early flight out on the last day of Paris Fashion Week. Jacobs's euphoric shows for Louis Vuitton boasted the kind of Ziegfeldian showmanship that is only possible when a man with a passion to match his talent is given a blank check and full creative rein. For Vuitton, Jacobs would set the stage in a massive clear tent in the Louvre's front courtyard, the Cour Carrée. He once erected a fountain so elaborate that, had it stayed, tourists would be throwing coins in it daily. He built and appointed

a carousel no state fair or Neverland Ranch could better. And he installed a quartet of rococo-framed elevators that opened into a world of erotica so menacing you were sure Belle de Jour had a room down the hall.

But Jacobs's masterstroke was the Louis Vuitton Express, which ran during fall/winter 2012 Paris Fashion Week, at the same time as the Musée des Arts Décoratifs staged an exhibition entitled *Louis Vuitton/Marc Jacobs*, contrasting the contributions of the two artists to this multibillion-dollar brand. While working on the installation, Jacobs became fascinated by "the obsession for travel people used to have. There was so much romance in how people thought about how to get there, what to take, how to pack it, what to pack it in, and how they should dress for the send-off."

Unlike other designers, who claim inspiration hit them while on safari, resulting in an entire collection of dashikis and wood jewelry, for Jacobs, a catalyst is just the start of his ongoing creative process. He says, "The glamour in those old ways got me thinking that, for me, travel is kind of melancholy and bittersweet but in a beautiful way. Am I leaving something? Am I going towards somebody? I often find myself crying, which brought me to [an] exhilaration of trains, because they move at [a] pace that enables you to see where you're headed or leaving from, which makes you more emotional and vulnerable. And who was more vulnerable and thrilling than Barbra [Streisand] in the scene in *Funny Girl* where she is on a B & O railroad car wearing her wide-collared tangerine coat, sable hat, and muff going off to see [Omar Sharif]—singing with her head out the window. So I said to my incredible collaborator Katie Grand, 'For the next show, let's have a train!'"

This romantic presentation began in Vuitton's massive clear tent as usual, but this time it was dark. Moody indigo spotlights revealed little more than Belle Époque trusses reaching the pitched ceiling and a massive amber-lit Louis Vuitton clock on the far wall. You felt as if you were in Paris's Gare du Nord station during a power outage. Fabric covered the floor area where a runway would normally go, and the audience was sternly cautioned to stay away.

At 10:05 A.M. on the Vuitton clock, the cloth on the floor was removed as the curtains behind the clock opened. A blasting train whistle sounded, and at once there was steam everywhere. When the steam partially cleared, it was apparent there was no runway under the fabric. There were train tracks.

Then came twice as much steam, and through its shadowy haze chugged the Louis Vuitton Express, an $8 million, navy-blue enamel and gold full-scale replica of a vintage train. In the elaborately detailed interior were Jacobs's models. Each sat on a numbered custom upholstery seat (corresponding to the number of the look she wore for

the show) with their accessories on an overhead brass luggage rack. By the time the stealthily moving locomotive came to a halt, the audience was delirious—and the fantasy hadn't even reached its final destination.

"We had gone so far on the runway with bags, which, of course, is the company's signature," says Jacobs. "We started with a dozen bags one season, then twenty, until finally every model was carrying a bag at shows. How do you top that? Well, what does every marvelous train like the Orient Express have plenty of? Porters."

As the girls alighted from the train to a sweeping symphonic Philip Glass score, they carried no bags but were accompanied by their own personal porter toting a combination of three or more suitcases, handbags, carry-ons, and hatboxes. The luggage was the most elaborate LV bags ever seen, lavishly crafted in kangaroo, ostrich, and other exotic fabrics; others featured LV-logo-embossed patents combined with weaves of leather, metals, brilliants, and bugle beads.

The elaborate period clothes would have fit right into Fanny Brice's trousseau. Fully cut A-lined coats in multicolored patterns or brocades with wide portrait collars and matching calf-length skirts and full pants, deep bouclé long cardigans over hand-painted chiffon florals, square-neck jacquard silk gowns, each under a massive Stephen Jones chapeau with feathers wide enough to shield any rain on your parade popping out of a brim.

Were the clothes in a style that most women could wear? Of course not. But the bags, totes, satchels, and trunks were what millions of Vuitton addicts live for, and there were waiting lists on styles before they ever reached the stores.

As for the train, it made its way to Shanghai for a restaging of the show. But as for the Vuitton's Belle Époque mood, by spring 2013, that trip was over. Instead, Jacobs presented a collection that riffed off op art, with massive canary-yellow-and-white straight coats, black-and-white-check shifts, and every skirt was a mini. "I can't stay on things too long," says Marc. "If I do that I get so bored. I've got to move on to something else." And we are right behind him. Waiting.

ACKNOWLEDGMENTS

I've lost count of how many times I've been introduced to someone at a party or charity event and heard my newfound acquaintance say, "You're a writer! Gosh, I would love to write. I've kinda thought about it . . . ." Naturally, I smile. Who doesn't love a compliment? But the irony of their cocktail chatter is that writing is a far less social occupation than being a Carmelite nun.

While toiling at magazines and newspapers for decades has enabled me to shut out most verbal distraction—from pithy debates over which evening clutch looks too chunky to fever-pitch morning after March Madness reassessments—ideally I prefer to write surrounded by silence. Television off. Playlist off (I just end up singing, or dancing). And people, most definitely, off-limits.

If I do venture from my chosen cloister, it's usually to a library, not exactly a hotbed of interaction. And though movies and videos, depending on their subject matter can provoke communal giggles, or, even better, a snuggly twosome, it's cruel and unusual punishment to engage the company of others when watching a film for a book such as this one, rewinding repeatedly, running scenes frame by frame, and then hitting pause to make notes.

Consequently, such self-imposed isolation inevitably breeds the delusion that I have written this book with no help from anyone. I did it all by myself, so, baby, take a solo bow!

But having reengaged with mankind and after reading the manuscript, I realize it's not exactly true.

I do admit with undue pride that I have a damn good memory—my husband purports mine to be among the world's largest repository of pop-cultural minutiae and semi-vital knowledge—and I've been lucky enough to have been present for many of the seismic and noteworthy occasions that appear in this book. But those who actually created many of these momentous events and entertainments cited here saw them from vantage points that gave them illuminating insights and observations beyond the reach of any mere eyewitness. Therefore, I am deeply indebted to the accessibility and razor-sharp total recall of designers Giorgio Armani, John Galliano, Marc Jacobs, Donna Karan, Calvin Klein, Michael Kors, Ralph Lauren, Bob Mackie, Isaac Mizrahi, and Vera Wang in helping to bring their specific histories alive once more.

Nor could any rock critic or enthusiast hope to match the vitality of Courtney Love in recounting her world and time with Kurt Cobain. Who better to tell me what it was like to be an object of unconsummatable desire than Will's true Grace, Debra Messing? I'm equally obliged to the wit, compassion, and humanity of *Will & Grace*'s cocreator David Kohan for sharing his delight and surprise as to how he changed our world.

For years, the folks at Chanel have listened to my ravings about how their short film for Chanel N° 5 starring Nicole Kidman is superior to its inspiration, director Baz Luhrmann's *Moulin Rouge,* so their generosity as well as Karl Lagerfeld's in providing so many exclusive sketches and photographs of this production is immensely gratifying. I will forever cherish Gianni Versace's friendship and counsel, and blush remembering his capacity for joy and mischief. South Beach was never more giddy than witnessing his daily stroll along Ocean Drive turn into a parade.

In response to that question celebrity interviewers love to hypothetically ask, "If you could have lunch with anyone living or dead who would it be?" it almost takes a bit lip to suppress smirking with contented arrogance, because I've already fished my wish—not once, but twice. Dining with Gene Kelly, then spending the afternoon at his home in Beverly Hills when I was men's style editor for the *New York Times Magazine* was like seeing the face of . . . Gene Kelly, actually, since watching *Singin' in the Rain* is my idea of heaven. And sitting across from Diane Keaton in a booth at the Beverly Hills Hotel not only allowed me to experience how a director can become bewitched by a muse but also turned this least star-struck person ever to work at a magazine all about celebrity (*InStyle*) into such a gushy fan, I kept a post-interview voice mail of Keaton's on my phone for nearly a year because it sounded so deliciously like an outtake from *Annie Hall*.

Not all phone calls are as sparkling. But some are far more necessary and essential in achieving one's goals. A little more than two years ago, I decided to upend my life, routine, and career in order to rekindle the enthusiasm and challenges that once made my workday such a rush. People do this all the time (as have I, on two other occasions), except usually when decades younger. It was a big deal. Repositioning and refocusing my life took more time than I first imagined it would— and this book's publication was delayed a year.

So thank you, Nicole Hyatt, my photo editor, for your unwavering support, good taste, and endurance.

Despite the image put forth in films like *All the President's Men* and *His Girl Friday,* editors so staunchly and steadfastly on a writer's side are more rare than honest reporting. I was so late in delivering this book that Elizabeth Viscott Sullivan could have cut me loose. But she didn't. Instead, the little lady dug in her heels, then dug into my psyche, and in constant rotation she pushed, encouraged, prodded, steered, badgered, rallied, hovered, hailed, insisted, and inspired in ways that induced high anxiety and generated the best in me. Her uncanny ability to keep pace with a writer in both enthusiasm and knowledge is astonishing, not because she's done her homework but due to the vast, inherent knowledge she already has at her disposal. Her unwavering clarity in visualizing and steering a book toward its intended mission is maddening and ass-saving. I handed her entries I loved. She handed them back and asked for more so that everyone else could love them as much as I do. A good editor helps assemble the book you hope to write. A great editor gives you the opportunity to create a better book than you originally imagined. Writers should beat down her door.

Finally, it's not much fun to live with a writer on deadline, who returns your affection with a quick kiss and the false promise of "I'm almost done"; who, for the moment anyway, chooses staring at a computer screen over looking into your eyes. While in my head I was having the best time ever writing this book, I was quietly informed by David Nickle that I had turned into "the dullest person alive." I abandoned the person I adore most, forcing him to seek the companionship with the unsettling misfits on the Syfy channel and psychopaths who run amok in James Patterson's parallel universe. He never complained. He only pouted once. I know I can't pull off this schedule again. No one can be this patient twice. But all he ever said was, "Don't stop, but don't rush" and "Make sure Elizabeth is happy." You've got to love a man like that. Do I ever.

—Hal Rubenstein
New York City, 2015

SELECT BIBLIOGRAPHY

Books

Andrews, Bart. *The "I Love Lucy" Book*. New York: Crown (reissue edition), 1985.

Brooks, Tim, and Earl Marsh. *The Complete Directory to Prime Time Network and Cable TV Shows, 1946–Present*. New York: Ballantine, 1988.

Burns-Ardolino, Wendy. *Jiggle: (Re)shaping American Women*. Lanham, MD: Lexington, 2007.

Burton, Richard and Chris Williams. *The Richard Burton Diaries*. New Haven, Yale University Press, 2012

Christie's. *The Collection of Elizabeth Taylor: The Complete Set*. New York: Christie's, 2011.

Goldsmith, Lynn. *New Kids*. New York: Rizzoli, 1990.

Hewitt, Paolo. *Fab Gear: The Beatles and Fashion*. New York: Prestel, 2011.

Landis, Deborah Nadoolman. *Dressed: A Century of Hollywood Costume Design*. New York: Harper Design, 2007.

Lang, Michael. *The Road to Woodstock*. New York: HarperCollins, 2009.

Magill, Frank Northern, Stephen L. Hanson, and Patricia King Hanson. *Magill's Survey of Cinema—English Language Films,* second series, volume 6. New York: Salem Press, 1981.

Mann, William J. *How to Be a Movie Star: Elizabeth Taylor in Hollywood*. London: Faber & Faber, 2009.

Maslon, Laurence. *The Sound of Music Companion*. New York: Fireside, 2006.

Mazzeo, Tilar J. *The Secret of Chanel N°.5: The Intimate History of the World's Most Famous Perfume*. New York: HarperCollins, 2010.

Nelson, Thomas Allen. *Kubrick: Inside a Film Artist's Maze*. Bloomington, IN: Indiana University Press, 2000.

Phillips, Gene D., ed, *Stanley Kubrick: Interviews*. Jackson, MS: University of Mississippi Press, 2001.

Reichert, Tom. *The Erotic History of Advertising*. New York: Prometheus Books, 2003.

Rubenstein, Hal. *100 Unforgettable Dresses*. New York: Harper Design, 2011.

Sandford, Christopher. *McQueen: The Biography*. New York: Taylor Trade, 2003.

Santopietro, Tom. *Considering Doris Day*. New York: St. Martin's Press, 2007.

Segal, Erich. *Love Story*. New York: Harper & Row, 1970.

Stam, Robert. *Reflexivity in Film and Literature: From Don Quixote to Jean-Luc Godard*. New York: Columbia University Press (reprint edition), 1992.

Truffaut, François. *Hitchcock*. New York: Simon & Schuster, 1967.

Van Noten, Dries. *A Golden Anniversary*. Antwerp: Belgium: Dries Van Noten, 2005.

Van Noy, Nikki. *New Kids on the Block: Five Brothers and a Million Sisters*. New York: Touchstone Books, 2012.

Versace, Gianni. *Signatures*. Milan: Leonardo Arte, 1992.

———. *Vanitas*. Milan: Leonardo Arte, 1994.

Versace, Gianni, and Donatella Versace. *South Beach Stories*. Milan: Leonardo Arte, 1993.

Young, Caroline. *Classic Hollywood Style*. London: Francis Lincoln, 2012.

Newspapers and Periodicals

Bohlen, Celestine. "A New 'Lolita' Stalls in Europe." *New York Times*, September 23, 1997.

Foley, Bridget. "Q&A: Ralph Lauren Now." *Women's Wear Daily*, April 14, 2014.

Canby, Vincent. "Screen: Perfection and a 'Love Story': Erich Segal's Romantic Tale Begins Run." *New York Times*, December 18, 1970.

Cartner-Morley, Jessie. "Boy Done Good." *Guardian US Edition,* September 19, 2005.

Crowther, Bosley. "The Screen: 'Pillow Talk.'" *New York Times*, October 7, 1959.

Galloni, Alessandra. "The Future of Armani." *Wall Street Journal*, May 23, 2012.

James, Caryn. "Revisiting a Dangerous Obsession." *New York Times*, July 31, 1998.

Dougherty, Steve. "The Heartthrobs of America." *People*, April 13, 1990.

Hawthorne, Mary. "All True Love Must Die: Richard Burton's Diaries." *New Yorker*, January 30, 2013.

Kael, Pauline. "'Bonnie and Clyde.'" *New Yorker*, October 21, 1967.

Kanner, Bernice. "The Bra's Not for Burning." *New York*, December 12, 1983.

Kehr, Dave. "Two Smooth Operators on the Line— 'Pillow Talk,'" *New York Times*, May 11, 2012.

Larocca, Amy. "The $1 Billion Girl." *New York,* February 13, 2011.

Marin, Rick. "Grunge: A Success Story." *New York Times,* November 15, 1992.

McGrath, Douglas. "No More Que Será Será; Give Day Her Due." *New York Times*, January 8, 2010.

McKay, Nellie. "Eternal Sunshine." *New York Times*, June 3, 2007.

"Mick Jagger Rocks His Own Wedding Reception in St. Tropez." *Rolling Stone*, June 10, 1971.

Morris, Bernadine. "Fireworks and the Finale." *New York Times*, August 14, 1994.

Morrison, Patt. "Patt Morrison Asks: Doris Day." *Los Angeles Times*, January 7, 2012.

Morrow, Lance. "Middle America's Answer to Philip Roth." *New York*, April 27, 1970.

Nussbaum, Emily. "Sex and the City: Was It Still Okay to Drink Cosmos?" *New York,* August 27, 2011.

Peiffer, Kim. "Jessica Simpson: Accidental Fashion Mogul." *People Style Watch*, February 14, 2011.

Rubenstein, Hal. "How They Stole the Story." *The New York Times*, October 24, 1993.

Sebba, Anne, and Imogen Fox. "Wallis Simpson Used Fashion as a Weapon." *Guardian US Edition*, September 2, 2011.

Specter, Michael. "The Fantasist: How John Galliano Reimagined Fashion." *New Yorker*, September 22, 2003.

Spindler, Amy M. "Style; It's All About Yves." *New York Times*, January 9, 2000.

Spoto, Donald. "Alfred Hitchcock and His Infatuation with Tippi Hedren: The Real Story." *Times of London*, November 24, 2012.

Tauber, Michelle, and Mary Green. "Brad & Angelina: They Do!" *People*, September 15, 2014.

Wallace, Amy. "Deep Inside Baz Luhrmann's Creative Chaos." *New York Times*, February 7, 2014.

Welsh, Kenneth T. "The 1960s: Polarization, Cynicism, and the Youth Rebellion." *U.S. News & World Report,* March 12, 2010.

Online Articles

Abraham, Tamara. "Forget music . . . How Jessica Simpson's Fashion Empire Is on Course to Break $1billion in Sales." *DailyMail Online*, December 7, 2010, http://www.dailymail.co.uk/femail/article-1336474/Jessica-Simpson-course-fashions-1billion-woman-label-sales-soar.html.

Adams, Erik, Donna Bowman, Phil Dyess-Nugent, Genevieve Koski, Ryan McGee and Todd VanDerWerff. "More Than 60 Years Ago, a Pregnant Lucille Ball Couldn't Call Herself 'pregnant.'" *A.V. Club*, July 24, 2013, http://www.avclub.com/article/more-than-60-years-ago-a-pregnant-lucille-ball-cou-100629.

Annabelle. "The 8 Wedding Dresses & 7 Grooms of Elizabeth Taylor." Historical Honey, May 6, 2014, http://historicalhoney.com/wedding-dresses-grooms-elizabeth-taylor/.

Basye, Ali, "Cinemode: Armani Makes His Move with *American Gigolo*." *On This Day in Fashion*, February 1, 2011, http://onthisdayinfashion.com/?p=10602.

———. "Cinemode: Rebel Without a Cause." *On This Day in Fashion*, October 27, 2010, http://onthisdayinfashion.com/?p=7350.

"The Beatles." http://www.edsullivan.com. Accessed December 31, 2014.

Bella. "What Is Kinderwhore?" Rag and Magpie, February 15, 2011, http://www.ragandmagpie.co.uk/blog/2011/02/how-to-dress-kinderwhore/.

Blanks, Tim. "John Galliano's Fall 1999 Dior Haute Couture Collection." http://www.dailymotion.com, December 18, 2014.

———. "John Galliano's Fashion Opera for Dior Couture." Style.com, December 5, 2013, http://video.style.com/watch/throwback-thursdays-with-tim-blanks-john-galliano-s-fashion-opera-at-christian-dior.

Blondeatthefilm. "Now, Voyager." *Blonde at the Film*, September 17, 2014, http://theblondeatthefilm.com/2014/09/17/now-voyager-1942/.

"Chanel N° 5: The Story Behind the Classic Fragrance." BBC News, May 29, 2011, http://www.bbc.co.uk/news/world-13565155.

"Cinema Style File: Steve McQueen Steals High Style in 1968's *Thomas Crown Affair*." *GlamAmor*, May 8, 2012, http://www.glamamor.com/2012/05/cinema-style-file-steve-mcqueen-steals.html.

"The Classic American Success Story." History of Schott NYC, https://www.schottnyc.com/about.cfm. Accessed November 25, 2014.

Cobain, Kurt. "Suicide note." http://kurtcobainssuicidenote.com/kurt_cobains_suicide_note_scan.html,. Accessed January 5, 2015.

Correze Tout de Suite Ailleur. "The Cistercian Abbey at Aubazine." http://www.tourismecorreze.com. Accessed December 8, 2014.

Dirks, Tim. "Filmsite Movie Review: 'Now Voyager' (1942)." AMC Filmsite, http://www.filmsite.org/nowv.html.

———. "Filmsite Movie Review: 'Romeo and Juliet' (1968)." AMC Filmsite, http://www.filmsite.org/rome.html.

Doyle, Jack. "The Love Story Saga." *Pop History Dig*, http://www.pophistorydig.com/topics/"the-love-story-saga"1970-1977/.

"The Duchess of Windsor and Her Dress." *The Royal Order of Sartorial Splendor,* June 26, 2013, http://orderofsplendor.blogspot.com/2013/06/wedding-wednesday-duchess-of-windsor.html.

Ebert, Roger. "Bonnie and Clyde." RogerEbert.com, September 25, 1967, http://www.rogerebert.com/reviews/bonnie-and-clyde-1967.

———. "Great Movie: Romeo and Juliet." RogerEbert.com, September 17, 2000, http://www.rogerebert.com/reviews/great-movie-romeo-and-juliet-1968.

———. "Interview with Sonny and Cher." RogerEbert.com, May 7, 1967, http://www.rogerebert.com/interviews/interview-with-sonny-and-cher.

"Enid Bissett, Ida Rosenthal & William Rosenthal: An Uplifting Idea." *Entrepreneur*, October 9, 2008, http://www.entrepreneur.com/article/197610.

"Flashback: The Beatles Rock Shea Stadium; Begin First Hamburg Residency." *K-SHE95*,

August 15, 2014, http://www.kshe95.com/
news/real-rock-news/flashback-beatles-rock-
shea-stadium-begin-first-hamburg-residency.

Foreman, Katya. "The Trench: A Coat for All
Seasons." BBC, October 24, 2013, http://www.
bbc.com/culture/story/20131024-the-trench-
coat-for-all-seasons.

Gager, Russ. "Jessica Simpson." Retail
Merchandiser, http://www.retail-merchandiser.
com/index.php/reports/licensing-reports/670-
jessica-simpson.

Gil-Curiel, Germán. "Dancing Tragedy: Alexander
McQueen's Aesthetics of Spectacle." SemiotiX,
http://fashion.semiotix.org/2013/02/dancing-
tragedy-alexander-mcqueens-aesthetics-of-
spectacle/.

Green, Mary, and Stephen M. Silverman.
"John Warner: Elizabeth Taylor 'Was a
Fox.'" People, March 26, 2011, http://
www.people.com/people/package/
article/0,,20261725_20476454,00.html.

Holgate, Mark. "Spring 2005 Ready-to-Wear:
Dries Van Noten." Style.com, October 6, 2004,
http://www.style.com/fashion-shows/spring-
2005-ready-to-wear/dries-van-noten.

Honey D. "I Dreamed I Was an Advertising
Student in my Maidenform Bra." Maidenform
Advertising, October 23, 2012, http://
maidenform-advertising.blogspot.
com/2012/10/i-dreamed-i-was-advertising-
student-in.html.

Katrina, "Maria's Wedding Dress Is Up for
Auction!" Edelweiss Patterns Blog, October
8, 2013, http://www.edelweisspatterns.com/
blog/?p=4194.

Kerr, Alison. "Style on Film: Now, Voyager." Style
Matters, October 14, 2010, https://alisonkerr.
wordpress.com/2010/10/14/style-on-film-now-
voyager/.

"King Edward VIII & Wallis Simpson." People
archive, February 12, 1996, http://www.people.
com/people/archive/article/0,,20102762,00.html.

Kingslover, Jay. "Ida Cohen Rosethal." http://jwa.
com. Accessed December 28, 2014.

Krupnick, Ellie. "Jessica Simpson: I Owe My
Fashion Success to a Pair of Daisy Duke Boots."
Huffington Post, December 4, 2013, http://
www.huffingtonpost.com/2013/12/04/jessica-
simpson-fashion-success_n_4384195.html.

LaSalle, Mick, "Replay: 'Flashdance.'" SFGate,
March 22, 2014, http://blog.sfgate.com/
mlasalle/2014/03/22/replay-flashdance/.

Laverty, Christopher. "American Gigolo: Armani
Gere." Clothes on Film, May 5, 2012, http://
clothesonfilm.com/american-gigolo-armani-
gere/13314/.

———. "Belle de Jour: Sex and Alienation."
Clothes on Film, October 13, 2009, http://
clothesonfilm.com/belle-de-jour-sex-and-
alienation/4470/.

———. "Catherine Deneuve in Potiche: Still Belle."
Clothes on Film, October 10, 2011, http://
clothesonfilm.com/catherine-deneuve-in-
potiche-still-belle/22594/.

———. "Doris Day in Pillow Talk: Couture
Allure." Clothes on Film, May 18, 2012, http://
clothesonfilm.com/doris-day-in-pillow-talk-
couture-allure/25632/.

———. "Flashdance: Jennifer Beals' Dance and
Casual Wear." Clothes on Film, July 13, 2009,
http://clothesonfilm.com/flashdance-jennifer-
beals-dance-casual-wear/1978/.

Lindbergs, Kimberly, "Fashion & Passion in The
Thomas Crown Affair." Cinebeats, September
30, 2008, https://cinebeats.wordpress.
com/2008/09/30/fashion-and-passion-in-the-
thomas-crown-affair/.

Lo, Danica. "20 Years Since Unzipped: 28 Ways
the Fashion Industry Has Changed Since
1994." Glamour Fashion, February 13, 2014,

http://www.glamour.com/fashion/blogs/dressed/ 2014/02/20-years-since-unzipped---28-w.

McKnight, Ralph. *The Films of Doris Day*, www. dorisday.net. Accessed November 8, 2014

Meranda, Yoel. "The Obsession with the Past in Hitchcock's *Vertigo*." *Ways of Seeing*, http:// www.waysofseeing.org/vertigo.html.

The Metropolitan Museum of Art. "Alexander McQueen: Savage Beauty, May 4–August 7, 2011." *Metropolitan Museum of Art* (blog), http://blog.metmuseum.org/ alexandermcqueen/. Accessed February 8, 2014.

Miller, Frank. "Behind the Camera on *Bonnie and Clyde*." *TCM* (blog), May 19, 2015, http://www.tcm.com/this-month/ article/24136%7C0/Behind-the-Camera-Bonnie-and-Clyde.html.

Mitchner, Stuart. "Revisiting Stanley Kubrick's 'Lolita' at 50: 'You Gasp as You Laugh.'" *Town Topics,* September 5, 2012, http://www. towntopics.com/wordpress/2012/09/05/ revisiting-stanley-kubricks-lolita-at-50-you-gasp-as-you-laugh/.

Mower, Sarah. "Spring 2004 Ready-to-Wear: Alexander McQueen." Style.com, October 10, 2003, http://www.style.com/fashion-shows/ spring-2004-ready-to-wear/alexander-mcqueen.

Nessymon. "Analyzing Advertising: No. 5, The Film." http://www.nessymon.com. Accessed November 14, 2014.

O'Connor, Claire, "Jessica Simpson's $1 Billion Retail Empire: 'I Understand Women.'" *Forbes*, May 16, 2014, http://www.forbes.com/sites/ clareoconnor/2014/05/16/jessica-simpsons-1-billion-retail-empire-i-understand-women/.

Osborne, Daniel. *A Million Dreams . . . One Bra: Maidenform—A Senior Thesis Submitted to the Faculty of the Department of History in Candidacy for the Degree in Bachelor of Arts in History at the University of North Carolina at Asheville.* http://toto.lib.unca.edu/sr_papers/ history_sr/srhistory_2008/osborn_daniel.pdf.

Phelps, Nicole. "Fall 2012 Ready-to-Wear: Louis Vuitton." Style.com, March 7, 2012, http:// www.style.com/fashion-shows/fall-2012-ready-to-wear/louis-vuitton.

"*Pillow Talk*—Classic Films Reloaded." *Classic Films Reloaded*, http://classicfilmsreloaded.com/ pillow-talk.html.

Pinsent, Ed. "Vertigo: A Beautiful Film with Disturbing Themes of Obsession and Control." *Under Southern Eyes*, April 9, 2011, http:// undersoutherneyes.edpinsent.com/vertigo-beautiful-film-with-disturbing-themes-of-obsession-and-control/.

Queenseyes. "The Fashion That Was: The Sixties and How It Influenced the Fashion World." *Buffalo Rising*, October 21, 2011, http:// buffalorising.com/2011/10/the-fashion-that-was-the-sixties-and-how-it-influenced-the-fashion-world/.

Raisbeck, Fiona. "Chanel No. 5: The Truth Behind the Iconic Fragrance." *Marie Claire UK*, October 16, 2013, http://www.marieclaire. co.uk/blogs/542484/chanel-no-5.html.

Russell, Lawrence. "*Vertigo*." *Culture Court*, http:// www.culturecourt.com/F/Noir/Vertigo.htm.

Ryersson, Scot D., and Michael Orlando Yaccarino. "The Official Site—The Marchesa Luisa Casati." http://www.marchesacasati.com. Accessed December 16, 2014.

Sebba, Anne. "The Truth about Mrs. Simpson: Why Wallis Never Wanted to Marry Her King." *Daily Mail Online*, August 8, 2011, http:// www.dailymail.co.uk/femail/article-2023590/ The-truth-Mrs-Simpson-Why-Wallis-wanted-marry-king.html.

———. "The Truth about Mrs. Simpson: Banished by the Royals, Wallis Wrote Secret Love Letters to the One Husband Who Made Her Happy." *Daily Mail Online*, August 9, 2011, http://

www.dailymail.co.uk/femail/article-2023983/
The-truth-Mrs-Simpson-Banished-royals-
Wallis-wrote-secret-love-letters.html.

Shine, Jacqui. "Bonfire of the Inanities." *The Awl*,
November 12, 2014, http://www.theawl.com/
2014/11/the-history-of-the-new-york-times-
styles-section.

Silver, Charles. "Luis Buñuel's *Belle de Jour*." *Inside/
Out*, April 22, 2014, http://www.moma.org/
explore/inside_out/2014/04/22/luis-bunuels-
belle-de-jour.

Snider, Eric D. "What's the Big Deal?: *Bonnie and
Clyde* (1967)." Film.com, April 6, 2010, http://
www.film.com/movies/whats-the-big-deal-
bonnie-and-clyde-1967.

"The Sonny & Cher Shows." *TV Party*, http://
www.tvparty.com/sonnycher.html. Accessed
November 25, 2014.

"Steve McQueen's Glen Plaid 3-Piece as Thomas
Crown." *BAMF Style*, May 28, 2013, https://
bamfstyle.wordpress.com/2013/05/28/
mcqueen-thomas-crown-1st-suit/.

"The Storytelling Wardrobe of Bette Davis in *Now,
Voyager*. *Chanelesque*, September 10, 2010,
http://chanelesque.livejournal.com/94910.html.

"The Style Essentials: Seems Like Old Times for
Diane Keaton's Iconic Style in *Annie Hall*."
GlamAmor, October 28, 2012, http://www.
glamamor.com/2012/10/the-style-essentials-
seems-like-old.html.

"Style in Film: Catherine Deneuve in 'Belle de
Jour.'" *Classiq*, November 30, 2011, http://
classiq.me/style-in-film-catherine-deneuve-in-
belle-de-jour.

"Style in Film: Richard Gere in *American Gigolo*."
Classiq, July 23, 2014, http://classiq.me/style-
in-film-richard-gere-american-gigolo.

Susman, Gary, "'Lolita': How Stanley Kubrick
Turned Vladimir Nabokov's Novel into a
Mainstream Hit." *Moviefone*, July 11, 2012,
http://news.moviefone.com/2012/06/11/lolita-
stanley-kubrick-vladimir-nabokov/.

Tannenbaum, Rob. "The Real Story Behind
Madonna's Iconic 'Like a Virgin' Performance
at the 1984 VMAs." *Billboard*, October 28,
2014, http://www.billboard.com/articles/
news/6296887/madonna-1984-mtv-vmas-
performance.

"*The Thomas Crown Affair*: The Wardrobe."
Feather Factor, April 14, 2014, http://www.
featherfactor.com/2014/04/the-thomas-crown-
affair-the-wardrobe.html.

Turner Classic Movies. "Casablanca." http://www.
tcm.com. Accessed November 14, 2013.

"Ultimate I Love Lucy Wiki." http://
ultimateIlovelucy.wikia.com. Accessed
September 17, 2014.

Vickers, Hugo, "Robbed, Abused, Sedated, and
Alone . . . the Desperate Last Days of the
Duchess of Windsor." *Daily Mail Online*,
March 20, 2011, http://www.dailymail.co.uk/
femail/article-1367933/Wallis-Simpson-
Robbed-abused-Duchess-Windsors-days.html.

Willman, Chris. "How Madonna's 1984
VMA Wedding Dress Wed Her to Pop
Culture Forever." *Yahoo! Music*, August 31,
2012, https://www.yahoo.com/music/bp/
madonna-1984-vmas-wedding-dress-wed-her-
pop-073524862.html.

"Woodstock 1969 Lineup and Songlist." http://
digitaldreamdoor.com. Accessed November 14,
2014.

PHOTOGRAPHY CREDITS

10,11: Courtesy Hal Rubenstein.
12, **14**, **15**: Courtesy Everett Collection.
17: Guzman for stocklandmartel.com.
19, **top left:** Kevin Cummins/Getty.
19, **top right:** Frank Micelotta/Getty.
20: Courtesy of The Advertising Archives.
23: Maria Valentino/MCV Photo.
24: © Doug Ordway.
25, **top** and **bottom:** Maria Valentino/ MCV Photo.
27: MTV/Courtesy Everett Collection.
28: Jamie McCarthy/Getty Images.
31: Courtesy Everett Collection.
33: Jerry Tavin/Everett Collection.
34, 37: Maria Valentino/MCV Photo.
38, 40–41: Bruce Weber/Courtesy Calvin Klein.
42: AP Photo.
44: Bill Eppridge/Getty Images.
45, **clockwise, from top left:** Bill Eppridge/ The LIFE Picture Collection/Getty Images; The LIFE Picture Collection/Getty Images; John Dominis/The LIFE Picture Collection/Getty Images; Elliott Landy/Redferns/ Getty Images; Fotos International/Getty Images; Bill Eppridge/Getty Images; Ralph Ackerman/Getty Images.
47: Blank Archives/Getty Images.
48–49: Courtesy Everett Collection.
51: Universal/Getty Images.
52, 55: MCV Photo.
56: Daniel Simon/Gamma/Getty Images.
57: MCV Photo.
58: Thierry Orban/Sygma/Corbis.
59: MCV Photo.
60: Paramount/Courtesy Everett Collection.
63: Paramount Pictures/Courtesy Neal Peters Collection.
65: Courtesy Donna Karan International.
66: Courtesy of The Advertising Archives.
68: Courtesy Everett Collection.
71: MGM/Kobal Collection.
73, 74: Miramax/Courtesy Everett Collection.
77: Paramount/Kobal Collection.
78, **top left:** Mary Evans/BHE Films/Dino De Laurentiis Cinematografica/Verona Prod/Ronald Grant/Everett Collection.
78, **top right:** Courtesy Everett Collection.
80: Paramount/Kobal Collection.
83, **clockwise, from top left:** CBS/Neal Peters Collection; CBS via Getty Images; mptvimages.com; mptvimages.com; © Gene Trindl/mptvimages.
85: mptvimages.com.

86: © Phil Stern, Courtesy of Fahey/Klein Gallery, Los Angeles.
88: Courtesy Everett Collection.
90, 92: © Photo Baz Luhrmann/Chanel.
93, **top**: © Photo Baz Luhrmann/Chanel.
93, **bottom**: © Chanel/Sketch Karl Lagerfeld.
94: © Chanel/Sketch Karl Lagerfeld.
95: © Photo Baz Luhrmann/Chanel.
97: Courtesy Everett Collection.
98: United Artists/Courtesy Neal Peters Collection.
100: Spelling/ABC/The Kobal Collection.
102: ABC Photo Archives/Getty Images.
104: United Artists/Courtesy Neal Peters Collection.
106–107: Courtesy Everett Collection.
108: United Artists/Courtesy Neal Peters Collection.
110, 112: Courtesy Ralph Lauren.
115: Richard Corkery/NY Daily News Archive via Getty Images.
116–117: Courtesy Everett Collection.
118: Mondadori\Everett Collection.
121: Popperfoto/Getty Images.
122: Paramount/Courtesy Everett Collection.
124: Mary Evans/Polygram Filmed Entertainment/Ronald Grant/Everett Collection.
125: Paramount/Courtesy Everett Collection.
126: Photo/Michel Euler.
129, **top right:** AP Photo/Michel Euler.
129, **top left:** Daniel Simon/Gamma/ Getty Images.
129, **bottom**, **left** and **right**: Gamma-Rapho/ Getty Images.
130–131: Pierre Verdy/AFP/Getty Images.
133: Courtesy Everett Collection.
134: Mary Evans/Paramount Pictures/ Ronald Grant/Everett Collection.
136: mptvimages.com.
137: Maria Valentino/MCV Photo.
139, 140: NBC/Getty Images.
143: Mary Evans/Robert et Raymond Hakim/Paris Film Productions/Five Film/ Ronald Grant/Everett.
144, 145, 147: Courtesy Everett Collection.
148: Courtesy Music World Entertainment and Columbia Records/Sony BMG.
150: Dana Edelson/NBC/NBCU Photo Bank via Getty Images.
151: Courtesy Music World Entertainment and Columbia Records/Sony BMG.
153, 154, 155: MGM/Courtesy Neal Peters Collection.
156–157: Everett Collection/Everett

Collection.
158: Mondadori/Getty Images.
161: Atelier Versace/Splash News/Corbis.
163: WPA Pool/Pool/Getty Images.
165, 167: Courtesy Everett Collection.
168,170–171: Express/Getty Images.
172, 174, 175, 177: Courtesy of The Advertising Archives.
179: Warner Bros./Getty Images.
180: Dan Farrell/NY Daily News Archive via Getty Images.
183: Mark and Colleen Hayward/Getty Images.
184: CBS via Getty Images.
187: Wenn.com.
188: Mary Evans/Ronald Grant/Everett Collection.
189: Paramount/Courtesy Everett Collection.
191: FPG/Getty Images.
192: Courtesy Desilu Productions/CBS.
195: Dirck Halstead//Time Life Pictures/ Getty Images.
197: Paramount/Getty Images.
198, 199: Paramount/Courtesy Everett Collection.
201: API/Gamma-Rapho via Getty Images.
202: AP Photo.
203: Popperfoto/Getty Images.
204: dpa /Landov.
205: AP Photo.
206: Wenn.com.
207: APIC/Getty Images.
209: © 1976 Bob Alyott.
211: Herb Ritts/Trunk Archive.
213: Katsumi Kasahara/AP Photo.
215: © 1990 Lynn Goldsmith.
217: John Kobal Foundation/Getty Images.
218: Courtesy Everett Collection.
219: mptvimages.com.
220: Courtesy Warner Bros.
221: Warner Bros./Neal Peters Collection.
222, 224–225: Maria Valentino/MCV Photo.
227, **top:** Courtesy Everett Collection.
227, **bottom:** Maria Valentino/MCV Photo.
229: Steve Granitz/WireImage.
230: AP Photo/Chris Carlson.
233: mptvimages.com.
234, 235: ©20th Century Fox/Courtesy Everett Collection.
236: Erik C Pendzich/Rex Features/ courtesy Everett Collection.
238: HBO/Courtesy Everett Collection
241, 242–243,244, **left**: Maria Valentino/ MCV Photo.
244, **right**:Victor Boyko/Getty Images.

THE LOOKS OF LOVE

HarperCollins books may be purchased for educational, business, or sales promotional use. For information please e-mail the Special Markets Department at SPsales@harpercollins.com.

First published in 2015 by
Harper Design
An Imprint of HarperCollins*Publishers*
195 Broadway
New York, NY 10007
Tel: (212) 207-7000
Fax: (855) 746-6023
www.hc.com
harperdesign@harpercollins.com

Distributed throughout the world by
HarperCollins*Publishers*
195 Broadway
New York, NY 10007

ISBN 978-0-06-227969-9

Library of Congress Control Number: 2013931916

Book design by Christine Heslin

Printed in China
First Printing, 2015

ABOUT THE AUTHOR

Hal Rubenstein is a writer, designer, and one of the founding editors at *InStyle* magazine, where he served as fashion director for fifteen years. In fall 2013, he launched his eponymous women's collection on the Home Shopping Network and formed Hal Rubenstein & Associates, which has provided private consultation to brands such as Gabriel & Co. jewelers, the Raleigh Hotel, Giorgio Armani, and American Express. In 2015, he launched his website, Halrubenstein.com, which focuses on popular culture and offers advice on leading a better life, and with model-designer Iman Abdulmajid, he introduced a new style show on Sirius Radio. The author of the bestselling *100 Unforgettable Dresses* (Harper Design, 2011) and *Paisley Goes with Nothing*, he is a special projects editor at *Architectural Digest*. He has also written cover stories and interviews, and served as a columnist on various pop culture topics for *The New Yorker*, *New York* magazine, *Interview*, *Elle*, *Vogue*, *Vanity Fair*, and *Details*. He has been a frequent red-carpet commentator for such shows as *The Today Show*, *Extra*, and *The View*. He lives in New York City with his husband, David Nickle, and his dog, Murray.

391.009   Rubenstein, Hal.
R
          The looks of love.

DATE			